More Praise for *Moral Intelligence 2.0*

"Lennick and Kiel demonstrate the critical importance of values-based leadership in building companies that last during difficult times.

—**Charles W. Sorenson**, M.D., President and CEO,
Intermountain Healthcare

"Lennick and Kiel reveal the moral leadership practices of successful organizations. It's fascinating to learn how moral intelligence drives business success at companies like Cardinal Health, American Express, and Hormel."

—**Andrew Doman**, President and CEO, Russell Investment Group

"*Moral Intelligence 2.0* has given me insights that will help us with the continued evolution of our business and will enhance our long-term survival and prosperity."

—**Joe Dedin**, Executive Director, Eagle Bluff
Environmental Learning Center

"Rarely do books come out that become required reading for members of all Boards. *Moral Intelligence 2.0* gives a masterly analysis of how to do the right thing in corporate life."

—**Peter Hogarth**, Former Director London Stock Exchange
and Senior Partner, LVA Partners

"I've discovered from this book that it is moral intelligence which I have found so critical to my years of leading others. This has surely been the formula for the success of my business."

—**Dale Larson**, Owner, Larson Doors, Inc.

"Lennick and Kiel have brought focus to a subject has been undervalued for years. I found that if my senior team held firmly to these principles, we would safely navigate the most challenging of times. I strongly recommend this book for every CEO and leader in the business world."

—**Richard Harrington**, Retired CEO, Thomson Reuters

"The value of emotional intelligence in leadership has been well documented, but in this book, Lennick and Kiel solidify the absolute correlation between moral intelligence and business performance. This should be required reading for leaders at all levels."

—**Bill Shaner**, President and CEO, Save-A-Lot Food Stores

"The authors show that rather than slowing down a business, moral intelligence is essential to success—even in the most difficult of times and when the competition is fiercest."

—**Gary Bhojwani**, President and CEO, Allianz Life Insurance Company of North America

"Lennick and Kiel provide a clear and compelling path for readers to understand the importance of strong moral values to their business and the way forward toward execution."

—**Michael E. LaRocco**, President and CEO, Fireman's Fund Insurance

"This important book challenges every leader, every citizen, to lead lives with purpose, intention, and a true north."

—**Roger Fransecky**, Ph.D., Founder and Senior Partner, LVA Partners

"Lennick and Kiel confront leadership's comfort levels with gritty questions such as whether alleged values are aligned with actual behavior. *Moral Intelligence 2.0* is a no nonsense book to be valued by those willing to invest effort to achieve integrity and success."

—**Michael Sabbeth**, Esq., Author of *The Good, The Bad, & The Difference: How To Talk With Children About Values*

"During these times of public mistrust and cynicism of government, corporate America, and mass media, this book is needed now more than ever. The companies highlighted by the authors are thriving examples that success and profit can be achieved without sacrificing integrity. Our business is our employees."

—**Yvonne K. Franzese**, Chief Human Resources Officer, Allianz of America

Moral
Intelligence 2.0

Enhancing Business Performance
and Leadership Success
in Turbulent Times

Doug Lennick • **Fred Kiel, Ph.D.**
with Kathy Jordan, Ph.D.

PRENTICE
HALL

Upper Saddle River, NJ • Boston • Indianapolis • San Francisco
New York • Toronto • Montreal • London • Munich • Paris • Madrid
Cape Town • Sydney • Tokyo • Singapore • Mexico City

The publisher offers excellent discounts on this book when ordered in quantity for bulk purchases or special sales, which may include electronic versions and/or custom covers and content particular to your business, training goals, marketing focus, and branding interests. For more information, please contact:

U.S. Corporate and Government Sales
(800) 382-3419
corpsales@pearsontechgroup.com

For sales outside the United States, please contact:

International Sales
international@pearson.com

Visit us on the Web: informit.com/ph

The Library of Congress Cataloging-in-Publication data is on file.

Copyright © 2011 Pearson Education, Inc.

ISBN-13: 978-0-13-249828-9
ISBN-10: 0-13-249828-6

Text printed in the United States on recycled paper at R.R. Donnelley in Crawfordsville, Indiana.
Second Printing June 2011

Associate Publisher: Tim Moore
Executive Editor: Jim Boyd
Development Editor: Russ Hall
Managing Editor: Kristy Hart
Project Editor: Jovana San Nicolas-Shirley
Copy Editor: Apostrophe Editing Services
Indexer: Erika Millen
Proofreader: Water Crest Publishing
Publishing Coordinator: Pamela Boland
Cover Designer: Chuti Prasertsith
Compositor: Nonie Ratcliff

To our wives, Beth Ann Lennick and Sandy Kiel, who have helped us fine-tune our own moral compasses over the years—and to our children, who always lovingly challenge us to live in alignment! Alan, Mary, and Joanie (Doug) and Kelly, Amy, Bryn, Anna, Jordan and Freda (Fred)— and to our parents, whose early nurturing provided our foundation— Albert and Martha Lennick and Orville and Mabel Kiel

Contents

Foreword by Richard Leider xiii

Foreword to Previous Edition
by Richard E. Boyatzis xvi

Introduction xxix

    Leaders Interviewed xxxiv
    Thought Partners xxxvii

PART ONE • MORAL INTELLIGENCE

1 Good Business 3

    Moral Stupidity Act 1 5
    What Does Moral Leadership Look Like? 15
    Endnotes 31

2 Born to Be Moral 35

    What the Best Leaders Believe 36
    A Visit to the Nursery 38
    Nature Versus Nurture 38
    Growing Up Moral 39
    Learning to Be Responsible 40
    When Things Go Wrong 41
    Inside Your (Moral) Brain 41

It's All in Your Head 42

The Moral Map of Your Brain 45

Why We're Good and Why We're Bad 46

So What Goes Wrong? 47

The Neuroscience of Moral Decision Making . . . 48

Can We Actually Change Our Brain? 52

Moral Software 53

Endnotes 54

3   Your Moral Compass 57

The Morality of Values 65

Put It in Writing 74

Frame 3: Behavior 75

Endnotes 80

4   Staying True to YourMoral Compass 81

Endnote 93

PART TWO • DEVELOPING MORAL SKILLS

5   Integrity 97

Acting Consistently with Principles,
Values, and Beliefs 98

Telling the Truth 100

Standing Up for What Is Right 106

Keeping Promises 109

6   Responsibility 113

Taking Responsibility for Personal Choices 115

Admitting Mistakes and Failures 117

Embracing Responsibility for Serving Others . . . 121

Endnotes 124

7   Compassion and Forgiveness **125**

Actively Caring About Others 126

Letting Go of Your Own Mistakes 129

Letting Go of Others' Mistakes 131

8   Emotions. **135**

Self-Awareness. 137

Understanding Your Thoughts. 140

Personal Effectiveness 141

Deciding What to Think 141

Self-Control. 142

Nurturing Emotional Health 143

Interpersonal Effectiveness. 147

Empathy 148

Misplaced Compassion 149

Respecting Others 151

Getting Along with Others 154

Endnote. 156

9   Making Moral Decisions **157**

How Roger Used the 4 Rs 158

Endnotes 178

PART THREE • MORAL LEADERSHIP

10   The Moral Leader. **181**

Performance Problems 195

Endnote. 196

11 Leading Large Organizations 197

The Fabric of Values 197

Is There Such a Thing as a Morally Intelligent
Organization? 199

The Morally Intelligent Organization—
An Aerial View 199

Morally Intelligent Policies 201

The Principles That Matter Most 202

Cultivating Organizational Integrity 203

The Responsible Organization 204

The Compassionate Organization 213

The Forgiving Organization 215

Recruiting for Values 217

Reinforcing Values Starts at the Top 218

The Power of Formal Rewards 219

Success Stories 221

Ideal Versus Real 221

Values and the Global Organization 222

Endnotes 222

12 Moral Intelligence for the
Entrepreneur 223

Moral Values in Small Organizations 228

Last Words About Business Start-Ups 242

Endnotes 242

Epilogue   Becoming a Global Moral
Leader 243

Raising the Stakes 244

Watch Your Wake 245

Give Back 246

Create the Future 247

A Global Business Opportunity 248

Conclusion 250

Endnotes 250

A   Strengthening Your Moral Skills 251

A Look in the Mirror 252

Using the MCI 252

The Right Frame of Mind for Completing
the MCI 253

Scoring and Interpreting Your MCI 253

Prioritizing Your Moral Development Efforts . . . 254

The Road Less Traveled 255

The 80/20 Rule 255

Your Moral Development Plan 256

Putting Your Moral Development Plan
into Practice 258

Breaking Bad Habits 258

Reward Yourself for Positive Change 259

Surround Yourself with Positive People 259

Do I Really Need to Change? 260

Books, Audio, and Video Media 261

Workshops 261

Personal Counseling 261

Executive Coaching 262

Endnote 262

B   Moral Competency Inventory (MCI) . . . 263

C   Scoring the MCI 271

Moral Competencies Worksheet 274

What Your Total MCI Score Means 274

D Interpreting Your MCI Scores **277**

    Total MCI Score (Alignment Score) 278

    Highest and Lowest Competency Scores 279

    Individual Item Scores 279

    Reality Testing 280

    Do Your Scores Matter? 281

    Now What? 282

Index **285**

Foreword

I find the wisdom of poets useful in my life and work. With a few words, the right poem at the right time can speak with a clear voice and help us see things new in the world.

This poem by William Stafford provides us with a helpful place to return if we feel confused about a moral choice or challenge in the world.

"The Way It Is"
There's a thread you follow. It goes among
things that change. But it doesn't change.
People wonder about what you are pursuing.
You have to explain about the thread.
But it is hard for others to see.
While you hold it you can't get lost.
Tragedies happen; people get hurt
or die; and you suffer and get old.
Nothing you do can stop time's unfolding.
You don't ever let go of the thread.
—William Stafford

Moral Intelligence 2.0 provides us with the helpful guidance to choose and to follow the "thread" of our own moral compass.

Each day we face a series of "moral moments"—personal choice points. These are moments that require some decisions to serve others

Credit: William Stafford, "The Way It Is," from *The Way It Is: New and Selected Poems*. Copyright (cr) 1998 by the Estate of William Stafford. Reprinted with the permission of Graywolf Press, Minneapolis, Minnesota, www.graywolfpress.org.

or to be self-absorbed. We are likely, at times, to find ourselves in moral dilemmas. Each choice we make can feel as if we are either holding on to or letting go of our thread.

We find the purpose path through our own life by following our own moral compass, holding on to our thread. How do we do such a thing? How do we follow some invisible thread that runs through our life? How can we even know it exists?

One of the most helpful answers I can give is to simply read this book. It will help you look at the story of how your own life of moral intelligence has unfolded. It will help you see the thread that, perhaps invisible at the time, helped you choose whether to say yes or no, right or left.

The authors have set out to illuminate a very complex subject—that of the moral compass in us all. And I found their insights revealing. Chapter 2 "Born to Be Moral" is worth the price of the book. I found myself again and again reflecting on the story, "A visit to the nursery." The notion of our inborn capacity of empathy struck a deep chord within me.

If we can trust that we are born "hardwired" to be moral, if we can trust that our hearts know how to recognize our thread, then this book will provide a blueprint, a manual of specifics to follow it.

What practices, what knowledge or resource do we turn to in order to find our way? First, as the authors show us, we begin by choosing to uncover and express our purpose. Next, we clearly define the distinction between "how" we make choices, and "why" we make them. How often have we allowed the how of our choices to overshadow why we made them?

Holding on to the thread, listening to your moral compass, may seem insignificant, but it is no small thing. It dramatically shifts the way we see, the way we choose, and the way we lead and live. It determines whether we lead a life of anxiety and stress or a spacious life of purpose and meaning. You don't ever let go of the thread.

Bottom-line thinking might now prevail, but the moral compass journey has deep roots. It also has deep resonance. One might say, in fact, that it's not so much an idea whose time has come, as an idea that has always been with us—it's just that we need to be reminded. I'm pleased that so many people's lives have already been changed for the better through this reminder and I hope that the 2.0 edition will add to the number of those who are on the purpose path.

—Richard Leider

Bestselling author of *The Power of Purpose* and *Repacking Your Bags*

Foreword
to Previous Edition
Building a Better Culture

There are few issues with more significant impact on life in and out of organizations today than that of moral action. Crusades and jihads are moral righteousness taken to harmful and even evil extents—hurting others and demanding homogeneity of beliefs. The moral righteousness involved in trying to fix, save, or punish others has led to some of the most horrible episodes in human existence. Beyond the tragic loss of life, there is the subjugation of the human spirit. There is the loss of dreams and possibilities—the loss of spirit. Ironically, this travesty of moral imperialism comes at the same time as people worldwide are voicing the need for more spirituality and religion.

Most of us know right from wrong. In hundreds of studies of the characteristics that differentiate outstanding from average leaders from their less effective counterparts (both average and poor performers), integrity has never appeared to distinguish high performers. Is this evidence of a morally bankrupt system? No. It is that the moments of "outtegrity" are so egregious and shocking that we become preoccupied with them. In the process, we miss the many tests of our morality and humanity that we face each day. For example, deciding how to promote a product or service is enacted in the context of one's values and an organizational culture that encourages consistency with a set of shared beliefs and norms.

The essential challenge of moral intelligence is not knowing right from wrong, but doing versus knowing. There are people who are suffering from mental illness and a small percentage of the population that are psychopaths or sociopaths. All of these people may not "know" right from wrong. But most of us are not in that category. So why don't we act appropriately more often? Most of us do—most of the time. Of the hundreds of decisions we make each day, most of us consider what is "right," what will be better and help our community, organization, and fellow humans. But we don't always agree on what is right.

Values and Operating Philosophy

This is where values and philosophy come into play. Our values are based on beliefs and determine our attitudes. A value typically includes an evaluation (i.e., good or bad designation) of an object or subject. Sets of values form proscriptions and prescriptions (i.e., statements of what *not* to do and what *to do*) that guide our daily life. Values also affect how we interpret and perceive things and events around us. But decades of research on values have shown little correlation to behavior.[1]

To understand people's actions, we have to look behind specific values to uncover how an individual determines value. This can be called a person's "operating philosophy." Research into typical operating philosophies has resulted in a test that allows us to measure a person's relative dominance among three different ways to determine the value of a act, a project, a decision, how to spend your time, and so forth.[2] Our philosophy is the *way* we determine values.

For example, a consultant lists "family" as a dominant value, but still spends five days a week away from his wife and two children, traveling for his job. He says he's enacting his value by providing enough money for his family's needs. By contrast, a manufacturing manager who also lists "family" as his dominant value has turned down promotions so he can have dinner each night with his wife and children.

The difference between those two men might be in how aware they are of their true values, how aligned their actions are with those values, or in the way they *interpret* their values. Accordingly, they reveal deep differences in how each values people, organizations, and activities. Such differences may reflect disparate operating philosophies—the most common of which are pragmatic, intellectual, and humanistic.[3] And although no one philosophy is "better" than another, each drives people's actions, thoughts, and feelings in distinctive ways.

The central theme of a pragmatic philosophy is a belief that *usefulness* determines the worth of an idea, effort, person, or organization.[4] People with this philosophy often measure things to assess their value, and believe that they're largely responsible for the events of their lives. No surprise, then, that among the emotional intelligence competencies, pragmatics rank high in self-management. Unfortunately, their individualistic orientation often—but not always—pulls them into using an individual contribution approach to management.

The central theme of an intellectual philosophy[5] is the desire to understand people, things, and the world by constructing an image of how they work, thereby providing them some emotional security in predicting the future. People with this philosophy rely on logic in making decisions, and assess the worth of something against an underlying "code" or set of guidelines that stress reason. People with this outlook rely heavily on cognitive competencies, sometimes to the exclusion of social competencies. You might hear someone with an intellectual philosophy say, for example: "If you have an elegant solution, others will believe it. No need to try to convince them about its merits." They can use a visionary leadership style, if the vision describes a well-reasoned future.

The central theme of a humanistic philosophy is that close, personal relationships give meaning to life.[6] People with this philosophy are committed to human values; family and close friends are seen as more important than other relationships. They assess the worth of an activity in terms of how it affects their close relations. Similarly, loyalty is valued over mastery of a job or skill. Where a pragmatist's philosophy might lead her to "sacrifice the few for the many," a humanistic leader would view each person's life as important, naturally cultivating the social awareness and relationship management competencies. Accordingly, they gravitate toward styles that emphasize interaction with others.

Each one of us believes in these three value orientations (i.e., pragmatic value, intellectual value, and human value). But most of us will prioritize three value orientations differently at different stages in our lives.

The point is that we have to be more aware both *of* our values and *how* we value—our philosophy. We need to be sensitive to those who have different values and different philosophies if we are to live together and make the world a better place. And we need to be sensitive to such differences if we are to have adaptive, resilient, and innovative organizations. Diversity brings us innovation, but only if we are open to it and respect it.

In this book, Doug Lennick and Fred Kiel define **moral intelligence** as, "the mental capacity to determine how universal human principles should be applied to our values, goals, and actions." They argue we are "hard wired" to be moral but often stray from the path. Within each of us are the values and basis for our moral compass. Each of us should pay attention to our moral compass often—more often than we do. Lennick and Kiel's exploration of this topic could not have come at a more important time.

Cultural Relativism and Moral Horizons of Significance

We are exposed to the vast differences in the world on the Internet, television, movies, and newspapers. We see it in our organizations and schools. We see it walking down the street of most cities of the world. Is every culture and subgroup within it assured that its values and philosophy are "OK" with the rest of us? Maybe not.

In his 1991 book, *The Ethics of Authenticity*, McGill University Professor and prominent philosopher, Charles Taylor, claimed that cultural relativism and postmodernism both violated basic ethical standards.[7] He claimed that cultural relativism ("everyone has their own morality based on their situation and culture") taken to its ultimate conclusion becomes moral anarchy. It breeds a form of egocentrism and selfishness. It suggests everyone is in their own world. Similar to the argument in *Moral Intelligence*, Taylor suggests that there are, among humans and society, "moral horizons of significance." These are the universals that Lennick and Kiel propose are so crucial to organizational success. We know it is wrong to kill another human. But we can be brought to that point by contingencies. Is it acceptable to kill someone to defend your family? To get food for yourself? To take their shirt or sneakers because you like them and cannot afford to buy them? Because they annoy you? Because they have insulted your faith? Taylor's concept is central to the application of the ideas in this book. How do we determine what exceptions to moral universals are justified and which show a lack of moral intelligence?

But this brings us back to whose values and philosophy are right or more right than the others? Without a high degree of moral intelligence, Lennick and Kiel illustrate in their book with marvelous and moving stories, we fall back into fighting to defend our own views as best—and imposing them on others.

In deconstructing the components of moral intelligence, Lennick and Kiel show us how four clusters of skills integrate to form this capability: integrity, responsibility, compassion and forgiveness, and emotions. They offer many ideas as to how we can use our moral intelligence to evoke moral intelligence in others. Their combined effect will be more effective organizations. Why? First, we will be proud of where we work and for what it stands. Therefore, we will feel more committed to the organization, its culture, and vision. Third, we will access and utilize more of our own talent (and that of others around us) because we are free from guilt and shame. And fourth, it is the right thing to do!

Believing and Belonging

There is another crucial business impact from values, philosophy, and collective moral intelligence—they form the basis of our organizational vision, purpose, and culture. We want to believe in what we are doing.

We want to feel that we are contributing and our work has some meaning. But looming labor pool demographics and skill shortages suggest that, as McKinsey and Company said, we are in a "war for talent."[8] This will become a battle for the hearts and minds (and even the spirit) of people your organization wishes to attract, keep, and motivate. Over the course of the next decades, an organization's vision, sense of purpose, and culture will become even more significant recruitment differentiators to discerning job applicants.

Moral Intelligence

In the following pages, you will be provoked into reflecting on your own beliefs and style of using them. You will be inspired by reading about effective executives with high moral intelligence. You will be ashamed and embarrassed reading about ineffective executives who do not seem to be able to spell moral intelligence, nonetheless, live it. The apparent simplicity of their argument and smoothness of their writing style should not be misunderstood. This material is deep and significant. The impact of moral intelligence is much more than the long-term success of your organization. It is the preservation of our civilization and species.

—Richard E. Boyatzis
Coauthor of *Primal Leadership*
January 31, 2005

Endnotes

1. Michael Hechter. "Values research in the social and behavioral sciences." In Michael Hechter, Lynn Nadel, and Richard E. Michod, (eds.). *The Origin of Values*. New York: Aldine de Gruyter, 1993.

2. Gordon W. Allport, P.E.Vernon, and Garnder Lindzey, *Study of Values*. Boston: Houghton Mifflin, 1960.; Chris Argyris and Don Schon, *Theory in Practice Learning*. San Francisco, CA: Jossey-Bass, 1982.; Clyde Kluckhohn. "Values and Value-Orientations in the Theory of Action." In Talcott Parson and E.A. Shils, eds. *Toward a General Theory of Action*. Cambridge, MA: Harvard

University Press, 1951. pp. 388-433.; Florence Kluckhohn and Fred Strodtbeck. *Variations in Value Orientations*. Evanston, IL: Row, Peterson & Co, 1961.; Milton Rokeach, *The Nature of Human Values*. New York: Free Press, 1973.; Shalom H. Schwartz, "Universals in the Content and Structure of Values: Theoretical Advances and Empirical Tests in 20 Countries," *Advances in Experimental Social Psychology,* volume 25. NY: Academic Press, 1992. pp. 1-65.; Michael Hechter, "Values Research in the Social and Behavioral Sciences," In Michael Hechter, Lynn Nadel, and Richard.E. Michod, eds. *The Origin of Values*. New York: Aldine de Gruyter, 1993. pp. 1-28.

3. "Assessing Your Operating Philosophy: The Philosophical Orientation Questionnaire" measures the relative dominance of each of these three for the person. Richard E. Boyatzis, Angela J. Murphy, and Jane V. Wheeler, "Philosophy as a Missing Link Between Values and Behavior," *Psychological Reports*, 86 (2000): pp. 47-64.

4. The Pragmatic Operating Philosophy emerged from "pragmatism" (as reflected in the works of John Dewey, William James, Charles Sanders Peirce, and Richard Rorty,), "consequentialism" (as reflected in the works of C.D. Johnson, and P. Pettit), "instrumentalism" (as reflected in the works of John Dewey), and "utilitarianism" (as reflected in the works of Jeremy Bentham, and John Stuart Mill). See the Boyatzis, Murphy, and Wheeler article cited earlier for the full references.

5. The Intellectual Operating Philosophy emerged from "rationalism" (as reflected in the works of Rene Descartes, Gottfried Wilhelm Leibniz, Benedict de Spinoza), and the various philosophers claiming rationalism as their etiological root, such as Georg Wilhelm Friedrich Hegel and Jurgen Habermas, as well as the philosophical structuralists (Claude Levi-Strauss and Jean Piaget), and post-modernists (Friedrich Nietzsche). See the Boyatzis, Murphy, and Wheeler article cited earlier for the full references.

6. The Human Operating Philosophy emerged from "communitarianism" (W. F. Brundage), "hermeneutics" (Hans-Georg Gadamer), "humanism" (Francesco Petrarch and R.W. Sellars), and "collectivism" (R. Burlingame and W.H. Chamberlin).

7. Charles Taylor. *The Ethics of Authenticity*. Cambridge: Harvard University Press, 1991.

8. Elizabeth Chambers, Mark Foulon, Helen Hanfield-Jones, Steven Hankin, and Edward Michaels, III. *The War for Talent. The Mckinsey Quarterly*, #3, 1998.

Acknowledgments

We wish to give a special thanks to Orlo Otteson, our original "cracker-jack" researcher who, over four years, helped us successfully tackle the mountainous job of reviewing the vast literature on this subject.

We wish to thank all our colleagues and friends who have been so important in helping us sharpen our thinking on moral intelligence. Just as important, they encouraged us to continue our research efforts when the word "moral" was not a word one easily used in public discourse.

These people also inspired us by their own demonstration on a day-to-day basis of what it means to live in alignment!

A partial list from Doug: Kay May, my office manager and friend for more than 30 years and now one of my business partners; John Wright, the best man at my wedding and my partner in launching my writing career more than 25 years ago with *The Simple Genius (You)*; the CEOs I have been fortunate to work for and learn from—in order of their appearance, they include Harvey Golub, Jeff Stiefler, Dave Hubers, Jim Cracchiolo, and Ken Chenault; my colleagues at Lennick Aberman—Rick Aberman, Jim Choat, Jim Jensen, Kay May, Kris Petersen, Judy Skoglund, Ben Smith, Chuck Wachendorfer, Chris Ambrose, Ryan Goulart, Teresa Hanratty, Ray Kelly, Elaine Larson, Teresa Lombard, and Leela Rao; the talented team of senior executives I was privileged to lead at American Express Financial Advisors before changing roles in September 2000—Teresa Hanratty, Brian Heath, Jim Jensen, Marietta Johns, Steve Kumagai, Becky Roloff, Sam Samsel, Norm Weaver, and Mike Woodward; Steve Lennick, my cousin, friend, and confidant; Carol Lennick, my sister; Bob Day and Tom Turner, the two men who took a chance on me when I was eager to start my business life at the ripe old age of 21—they trained and developed me; Roy Geer, Row Moriarty, Richard Leider, Larry Wilson, and Doug Baker Sr.—all five are mentors and friends for many years; and, very important, all the people I've had the opportunity to serve as either their leader or their follower or both.

A partial list from Fred: My partners Kelly Garramone, Richard Aldersea, Kim Merrill, and my other colleagues at KRW who have encouraged me on this journey: Randi Birk, Peg Howell, Nancy Bologna, Nikky Heidel, Cari Bixel, Heather Smallman, Mark Edwards, Donna Zajonc, Doug Bamford, Keith Taylor, Gayle Bunge, Heather Richetto-Rumley, Kathryn Williams, Glenn Schenenga, Tom Ferguson, and my close personal friends—Wayne and Joni Finnegan, Mark and Marsha Gorman, Keith and Kitty Baker, John Manz, Tom McMullen and the guys in my book club for 20 years, Dwight Cummins, Paul Harris, Bruce McManus, Michael Nation, Paul Brown, Ron Ellis, and Dave Strofferahn.

Finally, we wish to acknowledge each other, Esmond Harmsworth, and Jim Boyd. This book has been a labor of love, and we have loved laboring together.

About the Authors

Doug Lennick

Doug's career as an executive, a sales manager, and a developer of people is legendary. Today, in addition to his work as CEO and founding member of the Lennick Aberman Group, Doug continues to work directly with Jim Cracchiolo, CEO of Ameriprise Financial, formerly American Express Financial Advisors. Although no longer full time, Doug retains the title of EVP at Ameriprise Financial. As a senior advisor to Jim, Doug's focus is on workforce culture and performance. As a leader, a coach, and a mentor, Doug has taught thousands how to be successful in both their personal and professional lives.

Doug is a graduate of the University of Minnesota, Morris, with a degree in business management.

In the early 1990s, Doug was one of two (the other being Jim Mitchell) senior managers at American Express responsible for championing, developing, and implementing the Emotional Competence training program that was recognized by the Consortium for Research on Emotional Intelligence in Organizations as a model program. Doug's work and American Express's Emotional Competence program were recognized in Daniel Goleman's *Working with Emotional Intelligence* and in *Educating People to Be Emotionally Intelligent*, edited by Rueven Bar-On, J.G. Maree, and Maurice Jesse Elias, and in Tony Schwartz' *Fortune* magazine article on the same topic. In *The Power of Purpose,* Richard Leider referred to Doug as the "spiritual leader" of the company.

Doug lives in Edina, Minnesota, with his wife, Beth Ann. Their youngest daughter, Joan, attends graduate school at St. Mary's

University in Minneapolis and has an undergraduate degree from Stonehill College in Easton, Massachusetts. Their oldest daughter, Mary, has an undergraduate degree from the University of Minnesota and is a graduate student at Augsburg College in Minneapolis. Doug's son Alan is an actor and a manager/financial advisor for Ameriprise Financial and is living in Minneapolis with his teacher/actor wife Sari, and their son, Dylan.

lennickaberman.com
612-333-8791
dlennick@lennickaberman.com

Fred Kiel, Ph.D.

One of the pioneers in the field of executive coaching, Fred began challenging senior executives in the mid-1970s to improve their leadership skills. Trained as a Ph.D. counseling psychologist, he left the private practice world in the mid-1980s and has since devoted his full-time career as an advisor to CEOs and senior leaders in large organizations. In the late 1980s he co-founded KRW International, one of the durable and highly respected "boutique" firms in this space. He is also the founder and executive director of the KRW Research Institute, which is conducting research on the hidden beliefs and biases CEOs hold in their heads and hearts. These findings will be reported in a book scheduled for publication in 2012 and currently titled, *What CEOs Believe and How It Impacts the Bottom Line*.

Fred lives on his organic farm in Southeastern Minnesota, in the midst of cold running trout streams and Amish farms, along with his wife, Sandy. Sandy is the innkeeper for the Inn at Sacred Clay Farm—their country inn bed and breakfast with five luxury guest rooms and meeting space for small groups.

krwinternational.com
612-338-3020
kiel@krw-intl.com

Kathy Jordan, Ph.D.

Kathy was the collaborating writer with Doug Lennick and Fred Kiel for the first hardback and paperback editions of *Moral Intelligence*, and with Doug Lennick for his book *Financial Intelligence: How to Make Smart Values-Based Decisions with your Money and Your Life*. She is also co-author of *Becoming a Life Change Artist: 7 Creative Skills to Reinvent Yourself at Any Stage of Life*.

Kathy has a Ph.D. in counseling and human systems from Florida State University. After working for large organizations (AT&T Bell Laboratories and later Harvard Business School Publishing Corporation), she has flourished as an independent coach, consultant, and writer. Kathy lives in Saint Augustine, Florida, and Colorado Springs, Colorado, where she enjoys family time with her daughter Erin, son-in-law Doug, and granddaughter, Mackenzie Kathleen.

Introduction

In 2005 we were fortunate to publish the first edition of *Moral Intelligence.* In the book, we argued that sustainable business perform-ance was only possible when leaders and their organizations acted in concert with certain core universal principles, including integrity, responsibility, compassion, and forgiveness. We described the skills that were needed for leaders to behave in ways that were both moral and at the same time financially smart for their businesses. We demonstrated through the lives of some of the United States' most highly regarded leaders the essential relationship between moral competence and busi-ness success.

Still reeling from the corporate accounting scandals of the early 2000s, such as Enron and WorldCom, we hoped that *Moral Intelligence* would serve as a call to action for leaders to "do the right thing" for their stakeholders and themselves. Since the initial publication of *Moral Intelligence* six years ago, countless leaders have heeded that call to action. Sadly, other leaders continue to bury their moral compasses, choosing greed over integrity. In some cases, the choice to ignore moral principles and values has proved nearly catastrophic: By the fall of 2008, the global economy was about to implode. Much of the blame—though certainly not all—goes to financial services industry leaders who prioritized short-term financial gain for themselves and their firms over everything else, including their responsibility to customers, employees, and the survival of nations.

Mark Sheffert, Chairman and CEO of Manchester Companies, headquartered in Minneapolis, Minnesota, offers this perspective regarding the moral issues that underlie the financial crisis and global recession:

> I truly believe in my heart of hearts that the underpinning in the financial crisis was greed, power, and corruption with people grabbing for their unfair share of the economic pie. Financial institutions, Wall Street, Main Street, investors, rating agencies, people selling, people buying. Whether it was Ponzi schemes or backdating stock options or something else, it didn't matter. It was all justified somehow by the notion that 'I deserve it'. The country has lost its moral compass. The Johnson Institute did a study recently that revealed 56% of MBA students and 43% of law students admit they cheat, and 93% of them say cheating is justified, and more than 90% said they have no moral dilemma about doing so. Remember, these young cheaters and liars are our business leaders, politicians, and professionals of the future. Greed and lack of ethics have permeated every aspect of our society and it's a systemic issue. This greed and lack of ethics has resulted in an upside-down economy with massive unemployment, and it's not going to get better soon for a lot of reasons. Many companies went out of business and aren't even here to employ someone. Starting businesses in this environment is nearly impossible. Big companies are doing more with less. Six percent of the nation's GDP is related to the cost of dealing with fraudulent behavior. If your company generates $100 million in revenue, then your company is spending $6 million per year dealing with fraud and the lack of ethics.

Kim Sharan, chief marketing officer and President Financial Planning and Wealth Strategies for Ameriprise Financial, underscores Mark Sheffert's analysis of the financial costs of ignoring moral principles:

> Mistrust in the marketplace is very high. How do you reinforce to the consumer[s] that you're focused on doing what's right for them when every day there is a new scandal or fraud in the news? What has happened over the past three to five years is it has gotten harder to rise above the noise. I'm sure what happened to Enron at the turn of the century was felt by every energy company. What happened with Lehman and Bernie Madoff has created a halo effect that is felt by every company and everyone in the financial services industry. Because of the proliferation of social media, the viral nature of the situation has resulted in a high degree of mistrust of the entire [financial services] industry.

> For us at Ameriprise, we have to figure out how to show our clients that we have acted with integrity and excellence in all we do, doing the right thing for the consumer at every turn—all of that is critical. At the heart of building a brand is taking charge of delivering a great experience for the consumer. Every advisor and every employee has to deliver on certain principles every time. Those principles are *actively caring about the client, behaving with integrity, standing up for what is right,* and *accepting responsibility for serving them.* When it comes to moral intelligence, all of us have to be very real. It's always been critical for sustainable success, but it's more obvious now than at any other time.

With this edition of the book, *Moral Intelligence 2.0,* we intend to underscore the message that moral competence is critical not only to the success of individual leaders and business, but [also] to the survival of the global economy. For today's leaders, it is even more clear that moral competence is not a "nice to have;" it is a "must have."

The integrity crises of the first decade of the 21st century have been devastating. But they have not yet convinced enough leaders of the importance of morally intelligent leadership. How many wake-up calls do leaders need to get the message that their ultimate success depends on moral leadership? Will leaders get another chance to do the right thing? Given the precarious nature of today's global economy, we fear that this wake-up call to choose integrity over greed might very well be our last.

In a spring 2009 conversation with author Doug Lennick, American Express CEO Ken Chenault observed, "Business has focused too much on capitalism and profit versus capitalism and societal good." If the CEO of an iconic institution such as American Express thinks business should be paying a lot more attention to moral values, how can any leader afford to ignore the call to put moral values at the center of what they do? Leaders must hold themselves to a high standard, a *morally intelligent* standard.

Moral intelligence is not an issue only for American business leaders. It is a universal leadership imperative. For example, leaders at Deutsche Post, a global mail and logistics services provider, continually reinforce the importance of its corporate values: *to deliver excellent quality, to make our customers successful, to foster openness, to follow clear priorities, to be entrepreneurial, to act with integrity, and to accept social responsibility.* Deutsche Post has weathered tough times, including a large layoff in its U.S. based workforce in November 2008 as the world began to experience the impact of the financial crisis and a global recession. After suffering revenue losses in 2009, Deutsche Post rebounded in 2010 with 13.9% consolidated revenue growth by the end of the third quarter. It is no coincidence that Deutsche Post's commitment to its values and moral principles has contributed to its ongoing financial success.

Back in the mid-1990s, well before the early 2000 corporate accounting scandals, well before the dot.com bubble burst, and before we could have even imagined the global financial crisis that exploded in 2008, we had a conversation both authors vividly recall. Doug was then executive vice president, Advice and Retail Distribution for American Express Financial Advisors. Doug was well known for developing a high-performing sales force of approximately 10,000 financial advisors and was an early champion of emotional intelligence skills training at American Express. Fred, a pioneer in the field of executive coaching, was a psychologist and co-founder of a leading executive development company and then as now, actively engaged in helping senior executives improve their personal performance as leaders.

As we talked, we realized that we had some common ideas about the ingredients of high performance that we were both struggling to conceptualize. We agreed on the importance of emotional intelligence—the constellation of self-awareness, self-management, social awareness, and relationship management skills that are now commonly regarded as critical to success in the workplace. We discovered, though, that neither of us thought emotional intelligence was sufficient to assure consistent, long-term performance.

In the course of nearly 30 years, we had collectively worked as business executives, entrepreneurs, and leadership consultants to chief executives and senior leaders of Fortune 500 companies, large privately held companies, and start-ups. We had each coached hundreds of leaders. The most successful of them all seemed to have something in common that went beyond insight, discipline, or interpersonal skill. We also spoke about noted public figures with masterful emotional intelligence skills who would sway like reeds in the wind when faced with morally loaded decisions. We hypothesized that there was something more basic than emotional intelligence skills—a kind of moral compass—that seemed to us to be at the heart of long-lasting business success. Our ideas became the focus of the first edition of *Moral Intelligence*. In retrospect, we may have been ahead of our time: Given the financial crises of the late 2000s, our initial insights about the central importance of moral intelligence to business success seem more relevant than ever.

We offer this book as a roadmap for leaders to find and follow their moral compasses. In the pages ahead, you will hear from leaders who are committed to morally intelligent behavior. Although we believe that doing the right thing is right for its own sake, recent history has demonstrated that leaders who follow their moral compasses can find that it is the right thing for their organizations as well. In this book, we hope you find the tools to become the best leader you can be. You—and your organization—deserve nothing less.

Leaders Interviewed

We are deeply indebted to the large group of leaders who contributed to our thinking and research. Our interview subjects were especially generous with their time and candid in their self-assessments.

Douglas Baker	CEO, Ecolab Inc.
Dan Brettler	CEO and Chairman, Car Toys, Inc.
Kenneth Chenault	CEO and Chairman, American Express Company
Paul Clayton	Former CEO, Jamba Juice
Stan Dardis	CEO and President, Bremer Financial Corporation (retired)
Lon Dolber	President, American Portfolio Financial Services
Jeff Ettinger	CEO, Hormel Foods
Lynn Fantom	CEO, ID Media
Paul Fribourg	CEO and Chairman, Conti-Group Companies
Peter Georgescu	Chairman Emeritus, Young & Rubicam
Harvey Golub	Director, Campbell's Soup Company and Chairman and CEO (retired), American Express Company
Brian Hall	Former CEO, Thomson Legal & Regulatory Group

Don Hall, Jr.	CEO and Vice Chairman, Hallmark Cards
Dick Harrington	Chairman of The Cue Ball Group, former CEO, The Thomson Corporation
Brian Heath	Owner, Grape Creek Vineyards
David Hubers	CEO (retired), American Express Financial Advisors
Mike Hughes	President, Safeco Insurance
Sally Jewell	CEO, REI
Ken Kaess	Former CEO, DDB Worldwide, now deceased
David Kenny	President and Director, Akamai Technologies
Ken Krei	President Wealth Management Group, M&I Bank
Mike LaRocco	President and CEO, Fireman's Fund Insurance
Dale Larson	Owner and Chairman, Larson Manufacturing
Dan May	President, Advisor Net
Rowland Moriarty, Ph.D.	CEO and Chairman, Cubex Corporation; Founding Director, Staples; Founding Director, PetsMart
Don MacPherson	President, Modern Survey
Mark Oja	CEO, ACTIVEAID
Larry Pinnt	Chairman, Cascade Natural Gas
Michael Phillips	Former Chairman, The Russell Investment Group
Keith Reinhard	Former Chairman, DDB Worldwide
John Schlifske	President and CEO, Northwestern Mutual
Spenser Segal	CEO, ActiFi
Mayo Shattuck	CEO and Chairman, Constellation Energy
Mark Sheffert	Chairman and CEO, Manchester Companies
Dale Sperling	Former CEO, Unico Real Estate Company
Jay Sleiter	Former CEO and Chairman, BWBR Architects
Lynn Sontag	President, Menttium Corporation
Kim Vappie	CEO, Menttium Corporation
Charlie Zelle	CEO and Chairman, Jefferson Bus Lines
Roger Arnold	EVP and Chief Distribution Officer, Wealth Enhancement Group LLC

Brenda Blake	Senior Vice President, Global Leadership; Marketing, American Express
Walt Bradley	Financial Advisor, Thrivent Financial for Lutherans
Sam Bronfman	Former Senior Vice President, Seagrams, Inc.
George Brushaber	Former President, Bethel University
Cindy Carlson	Former President, Capital Professional Advisors
Michael Connolly	Operating Partner, Legal Tube; Managing Partner, Atlas Digital Partners; Chairman, Table Trac
Dave Edwards	Senior Vice President, Client Experience, TIAA Creft
Patrick Grace	Former Senior Vice President, The Grace Corporation
M'Lynn Hoefer	Principal, Tapaidra
Lori Kaiser	Former Senior Vice President, Cray Computer Co.
Gary Kessler	Senior Vice President of Human Resources, Honda America
Diane Kozlak	Vice President Sales, Modern Survey
Karen Lane	Former Governor's Staff, State of Washington
Harvey Leuning	Associate Pastor, Gloria Dei Lutheran Church, St. Paul, MN
Ann Levinson	Deputy Director, Seattle Monorail Authority
Pam Moret	Senior Vice President, Strategic Development, Thrivent Financial for Lutherans
Gary O'Hagan	President of Coaches Division, IMG
Carla Paulson	EVP, Chief Human Resources Officer, Bremer Financial Group
Tom Perrine	Senior Vice President IT, Cardinal Health
Mark Phillips	SVP Distribution, UnitedHealthcare Medicare and Retirement (United Health Group)
David Risher	Former Senior Vice President, Amazon.com
Pat Roraback	Senior Vice President, M&I Bank
Jim Ruddy	Former CLO, Safeco Insurance (Retired)
Joe Schlidt	Private Family Office Director, Godfrey & Kahn SC
Tom Schinke	Financial Advisor, Thrivent Financial for Lutherans

Kim Sharan	President Financial Planning and Wealth Strategies and Chief Marketing Officer, Ameriprise Financial
Ben Smith	Partner, Lennick Aberman Group; former CEO, American Partners Bank
Caroline Stockdale	SVP and Chief Talent Officer, Medtronic
Jim Thomsen	Senior Vice President of Distribution, Thrivent Financial for Lutherans
Michael Wilson	Chief Operating Officer, Comerica Wealth Management
Mike Woodward	Senior Vice President, Marketing & Communications, Ducks Unlimited

Thought Partners

We greatly appreciate our many colleagues and mentors whose input has helped sharpen our thinking about the moral dimensions of leadership. They include the following:

Rick Aberman, Ph.D.	Psychologist, emotional intelligence expert, and co-author of *Why Good Coaches Quit—and How You Can Stay in the Game*
Reuven Bar-On, Ph.D.	University of Texas Medical Branch, in the Department of Psychiatry and Behavioral Sciences, where he directs research in emotional and social intelligence
Richard Boyatzis, Ph.D.	Professor and Chair of the Department of Organizational Behavior at the Weatherhead School of Management at Case Western Reserve University, and co-author of *Primal Leadership: Realizing the Power of Emotional Intelligence*
Kate Cannon	President, Kate Cannon and Associates
Robert Caplan, Ph.D.	Director, Beach Cities Health District, an organization charged with promoting mental and physical wellness in three adjacent communities in Southern California

Cary Cherniss, Ph.D.	Director of the Rutgers University Organizational Psychology Program, professor of Applied Psychology and co-author of *The Emotionally Intelligent Workplace*
Stephen Covey, Ph.D.	Author of *The 7 Habits of Highly Effective People* whose conversations with Doug in the early 1990s reinforced early versions of our alignment model
Vanessa Druskat	Associate Professor, University of New Hampshire, Whittemore School of Business and Economics
Robert Emmerling, Ph.D.	Consultant and researcher specializing in the application of emotional intelligence concepts in the workplace
Jim Garrison	President and co-founder (with Mikail Gorbalhev) of the State of the World Forum and author of *America as Empire*
Roy Geer, Ph.D.	Psychologist, consultant, and co-author (with Doug Lennick) of *How to Get What You Want and Remain True to Yourself*
Daniel Goleman, Ph.D.	Co-director of the Consortium for Research on Emotional Intelligence in Organizations at Rutgers University, author of *Emotional Intelligence*, *Working with Emotional Intelligence*, and co-author of *Primal Leadership: Realizing the Power of Emotional Intelligence*
Marilyn Gowing, Ph.D.	Vice President for Public Sector Consulting and Services with the Washington office of AON Consulting
Darryl Grigg, Ph.D.	Psychologist
Jennifer Hugstad-Vaa, Ph.D.	Professor, St. Mary's University Minnesota
Dorothy Hutcheson	Head of School, Nightingale-Bamford School for Girls
Ruth Jacobs	Director of Research and Technology at McClelland Center for Research and Initiatives, The Hay Group

Stuart Kantor, Ph.D.	Co-founder and principal of Red Oak Consulting, an executive development firm
Stephen Kelner, Jr.	Global Knowledge Manager, Egon Zehnder International, Inc.
David Kidd	Partner, Egon Zehnder International, Inc.
Carol Keers	Co-founder, Change Masters, Inc.
Art Kleiner	Editor-in-Chief, *Strategy + Business Magazine*
Kathy Kram, Ph.D.	Professor of Organizational Behavior at the Boston University School of Management
Richard Leider	Founding partner of The Inventure Group and author of *Repacking Your Bags, the Power of Purpose, and Life Skills*
Jim Loehr, Ph.D.	Performance psychologist and co-author of *The Power of Full Engagement: Managing Energy, Not Time, Is the Key to High Performance and Personal Renewal* and author of *Stress for Success*
Fred Luskin, Ph.D.	Senior Fellow at the Stanford Center on Conflict and Negotiation, co-founder of the Stanford University Forgiveness Project, and author of *Forgive for Good*
Matthew Mangino	Consultant Director, Johnson & Johnson
Jim Mitchell	Executive Fellow, Leadership at the Center for Ethical Business Cultures in Minneapolis
Tom Mungavan	President and co-founder, Change Masters, Inc.
John Nicolay, MBA	MBA instructor, University of Minnesota
Hy Pomerance, Ph.D.	Co-founder and principal of Red Oak Consulting, an executive development firm
Richard Price, Ph.D.	Professor of Psychology and Business Administration at the University of Michigan, and Senior Research Scientist at the Institute for Social Research
Helen Reiess, M.D.	Director, Empathy Research and Training, Associate Clinical Professor, Harvard Medical School
Fabio Sala, Ph.D.	Associate Director, Learning and Development, Millennium Pharmaceuticals, Inc.

Jeffrey Schwartz	Psychiatrist, neuroscientist, and author, *The Mind and the Brain: Neuroplasticity and the Power of Mental Force,* Harper Perennial, 2003
Tony Schwartz	Co-author of *The Art of the Deal* and *The Power of Full Engagement: Managing Energy, Not Time, Is the Key to High Performance and Personal Renewal* and author of *What Really Matters: Searching for Wisdom in America*
Hersh Shefrin, Ph.D.	Professor of Finance at the Leavey School of Business, Santa Clara University, and author of *Beyond Greed and Fear*
Judy Skoglund	Partner, Lennick Aberman Group
Lyle Spencer, Ph.D.	President, Spencer Research and Technology, co-founder of Competency International, Cybertroncis Research Fellows, Director, Human Resource Technologies
Thérèse Jacobs Stewart, Ph.D.	Master Psychologist
Jeff Stiefler	Former CEO, Digital Insights
Redford Williams, Ph.D.	Professor of Psychiatry and Behavioral Sciences, Professor of Medicine, and Director of the Behavioral Medicine Research Center at Duke University Medical Center
Larry Wilson	Founder of Wilson Learning and Pecos River Learning Center, author of *The One Minute Sales Person and Changing the Game: The New Way to Sell* and co-author of *Stop Selling, Start Partnering*
Lauris Woolford	EVP, Fifth Third Bank

PART I

MORAL INTELLIGENCE

1

Good Business

Jim Thomsen, senior vice president of Member Services for Thrivent Financial, a membership-based financial services company, recalls the financial meltdown in September 2008 all too well: "I was really mad at our industry," Jim said, "but initially I wasn't worried about our company." Thrivent's solid standing compared to its competitors at the end of 2008 was well earned. In the several years leading up to the economic crisis, when "everything was hot," some members of Thrivent's field sales force had put a lot of pressure on company management and the Thrivent Bank to be more aggressive and to do some of the things other firms were doing. But Thrivent management resisted.

> **When it came to home lending, for example, we stayed with the fundamentals that have worked over time. We actually required things like 20% down payments for homes, and we used independent appraisers to determine property values. We had no subprime mortgages in our portfolio. It was**

hard to maintain that position when so many other companies were being aggressive and making lots of money doing so, but it was the right thing to do, and we did the right thing.

Jim thought that Thrivent had dodged a bullet thanks to its more conservative investment practices. But not completely. As Jim describes it

It was near the end of 2008. I had just been through a week where our executive team had been meeting, and we had just gotten a lot of good news. We had very little exposure to Lehman. We were well capitalized. We had no reliance on short-term debt. We were in a really strong position and prepared to weather a very difficult storm. I was feeling pretty good.

Later that evening, Jim attended a charity event at the famous Depot in downtown Minneapolis.

I was walking around the silent auction with a neighbor of mine, and he introduced me to an acquaintance of his who was an executive with another company. He asked me what I did for a living. I told him I was in the financial services industry, and he said, 'That used to be an honorable profession!' When he said that it was like a slap in the face. That comment to me was really an eye opener. I had been thinking we were immune because we had done the right thing, but I realized then we were going to be judged guilty by association. And I thought 'If I'm feeling this way, [then] the men and women meeting with our clients every day must really be feeling it.'

Jim realized in that moment that Thrivent would have to work hard to differentiate itself from its industry peers:

My personal reputation and the reputation of the firm [were] taken into the cesspool along with our industry. This was very hard on our employees and our representatives, and I realized I personally needed to take responsibility and serve their needs for information and understanding. I had to support our representatives and give them the confidence to be proactive and make contact with their clients and our members. Other executives and I made sure our representatives understood why our clients could and should have confidence in the company and their representative. A lot of advisors in the industry went into hiding, but we went on the offensive and increased our communication and contact with clients.

To a large degree, the strategy Jim and his fellow Thrivent executives adopted in the wake of the financial crisis has been successful. "We've actually had three of our best years ever," says Jim, *"because we had the courage not to follow the lemmings.* We really do make decisions with the best long-term interests of our clients in mind."

Jim's biggest fear today? "I worry that the world has short-term memories. Some of the leaders who took the industry down are gone, but I'm seeing some of the same behavior again that hurt the industry."

Moral Stupidity Act 1

Jim Thomsen's fear is well taken. In the last ten years, the corporate landscape has been through two waves of major financial misdeeds. The first part of the decade was marked by corporate accounting scandals that all had their roots in moral weakness on the part of corporate executives:

Former energy company Enron became the poster child for corporate corruption in 2001 when it was revealed that its financial status was fabricated through deliberate and extensive accounting fraud. In May 2006, former CEOs Ken Lay and Jeffrey Skilling were convicted of criminal fraud and conspiracy. In a dramatic twist, Ken Lay died—before he could be sentenced—in July 2006 of "natural causes" related to cardiovascular disease. In October 2006, Skilling was sentenced to 24 years and four months in prison. Ex-Enron CFO Andrew Fastow had pleaded guilty to fraud in 2004 in exchange for a ten-year prison sentence. In November 2006, Enron executives Andrew Fastow and his former chief aide Michael Kopper, received sharply reduced sentences because of their cooperation with prosecutors to help convict Ken Lay and Jeffrey Skilling. Between 2004 and the end of 2009, Enron Creditors Recovery Corporation paid out about $21.6 billion to Enron's creditors and litigation related to Enron's collapse continues.

In July 2004, cable company Adelphia founder and former CEO, John Rigas, and his son Timothy were found guilty of conspiracy, securities fraud, and bank fraud. Charges against them included concealing $2.3 billion in loans and embezzling, bankrupting what was then the nation's fifth-largest cable company.

In 2004, the Securities and Exchange Commission charged Lucent Technologies (later acquired by French telecommunications equipment-maker Alcatel) with fraudulently recognizing more than $1 billion in revenues and $470 million in pretax income during fiscal 2000. It also charged individual executives for their alleged roles in the case. Lucent settled the SEC Enforcement Action in May 2004, paying a $25 million penalty. Ten executives who were charged in the matter reached individual settlements involving sizable penalties over the course of the ensuing two years.

In 2005, HealthSouth former CEO Richard Scrushy was acquitted in a $2.5 billion fraud scheme to overstate earnings and inflate stock prices during a period between 1996 and 2002. The acquittal was surprising to many because there had been extensive testimony that he was knowledgeable about the fraud, and because 15 former executives had already pleaded guilty and a 16th had been convicted by jurors. But Scrushy's legal woes were not over. In August 2006, the Alabama Supreme Court ruled that Scrushy must repay $48.8 million in bonuses he received during the period of the fraud— at a time when the company was sustaining massive operating losses.

In 2006, antivirus and security software provider McAfee fired President Kevin Weiss, and its CEO and Chairman George Samenuk retired after a stock options investigation found accounting problems required financial restatements.

David C. Wittig, the former CEO of Kansas utility company Westar Energy, Inc., was sentenced in April 2006 to 18 years in prison for conspiracy, wire fraud, money laundering, and circumventing internal controls. Wittig served 13 months in prison before he was released on bond in January 2007, following a Federal appeals court reversal of several convictions.

Moral intelligence could have kept each of these companies, and their leaders, out of the courts. Instead companies, employees, and shareholders all suffered. Despite the damage caused by this raft of corporate corruption, despite the photos of executives being carried off in handcuffs, it seems that corporate America still hasn't learned the lessons of moral intelligence. Such corporate scandals represent just the tip of the iceberg for bad business behavior.

Financial Services Take the Stage

Nowhere has the absence of moral competence been more glaring than in the financial services industry. Looking at financial services with a moral lens, a financial services firm is supposed to exist to serve the financial needs of its clients, thereby generating profits for itself. But during the last decade, many financial services firms turned that mission on its head. It certainly appears they prioritized their own financial gain, often at the expense of the clients whose financial objectives they had a responsibility to serve. In looking back over the last few years, Ken Krei, president of the Wealth Management Group of M&I Bank observes:

> **There's been a great deal of momentum for the industry to sell the product that is easiest to sell, bonds, now and option rate securities earlier. Companies try to drive revenue with this momentum, but it hurts the seller eventually because eventually what's easiest to sell is not necessarily what's best for the buyer.**

Dale Larson, CEO and president of Larson Manufacturing Company, the largest U.S maker of storm doors, echoes Krei's sense about Wall Street's priorities:

> **I'm kind of cynical about Wall Street. They think the more complicated they make the product, the easier it is to sell and everyone will think they're smarter than anybody else. I think the derivative investments were way over the top. I think a lot of people knew what they were selling and didn't care. In the 1950s, only 6% of profits were made by financial institutions. Now it's about 35%, so a lot of people are making money by passing paper around.**

By fall of 2008, a growing number of industry observers were convinced that greedy executives in the financial services industry were not just cheating individual clients—they were likely major perpetrators of a massive economic crisis that threatened to take down the entire global economy. In contrast to the fate of the previous generation of corporate lawbreakers, most architects of the worst financial downturn since the Great Depression of the 1920s and 1930s have so far escaped prosecution or any major sanctions.

Former mortgage lender Countrywide CEO Angelo Mozilo has been widely reported in the media as a prime suspect in the economic crisis that began to brew by 2007. On June 4, 2009, the SEC filed charges against Mozilo and two other Countrywide executives. According to an October 15, 2010 Securities and Exchange (SEC) press release:

> **...they[Countrywide executives] failed to disclose to investors the significant credit risk that Countrywide was taking on as a result of its efforts to build and maintain market share. Investors were misled by representations assuring them that Countrywide was primarily a prime quality mortgage lender that had avoided the excesses of its competitors. In reality, Countrywide was writing increasingly risky loans and its senior executives knew that defaults and delinquencies in its servicing portfolio as well as the loans it packaged and sold as mortgage-backed securities would rise as a result.**

The SEC's complaint further alleged that Mozilo engaged in insider trading in the securities of Countrywide by establishing four 10b5-1 sales plans in October, November, and December 2006, while he was aware of material, nonpublic information concerning Countrywide's increasing credit risk and the risk regarding the poor expected performance of Countrywide-originated loans.[1]

In September 2010, *Daily Finance* reported the following:

> **During the 2008 mortgage meltdown, Mozilo's remarkable copper-colored visage became synonymous with executive excess. In addition to his impressive yearly salary and company-funded memberships at three country clubs, Mozilo also received millions of dollars in Countrywide stock, more than $406 million of which he liquidated to increase his bottom line. Over $140 million worth of these shares went on the block in 2006 and 2007.**

While Mozilo was getting rid of his Countrywide shares, the company was also loosening its mortgage guidelines, getting deeper and deeper into the risky subprime mortgages that later proved its downfall. These relaxed standards proved very helpful to Mozilo's friends—including Ed McMahon, Senator Christopher Dodd, and dozens of Fannie Mae employees—who received sweetheart mortgage deals from Countrywide. They were less helpful to stockholders, who were left holding the bag when Countrywide failed.[2]

In October 2010, Mozilo avoided trial on charges of fraud and insider trading by striking a deal to pay the SEC $67.5 million, the largest sum ever paid by a public firm senior executive in an SEC case. Those funds will be used to help repay harmed investors.

Prior to its collapse and sale to JPMorganChase in 2008, former financial giant Bear Stearns had been recognized multiple times as the "Most Admired" securities firm in *Fortune* magazine's "America's Most Admired Companies" survey, and second overall in the security firm section. The annual survey is a prestigious ranking based on employee talent, quality of risk management, and business innovation. *Fortune* magazine reported that in July 2007, while two Bear Stearns hedge funds holding toxic mortgage-backed securities were nearing collapse, CEO James "Jimmy" Cayne was playing bridge in Nashville. In March 2008, while the company was on the verge of bankruptcy, Cayne was again playing bridge—this time in Detroit. Two weeks later, right after JPMorgan raised its bid for the company, Cayne sold all his equity in the company, earning $60 million. Bear Stearns clients were not so lucky. Cayne later admitted some responsibility for the downfall of the once stellar firm. "I didn't stop it. I didn't rein in the leverage," he told *Fortune* magazine.[3]

According to Peter Chapman, author of a 2010 history of Lehman Brothers, "Lehman Brothers died when over 150 years later a once proud institution was caught peddling junk to the world."[4] Lehman's former CEO Dick Fuld, who presided over the death of one of Wall Street's most esteemed firms, has infuriated former clients and the general public alike. Fuld is especially reviled for refusing to apologize for his responsibility for the Lehman bankruptcy (the largest in U.S. history with $613 billion in outstanding debt), As one commentator pointed out "Even Bernie Madoff said he was sorry."[5]

Ken Lewis, former CEO of Bank of America, who helped orchestrate the acquisition of Merrill Lynch, was reported by numerous media outlets to have concealed information about huge bonuses that subsequently went to Merrill employees—bonuses funded by federal TARP funds. In February 2010, following an investigation by the SEC and New York Attorney General Andrew Cuomo, Cuomo sued Bank of America for defrauding investors and the government when buying Merrill Lynch & Co when it failed to disclose the Merrill bonus agreement. The bank agreed to pay a $150 million fine to settle a related lawsuit by U.S. regulators.[6]

Goldman Sachs initially seemed like the shining exception to the epidemic of greed that had unraveled other investment firms such as Lehman, Bear Stearns, and Merrill Lynch. But it may turn out Goldman Sachs is not immune to the moral lapses that have infected so many other firms. While the rest of the financial services industry might have felt reassured by Goldman Sachs' capability to pay out big bonuses in the midst of epic Wall Street failures, United States government officials were puzzled about its success. On April 16, 2010, the Securities and Exchange Commission charged Goldman Sachs with fraud in structuring and marketing collateralized debt obligations (CDOs) tied to subprime mortgages. According to the SEC announcement:

The SEC alleges that Goldman Sachs structured and marketed a synthetic collateralized debt obligation (CDO) that hinged on the performance of subprime residential mortgage-backed securities (RMBS). Goldman Sachs failed to

disclose to investors vital information about the CDO, in particular the role that a major hedge fund played in the portfolio selection process and the fact that the hedge fund had taken a short position against the CDO.

"The product was new and complex but the deception and conflicts are old and simple," said Robert Khuzami, director of the Division of Enforcement. "Goldman wrongly permitted a client that was betting against the mortgage market to heavily influence which mortgage securities to include in an investment portfolio, while telling other investors that the securities were selected by an independent, objective third party."

Kenneth Lench, chief of the SEC's Structured and New Products Unit, added, "The SEC continues to investigate the practices of investment banks and others involved in the securitization of complex financial products tied to the U.S. housing market as it was beginning to show signs of distress."

The SEC alleges that one of the world's largest hedge funds, Paulson & Co., paid Goldman Sachs to structure a transaction in which Paulson & Co. could take short positions against mortgage securities chosen by Paulson & Co. based on a belief that the securities would experience credit events.

According to the SEC's complaint, filed in U.S. District Court for the Southern District of New York, the marketing materials for the CDO known as ABACUS 2007-AC1 (ABACUS) all represented that the RMBS portfolio underlying the CDO was selected by ACA Management LLC (ACA), a third party with expertise in analyzing credit risk in RMBS. The SEC alleges that undisclosed in the marketing materials and unbeknownst to investors, the Paulson & Co. hedge fund, which was poised to benefit if the RMBS defaulted, played a significant role in selecting which RMBS should make up the portfolio.

The SEC's complaint alleges that after participating in the portfolio selection, Paulson & Co. effectively shorted the RMBS portfolio it helped select by entering into credit default swaps (CDS) with Goldman Sachs to buy protection on specific layers of the ABACUS capital structure. Given that financial short interest, Paulson & Co. had an economic incentive to select RMBS that it expected to experience credit events in the near future. Goldman Sachs did not disclose Paulson & Co.'s short position or its role in the collateral selection process in the term sheet, flip book, offering memorandum, or other marketing materials provided to investors.

The SEC alleges that Goldman Sachs Vice President Fabrice Tourre was principally responsible for ABACUS 2007-AC1. Tourre structured the transaction, prepared the marketing materials, and communicated directly with investors. Tourre allegedly knew of Paulson & Co.'s undisclosed short interest and role in the collateral selection process. In addition, he allegedly misled ACA into believing that Paulson & Co. invested approximately $200 million in the equity of ABACUS, indicating that Paulson & Co.'s interests in the collateral selection process were closely aligned with ACA's interests. In reality, however, their interests were sharply conflicting.

According to the SEC's complaint, the deal closed on April 26, 2007, and Paulson & Co. paid Goldman Sachs approximately $15 million for structuring and marketing ABACUS. By Oct. 24, 2007, 83% of the RMBS in the ABACUS portfolio had been downgraded and 17% were on negative watch. By Jan. 29, 2008, 99% of the portfolio had been downgraded. Investors in the liabilities of ABACUS are alleged to have lost more than $1 billion.[7]

In the wake of the SEC charges, on April 27, 2010, Goldman Sachs was called to testify before the Senate Permanent Subcommittee on Investigations because of concern that Goldman Sachs had been "setting up the firm's own securities to fail and betting secretly against those securities, or helping clients do so."[8]

Behavior such as that alleged against Goldman Sachs may not be illegal, but according to many industry leaders, it is certainly unethical. Christopher Whalen, managing director of financial research firm Institutional Risk Analytics, summed up the significance of the SEC charges against Goldman Sachs in this way: "Once upon a time, Wall Street firms protected clients. This litigation exposes the cynical, savage culture of Wall Street that allows a dealer to commit fraud on one customer to benefit another."[9]

Although Dan May, president of AdvisorNet Financial, a leading U.S. distributor of financial products, believes, "It's appalling to think that firms in the industry with 150-year reputations responded as they did with the pressure to make more money." He also insists that individual financial advisors, not just big firms, bear some of the responsibility for unethical sales practices:

> **I do believe financial advisors have some culpability. There's no way we can control the market but advisors could have better prepared people for the certainty of uncertainty. Advisors have to ask [critical] questions and must have the integrity to lose a client if it means doing the right thing. We have to expect more out of ourselves. We have to make sure this never happens again.**

More Fallout

But it isn't only Wall Street's customer base, the investor, that has suffered from greed in the financial services industry. As of 2011 in New York State alone, the economic collapse will have caused the loss of almost 300,000 jobs in the financial sector, with most of them focused in the combined sales and related/office and administrative support occupational category. In other words, lower-paid employees in financial services firms have borne the brunt of the mistakes made by their highly compensated superiors.[10]

When it comes to causing a potentially catastrophic meltdown of the global economy, you could argue there is a lot of blame to go around: greedy Wall Street executives, corrupt politicians, and derelict regulators. If all these allegations prove to be true, it will be obvious that what they all have in common is a shortage of moral competence. And though the jury is still out on the legal responsibility of numerous financial industry leaders for exposing all of us to an economic catastrophe, one thing is undeniably clear: The global financial woes we are still experiencing could not have happened if more financial industry leaders had been paying attention to the moral consequences of their business decisions. And it's also clear that the economic crisis in which we are still engaged is not the responsibility of a "few bad apples." What has led us to the brink of economic disaster is more like an epidemic of moral incompetence by business leaders, regulators, politicians, and yes, even consumers. But it is our business leaders who bear special responsibility for managing their enterprises within a moral framework. What has gone wrong? It's as though corporate leaders have turned the switch off on their moral intelligence. There's been a major power failure, and only a return to moral principles by our nation's corporate leaders can turn the lights back on. Only a renewed emphasis on the importance of moral intelligence will restore public confidence in big business in general, and in the financial services industry in particular.

What Does Moral Leadership Look Like?

Despite the crowd of morally compromised executives who have dominated the news of the last decade, there are many examples of morally intelligent leaders to inspire us. Thrivent's Jim Thomsen, whom we met at the beginning of the chapter, illustrates the importance of doing the right thing in the face of pressure to "follow the lemmings." Such moral courage doesn't develop overnight. Most successful leaders are morally gifted, but few of them are moral geniuses. They all make mistakes from time to time and, earlier in their careers, they typically made moral mistakes more often. But because of their high moral intelligence, they were quick studies. They held themselves accountable for their moral lapses, learned from them, and moved on. Consider Jay Coughlan's story. Today, Coughlan is chairman and CEO of XATA and until 2005, was CEO of Lawson Software, Minnesota's largest software company. But no one would have predicted his rise to that top spot back in 1998 after he fell asleep while driving intoxicated, causing a devastating accident that left him seriously injured and his father dead. The accident was the beginning of a remarkable personal transformation marked by a reawakening of his religious faith, a stronger relationship with his family and involvement in the community, and an intensive commitment to Lawson. Coughlan pleaded guilty to vehicular homicide and was sentenced to one month in jail, five months of house arrest, and ten years of probation. But because of Coughlan's honesty and the support of the community, the judge reduced his offense to a misdemeanor after he had served more than three months of his sentence. Meanwhile, during his absence from Lawson, the health care division that Coughlan had launched was flourishing. "That's when I learned I actually was successful as a leader," he told *The Wall Street Journal*, "when you can pull yourself out of the machine and it can still run."[11]

Coughlan's financial results were impressive and likely were the most significant factor in his subsequent promotions. The accident would have been a career-ending event for most people in Coughlan's shoes, but his response to the accident was extraordinary. "Jay, to his credit, stood right up and took responsibility; there was no hesitation," says Richard Lawson, the company's co-founder and co-chairman of the Board of Directors. "To me that is what counts. It's not the mistakes you make, it's how you react to those mistakes."

Gary O'Hagan's story offers yet more evidence of how adversity can contribute to our growth as moral leaders. Gary O'Hagan is president of the Coaches Division of the International Management Group, the world's largest sports marketing and talent representation agency.

Gary is an intense, competitive, and imposing man who looks like the football player he once was. As a young man, he was drafted, then cut by the San Francisco 49ers, and then picked up and cut by the New York Jets. Gary was devastated but determined to find another route to high achievement. He got a job as a financial trader with Solomon Brothers and attended law-school classes every weekday night. When his grandfather died, Gary was expected to attend the wake, the funeral, and represent the agency. Gary was anxious about falling behind at work and school, so he thought he could attend the funeral, make a quick appearance at the after-funeral lunch, after which he'd head back to work. But when he got to the restaurant, the significance of his family's loss finally registered, and Gary realized that his priorities were out of whack. He called his boss and told him he wasn't coming in to work. His boss was concerned and upset, but Gary stayed. He knew that if he didn't have the compassion to help his family in that moment, he would never amount to much either personally or professionally.

Lynn Fantom, CEO of ID Media, the largest direct response media service company in the United States, is another morally gifted leader. It is late in the afternoon one cool spring day when Lynn walks back to her corner office in a New York City skyscraper. The Empire State Building is visible out one window, the Met Life and Flat Iron building out the other. Lynn barely notices the spectacular view. She goes straight to her desk and opens an email from a human resources manager at her parent company, Interpublic. HR, it seems, is worried about how overloaded she is. They wonder if it is the best use of her time to respond to the employee comments and questions she gets on the "Ask Lynn" column on the company's intranet. Her public relations folks are also concerned about her schedule. They've recommended that she stop spending precious time posting her thoughts on media and marketing trends on the intranet. But Lynn thinks her personal responses to employees are an important part of the ID Media culture. She thinks that "Ask Lynn" gives her an opportunity to demonstrate that she cares about her workforce. She thinks that she has a responsibility to her workforce to share her business insights. To her, it's time well spent. Lynn is certain that employees like knowing they can ask her about anything and that she will give them an honest response. They also like knowing that she understands market trends and shares her understanding with them. "In exchange," says Lynn, "I really get their commitment to help us succeed." Lynn is sticking to her principles. She won't be giving up her intranet contributions anytime soon.

Jay, Lynn, and Gary are only a few of the many leaders we know with high moral intelligence, those who do their best to follow their moral compass. They do it because they believe it's the right thing to do. A funny thing happens when leaders consistently act in alignment with their principles and values: They typically produce consistently high performance almost any way you can measure it—gross sales, profits, talent retention, company reputation, and customer satisfaction. We think this is no accident. The successful leaders we know invariably attribute their accomplishments to a combination of their business savvy *and* their adherence to a moral code.

Doug Baker, CEO of Ecolab, a $4 billion dollar cleaning-products manufacturer, tells us that "living by my personal moral code is one of the key reasons I have this job." Ed Zore, former chairman and CEO of Northwestern Mutual, says, "Being moral—which to me means being fair, predictable, up-front, and not devious—all of this has been very important in my career. Everybody knows what I stand for. People know that we will never, ever be deceitful. We won't leave a nickel on the table, but in the end our word is our bond, and this is a real advantage in business." Gary Kessler, senior vice president of Human Resources, Administration and Corporate Affairs, at American Honda Motor Co., Inc., credits his principles and values for his career success. "I was VP of a business unit at Bausch and Lomb when I was 36 and at Honda when I was 45. I think I had the good fortune of working with people who recognized that I had sincerity and a conviction to do the right thing along the way."

A Special Kind of Intelligence

Most of the leaders you meet throughout the rest of this book are morally gifted. They are high in moral intelligence. Most of us are familiar with other kinds of intelligence, such as our cognitive intelligence (IQ) and our technical intelligence. IQ and technical intelligence are undeniably important to a leader's success. Leaders need to be good learners (IQ) who have expertise about their particular business (technical) areas. We call cognitive and technical intelligence *threshold competencies* because they are the price of admission to the leadership ranks. They are necessary but not sufficient for exceptional performance. They don't help you stand out from the competitive crowd because your rivals' leadership teams have as much basic intelligence and business savvy as you do.

Intelligence That Makes the Difference

To outpace your competition, you need to cultivate different kinds of intelligence we call *differentiating competencies. Moral intelligence* and *emotional intelligence* are two types of intelligence that are difficult for your competition to copy. Many corporate leaders ignore these differentiating competencies because they are often considered "soft skills" that are difficult to measure. In recent years, however, an increasing number of organizations have realized the performance benefits of emotional intelligence. Daniel Goleman deserves enormous credit for bringing emotional intelligence out of the academic closet and into the tough-minded halls of commerce. His books on emotional intelligence provide a rich and compelling case for the importance of emotional skills to corporate leaders.[12]

Although emotional intelligence is widely recognized as a business tool, its definition is still evolving. In 1990, Professors Peter Salovey of Yale University and John Mayer of the University of New Hampshire first coined the term. Their original definition of emotional intelligence

was "the ability to monitor one's own and others' feelings, to discrimi-
nate among them, and to use this information to guide one's thinking
and action."[13] They identified the components of emotional intelligence:

- Appraising emotions in self and others

- Regulating emotions in self and others

- Using emotions adaptively

Salovey later expanded those into five domains, which Dan Goleman
adapted in 1995 in *Emotional Intelligence: Why It Can Matter More
Than IQ*:[14]

- Knowing one's emotions (self-awareness)

- Managing emotions

- Motivating oneself

- Recognizing emotions in others

- Handling relationships

In 1997, Salovey and Mayer recharacterized emotional intelligence as
"the ability to perceive, appraise, and express emotion accurately and
adaptively; the ability to understand emotion and emotional knowledge;
the ability to access and/or generate feelings when they facilitate
thought; and the ability to regulate emotions in ways that assist
thought." The revised components became:

- Perceiving and expressing emotion

- Using emotion in cognitive activities

- Understanding emotions

- Regulation of emotions[15]

Other experts in the field of emotional intelligence offer slightly different twists, but the definitions are consistent with those of Salovey,

Mayer, and Goleman. For instance, Barbara Fredrickson's recent book *Positivity: Groundbreaking Research Reveals How to Embrace the Hidden Strength of Positive Emotions, Overcome Negativity, and Thrive* offers scientific evidence on the importance of positive thoughts in boosting emotional intelligence and enhancing personal and professional performance.[16]

Moral intelligence is new to the playing field. Just as emotional intelligence and cognitive intelligence are different from one another, moral intelligence is another distinct intelligence. Moral intelligence is our mental capacity to determine how universal human principles—like those embodied by the "golden rule"—should be applied to our personal values, goals, and actions. This book focuses on four principles that are vital for sustained personal and organizational success:

- Integrity

- Responsibility

- Compassion

- Forgiveness

Integrity is the hallmark of the morally intelligent person. When we act with integrity, we harmonize our behavior to conform to universal human principles. We do what we know is right; we act in line with our principles and beliefs. If we lack integrity, by definition, we lack moral intelligence.

Responsibility is another key attribute of the morally intelligent person. Only a person willing to take responsibility for her actions— and the consequences of those actions—can ensure that her actions conform to universal human principles. Compassion is vital because caring about others not only communicates our respect for others, but also creates a climate in which others will be compassionate toward us when we need it most. Forgiveness is a crucial principle, because without a tolerance for mistakes and the knowledge of our own imperfection, we are likely to be rigid, inflexible, and unable to engage with others in ways that promote our mutual good.

Compassion and forgiveness operate on two levels: first in how we relate to ourselves and second, in how we relate to others. Because we have yet to meet a person with *perfect* moral intelligence, putting principles into action requires that when we make inevitable mistakes, when our behavior fails to conform to universal human principles, we need to treat ourselves with compassion and forgiveness. If we are not gentle and forgiving of ourselves, we will not have the energy to move forward to build our moral capacity. Similarly, to inspire others to enhance their moral intelligence, we need to treat others with compassion and forgiveness.

Research tells us that emotional intelligence contributes more to life success than intellectual or technical competence. Emotional intelligence can help you behave with great self-control and interpersonal savvy. But emotional intelligence alone won't keep you from doing the wrong thing. Moral incompetence surfaces in moments when personal or business goals conflict with core values. Just about everyone has worked with someone who had great interpersonal skills but dropped the ball on a moral issue—perhaps an employee who let a colleague take the blame for something that was undeserved or a manager who gave an inflated performance rating to the boss' nephew. But until now, no one has paid much attention to systematically developing moral intelligence—even though the best leaders know it's their secret weapon for lasting personal and organizational performance.

Some competencies that appear on lists of emotional competencies have a definite moral flavor, such as the ones listed here (from Daniel Goleman's *Working with Emotional Intelligence*[17]):

- Have a guiding awareness of (personal) values and goals.
- Voice views that are unpopular and go out on a limb for what is right.

- Act ethically and are above reproach.

- Build trust through their reliability and authenticity.

- Admit their own mistakes and confront unethical actions in others.

- Take tough principle stands even if they are unpopular.

We believe it is more accurate to describe them as moral competencies. They are aspects of the four principles we describe and, in this book, we explore these attributes and the other competencies we see present in integrity, responsibility, compassion, and forgiveness. Perhaps it has been safer to think of these clearly moral competencies as emotional competencies because the culture of business in the last half century has discouraged all of us from talking about the "m" word. If there is a silver lining to the recent corporate scandals, it is that moral lessons are inescapable. The time has come to openly acknowledge the contribution of moral intelligence to effective leadership and sustainability.

Although both emotional intelligence and moral intelligence come into play when moral decisions are at stake, they are not the same. Emotional intelligence is values-free. Moral intelligence is not. Emotional skills can be applied for good or evil. Moral skills, by definition, are directed toward doing good.

Emotional intelligence and moral intelligence, though distinct, are partners. Neither works in a truly effective way without the other. In *Primal Leadership: Realizing the Power of Emotional Intelligence*,[18] Goleman and his co-authors, Richard Boyatzis and Annie McKee, tackle the boundary between emotional and moral intelligence when they discuss how good and bad leaders can use the same emotional competencies:

Given that adept leaders move followers to their emotional rhythm, we face the disturbing fact that throughout history, demagogues and dictators have used this same ability for deplorable ends. The Hitlers and Pol Pots of the world have all rallied angry mobs around a moving—but destructive—message. And therein lies the crucial difference between resonance and demagoguery:

Demagoguery casts its spell via destructive emotions, a range that squelches hope and optimism as well as true innovation and creative imagination (as opposed to cruel cunning). By contrast, resonant leadership grounded in a shared set of constructive values (our emphasis) keeps emotions resounding in the positive register. It invites people to take a leap of faith through a word picture of what's possible, creating a collective aspiration.[19]

Without a moral anchor, leaders can be charismatic and influential in a profoundly destructive way. As *Primal Leadership* emphasizes, truly effective leadership is "grounded in a shared set of constructive values." Without knowledge of those values—in other words, moral intelligence—the skills of emotional intelligence are ultimately ineffective in promoting high performance.

Moral intelligence is not just important to effective leadership—it is also the "central intelligence" for all humans. Why? It's because moral intelligence directs our other forms of intelligence to do something worthwhile. Moral intelligence gives our life purpose. Without moral intelligence, we would do things and experience events, but they would lack meaning. Without moral intelligence, we wouldn't know why we do what we do—or even what difference our existence makes in the great cosmic scheme of things.

A Renewable Asset. The more you develop your moral intelligence, the more positive changes you will notice, not only in your work but also in your personal well-being. Staying true to your moral compass will not eliminate life's inevitable conflicts. Will you have to compromise sometimes between your beliefs and the demands of your work environment? Yes! Will you make mistakes? Will you sometimes say the wrong thing out of jealousy or greed? Definitely! But staying the moral course will give you singular personal satisfaction and professional rewards.

Your "Moral Positioning System." Think of moral intelligence as a "moral positioning system" for your life's journey, analogous to the global positioning system used in some cars as a navigational tool. You can be a great driver, and your car can have a powerful engine and four-wheel drive, but when it's dark and you've never been in this neck of the woods before, you have directions that were given you by someone who doesn't know street names, and you cannot see the map you got from AAA, you are lost. Despite all your tools and resources, you have no idea if you are headed in the right direction. But if your car had a global positioning system, it would be virtually impossible for you to get lost. Like having a GPS for your car, your moral intelligence enables you to better harness all your resources, your emotional intelligence, your technical intelligence, and your cognitive intelligence, to achieve the goals that are most important to you—whether on the job or in the rest of your life. Unlike today's GPSs, moral intelligence is not optional equipment. It is basic equipment for individuals who want to reach their best creative potential and business leaders who want to capture the best efforts of their workforce.

Moral Intelligence and Business Success. Though leaders may attribute their companies' success to their commitment to moral principles, their evidence is based only on their personal experiences. So far, there has been no quantitative research that specifically studied the business impact of moral intelligence. But there are objective indications that moral intelligence is critical to the financial performance of your business. One measure of the influence of moral intelligence on business results comes from Ameriprise Financial (formerly American Express Financial Advisors) that implemented a highly effective emotional competence training program. American Express Financial Advisors defined *emotional competence* as "the capacity to create alignment between goals, actions, and values." The program emphasized development of self-leadership and interpersonal effectiveness and demonstrated how those emotional skills led to business and personal success. The bottom-line impact of the program was impressive, with participants in a pilot group producing sales that were 18 percent higher than a control group that didn't have the benefit of the training—no small change in a company that managed or owned assets in excess of $232 billion at the time. At the heart of the program was a special subset of skills that helped people to discover their principles and values and then create goals and action steps that flowed from those deeply held principles and values. American Express Financial Advisors' leaders realized that it was this overriding moral framework, that is, the emphasis on *principles* and *values*, which accounted for much of the success of the program. American Express Financial Advisors had already found from internal studies that the most successful advisors were highly confident, resilient under adverse circumstances, and, most important, acted from a strong core of principles and values. To form trusting partnerships with clients, advisors needed to be genuinely trustworthy. To be seen as trustworthy, advisors had to act in accordance with worthwhile personal values. If advisors practiced the self-management and social skills they learned in the training, but failed to operate from moral principles and values, they would fall short of sustainable success.

Although American Express Financial Advisors' data demonstrates the importance of an individual advisor's moral intelligence to financial performance, other businesses have discovered that they produce the best results when their company overall is known for its moral intelligence. Market research tells us that consumers judge a company's reputation mainly on the basis of its perceived values. A company's reputation translates straight to the bottom line: A recent study jointly conducted by Cone and Duke University provides behavioral proof that consumers prefer to make purchases from companies that are known for their ethical practices.[20]

The business case for moral intelligence gets another boost from a study done at DePaul University in Chicago. Researchers from the School of Accountancy and MIS compared the financial performance of 100 companies selected by *Business Ethics* magazine as "Best Corporate Citizens" with the performance of the rest of the S&P 500. Corporate citizenship rankings were based on quantitative measures of corporate service to seven stakeholder groups: stockholders, employees, customers, community, environment, overseas stakeholders, and women and minorities. The study found that overall financial performance of the 2001 Best Corporate Citizen companies was significantly better than the rest of the S&P 500. The average performance of the Best Citizens, as measured by the 2001 *Business Week* rankings of total financial performance, was more than 10 percentile points higher than the mean rankings of the rest of the S&P 500. According to *Strategic Finance* magazine, which reported the study, "It casts doubt on the persistent myth that good citizenship tends to lead to additional costs and thus negatively impacts a firm's financial results."[21]

Moral Intelligence and the War for Talent. Everyone agrees that talent is a key corporate asset, no matter what the state of the economy. A company's best employees can walk out the door at any time. They are much more likely to take their expertise and potential elsewhere if they don't like the ethical or moral tenor of their workplace.[22] Nancy Jones, chief marketing officer, Allianz Life Insurance Company of North America, believes that when the job market recovers from the Great Recession, companies that aren't treating employees with integrity and compassion now won't keep them later:

> **The environment of constant sacrifice being expected of employees these days is not sustainable. People get burned out and start looking for other jobs. Leaders have to establish a balance between *what* the business result is and *how***

business gets done. Otherwise productivity suffers and eventually you lose talent. As the economy improves, companies will discover that they can't maintain so much pressure on their people. Today people stay where they are if they can because there are no other options. But when the opportunity comes up, people will start looking for better hours, the chance to be more creative, make more money, or whatever. Then belatedly, companies will try to create incentives to get people to stay, and it won't work."

Don MacPherson, president of Modern Survey, underscores the scope of the problem, noting: "In a survey we conducted and released in 2010 we learned that the level of workforce disengagement in America is at or near historic highs across virtually all industries. And it is especially high in the financial services industry."

When good employees leave, sometimes it is a reaction to an entire organization that lacks a climate of moral intelligence; at other times, employees leave simply because their immediate supervisor or boss is lacking in moral competence. A number of years ago, a young man we know abruptly quit a job that he had been thrilled to get only a few months before. He loved the work and loved the product—selling sports hospitality packages of high-profile sports events to large corporations—but couldn't tolerate the moral climate. Some years before beginning his job, his company had run afoul of a major sports association for using misleading and unethical tactics to get people to buy tickets for a major golfing competition and was now under a court order that prevented them from lying to get people to buy tickets. The company's solution was to create two sales scripts for the golfing competitions—an "official" sales script for marketers to keep by the phone and show to the CEO if he stopped by. The actual sales script used by the marketers was the same kind of misleading pitch that had gotten the company into hot water in the first place. The final straw for this young man came when he was asked to start selling tickets for a major tennis event using the same misleading pitch.

It's not just current employees who yearn for a morally intelligent workplace. First-time job seekers increasingly rate the ethical character of prospective employees as a consideration in their decisions about where to work. Patrick Gnazzo, vice president of business practices for the manufacturer United Technologies Corp. in Hartford, Connecticut, reported in *The Wall Street Journal* article that a growing number of their job candidates apply for positions with UTC based on the job seekers' research into the company's ethics program.[23] Since 2005, United Technologies Corp. has worked diligently to create the kind of ethical climate that inspires employees' best efforts and strong business results. Today it boasts an unusually robust corporate ethics program, and in 2010 UTC received the Ethics Resource Center's prestigious annual Leadership in Ethics award in 2010.[24]

Moral Intelligence and the Consumer. Most perpetrators of the recent economic meltdown have escaped legal prosecution. However, they haven't escaped moral condemnation in the eyes of the public. The business impact of bad behavior in the financial services industry of moral incompetence is substantial. According to a 2009 survey, 59% of investors state that they have been let down by the financial markets; 48% now distrust financial institutions in general; and nearly half of investors have lost trust in government.[25] Imagine how investor confidence will impact the health of financial services firms over the long term. If investors can't trust the financial services industry in general, to whom will they turn for financial advice? If they haven't given up on the whole industry, it's likely that investors will be checking out their financial advisors much more carefully in the future to ensure that their financial well-being is in the hands of professionals with high integrity. Lack of trust in government, another key player in the recent economic disaster, was a major factor in the outcome of the November 2010 United States mid-term elections. Many formerly "safe" political incumbents, especially Democrats, were defeated in a populist wave of antigovernment sentiment. Voters appeared to be particularly upset about the governing Democratic Party's inability to make a dent in an exceptionally high unemployment rate. First-time Republican candidates for Congress helped the Republicans regain control of the House of Representatives.

If the public doesn't trust you, it will vote you out, no matter what business you are in. Business leaders across industries should not rest easy about their reputations. Last year's annual Gallup poll on Honesty and Ethics showed that only 12% of the public rates business executives' ethical standards as high or very high.[26]

Today, more than ever, consumers are likely to shun unethical companies, and they won't hesitate to make their displeasure known. More than 70% of American consumers have, at some point, punished companies they view as unethical, either by avoiding a company's products or speaking negatively about the company to others. A recent study demonstrated that consumers punish unethical practices more than they reward ethical practices. Automobile manufacturer Mitsubishi felt the effects of consumer punishment when its Japanese sales dropped 40% in fiscal year 2005 after it was discovered that company officials had suppressed information about widespread vehicle defects. The rapid rise of social networking sites such as Facebook and Twitter has turbocharged consumers' ability to use word of mouth to reward ethical companies and punish unethical ones.

The evidence is clear—moral intelligence plays a big part in sustainable corporate success. Without it, your organization risks devastating financial failure. What are the implications for your personal leadership effectiveness? If you pay attention to your own moral intelligence as a leader and encourage development of moral intelligence throughout your organization, you will inspire trust in your customers and vendors, as well as the best efforts of your workforce. That's the formula for ensuring sustainable optimal performance. It is possible to get ahead *without* moral intelligence: The corporate accounting villains and disgraced financial industry executives who have caused so much pain in the last decade are proof that you can do well despite moral lapses—for a while. But without moral intelligence, long-term business success is ultimately not sustainable.

Obviously, moral intelligence isn't the only determinant of sustainable business performance. You also need solid business skills, and you need a product or service that people want to buy. It's hard not to wonder what the financial services industry and the economy in general might be like today if more industry leaders had used both their business smarts and their moral smarts to execute their firms' strategy.

Moral intelligence won't completely immunize your company from the financial ups and downs of doing business in a volatile economy. But you need it to *stay* in business over the long haul. So, take your leadership to the next level—go beyond the usual formulas for leadership success.

But how do you begin? Exactly how does moral intelligence produce better business performance? What are the specific moral skills you need to inspire the best efforts of your workforce? How can your organization—whether large or small—use moral intelligence to create high-performing work environments? You find answers to these questions in the pages that follow.

Endnotes

1. http://www.sec.gov/news/press/2010/2010-197.htm.
2. Bruce Watson, "Where Are They Now? Seven Villains of the Financial Crisis," *Daily Finance*, September 15, 2010. http://srph.it/9bTrGJ.
3. William D. Cohan, "The rise and fall of Jimmy Cayne," *Fortune*, August 25, 2008. http://money.cnn.com/2008/07/31/magazines/fortune/rise_and_fall_Cayne_cohan.fortune/index.htm.
4. Peter Chapman, *The Last of the Imperious Rich: Lehman Brothers, 1844–2008*, Penguin, September 2010.
5. Gary Weiss, "No Need to Apologize," Portfolio, September 7, 2010. http://www.portfolio.com/views/columns/2010/09/07/no-regret-from-former-lehman-ceo-dick-fuld/#ixzz14L75yUtB.

6. Karen Freifeld and David Scheer, "Ken Lewis, Bank of America Sued by Cuomo for Fraud (Update5)," *Bloomberg Business Week*, February 4, 2010.

7. http://www.sec.gov/news/press/2010/2010-59.htm.

8. John D. McKinnon and Susanne Craig, "Goldman Is Bruised, Defiant in Senate," *The Wall Street Journal*, April 28, 2010.

9. Stevenson Jacobs, "Guilty or not, Goldman's reputation takes a hit," *Associated Press*, April 18, 2010.

10. "Turmoil on Wall Street: The Impact of the Financial Sector Meltdown On New York's Labor Market," New York State Department of Labor Division of Research and Statistics Bureau of Labor Market Information, June 2009. http://www.labor.ny.gov/stats/pdfs/wall_street.pdf.

11. Reported by Marcelo Prince, "Manager Discovers Leadership in an Accident's Aftermath," *The Wall Street Journal*, April 5, 2002.

12. For example, Daniel Goleman, *Emotional Intelligence: Why It Can Matter More Than IQ*. New York: Bantam, 1995, and *Working with Emotional Intelligence*. New York: Bantam, 1998.

13. Salovey, P., & Mayer, J. (1990). "Emotional intelligence." Imagination, cognition, and personality, 9(3), 185–211.

14. Daniel Goleman, *Emotional Intelligence: Why It Can Matter More Than IQ*. New York: Bantam, 1995.

15. Mayer, J. D. and Salovey, P. (1997). What is emotional intelligence? In P. Salovey and D. Sluyter (Eds). *Emotional development and emotional intelligence: Implications for educators* (pp. 3–31). New York: Basic Books.

16. Barbara Fredrickson, *Positivity: Groundbreaking Research Reveals How to Embrace the Hidden Strength of Positive Emotions, Overcome Negativity, and Thrive*, Crown Archetype, 2009.

17. Daniel Goleman, *Working with Emotional Intelligence*. New York: Bantam, 1998.

18. Daniel Goleman, Richard Boyatzis, Annie McKee, *Primal Leadership: Realizing the Power of Emotional Intelligence*. Harvard Business School Press, 2002.

19. Ibid.

20. For example, the 2008 Cone/Duke University Behavioral Cause Study and the 2008 Cone Cause Evolution Study. http://www.coneinc.com/stuff/contentmgr/files/0/8ac1ce2f758c08eb226580a3b67d5617/files/cone25thcause.pdf.

21. Curtus C. Verschoor, "Best Corporate Citizens Have Better Financial Performance," *Strategic Finance*, Vol. 83, No. 7, p. 20, January 2002.

22. Reported by Kris Maher, "Wanted: Ethical Employer: Job Hunters, Seeking to Avoid an Enron or an Andersen, Find It Isn't Always Easy," *The Wall Street Journal*, July 9, 2002.

23. Ibid.

24. "United Technologies Corp. and CEO Louis Chênevert Win ERC's 2010 Pace Award for Leadership in Business Ethics," Ethics Resource Center (ERC), October 28, 2010. http://www.ethics.org/news/pace2010.

25. Sullivan Insight on Affluent Investors for Financial Marketers, 2009.

26. Gallup, 2009, Honesty and Ethics of Professions poll. http://www.gallup.com/poll/124625/Honesty-Ethics-Poll-Finds-Congress-Image-Tarnished.aspx.

Born to Be Moral

What makes a leader effective? Turns out, the best leaders are not the charismatic or heroic types lionized in years past. According to the latest research, they are "quiet leaders" who accomplish great things modestly and without fanfare.[1] Leaders at the helm of the perennially great companies all share a common trait—humility.[2] They inspire high performance in others through their sensitivity to their followers' needs.[3] The best leaders think "we," not "I."[4] They are, quite simply, good people who consistently tap into their inborn disposition to be moral. They follow a moral compass—even when it's tempting not to. They make hard choices between right and wrong, or even between two different "rights." Great people—and great leaders—share common moral values. They believe in honesty and in being responsible for themselves and others. They show compassion for their fellow humans and know how to forgive others—and just as important—themselves.

What the Best Leaders Believe

The most effective leaders hold to a common set of principles and con-sistently use those principles to guide their day-to-day actions. They don't make up their values as they go along; they listen carefully to the call of moral values that already lie within all of us. The principles busi-ness leaders follow *are the same set of principles that all human soci-eties throughout time have believed to be "right."* These fundamental beliefs have been embedded in human society for so long that they are now widely recognized as *universal.*

Our extensive work with senior leaders of major corporations sup-ports the notion that there are principles we all share in common. Our results echo that of noted anthropologist Donald E. Brown, who found in his research that the moral codes of all cultures include recognition of responsibility, reciprocity, and ability to empathize.[5]

Other studies have confirmed Brown's findings. Genuine differ-ences in behavior in different cultures may distract us from what we have in common with all people—*a universal moral compass.* Consider a study that compared children in India with American children.[6] The differences in values were predictable: Indian children displayed more deference to elders and acceptance of tradition, whereas American chil-dren valued personal autonomy and freedom. But their moral codes were virtually identical. Both groups of children believed that it was wrong to lie, cheat, or steal, and both thought that it was important to treat the sick or unfortunate with kindness.

In another study, researchers Richard T. Kinnier, Jerry L. Kernes, and Therese M. Dautheribes identified a short list of universal princi-ples by analyzing earlier lists and examining the official tenets of major world religions.[7] Their rationale was that the principles held in common by major world religions are the ones most likely to be universal and enduring. They found the following principles espoused in common by all or most religions, and by secular organizations including American

Atheists, Inc., the American Humanist Association, and the United Nations Declaration of Rights:

- Commitment to something greater than oneself

- Self-respect, but with humility, self-discipline, and acceptance of personal responsibility

- Respect and caring for others (that is, the Golden Rule)

- Caring for other living things and the environment

Stephen Covey, author of *The Seven Habits of Highly Effective People*, offers more evidence of universal principles. "From my experiences in working with different people and cultures," he says, "I find that if certain conditions are present when people are challenged to develop a value system, they will identify essentially the same values. Each culture may express those values differently, but the underlying moral sense is always the same."[8]

Finally, noted psychologist Martin Seligman and his colleagues in the field of Positive Psychology have conducted research that led them to identify six universal virtues honored in all cultures in the world: wisdom, courage, humanity, justice, temperance, and transcendence.[9] Although the labels might vary slightly and though each culture may express these principles differently, the underlying moral sense is always the same. We believe that these universal principles exist, even though we know they are not universally applied. We believe that living in alignment with these principles is crucial to our individual and organizational survival and success.

Good leadership is not a function of some rare talent for inspiring others. Each one of us can be a good person and a great leader because we are all "hard-wired" to be moral. We were born that way. A glance at the news headlines might make that hard to believe, but here's why we think it is so.

A Visit to the Nursery

Walk into a hospital nursery, and you enter another world. It's bright and bustling, and its residents—most not more than a day or two old— are amazingly social. In the nursery, there is no such thing as one cry- ing infant. When one begins to cry, the others join in. Psychologists who study newborn behavior call this *neonate responsive crying*. The newborn is crying in reaction to another person's distress. How can a baby only a few hours old respond to someone else's pain? Researchers aren't sure how, but they have ruled out other explanations for the infant's response. It seems newborns don't cry when they hear a record- ing of their own crying—so it can't be the noise itself that's bothering them. Many psychologists believe that neonate responsive crying is the first indication of an inborn capacity for empathy. To become compas- sionate moral beings, we first need the ability to see the world through others' eyes (or hear their world through their cries!). Empathy is a key step in which infants appreciate that others exist independently of them and that others have their own separate needs. Yet the simple apprecia- tion that others have emotions and physical needs and are completely separate from us is not sufficient to make us moral beings. We can still, as many children (and adults) do, decide that the search for our own pleasures justifies our causing others pain.

Nature Versus Nurture

The explanation? Moral hard-wiring is not enough. We also need *moral software*, the programming that our moral hardware relies on to make moral choices. Like any other human capacity, morality is a combina- tion of our biology (our nature) and our experiences (our nurture). Take language, for example. You speak at least one language fluently. But you couldn't speak a word when you were born. You had to learn to speak. We know that speech is a learned proficiency because children invariably speak the language of their caregivers. But we also know that language requires an inborn capacity to speak and comprehend. Development of our morality follows a similar path. No one could teach us right and wrong unless we were wired to acquire, and act on, a moral compass. But just as we don't come out of the womb spouting Shakespeare, we are not born with a fully operational moral compass. It takes time—and the right set of experiences—to become fully moral. Noted UCLA neuroscientist and author Jeffrey Schwartz puts it this way: "As a young child you're taught the moral values of society. We wire our brains with them by paying attention to them."[10]

Growing Up Moral

Let's pick up the story of our moral development as we leave the nursery. Our newborn crying response sets the stage for a more mature empathy that emerges gradually during our early childhood. By the time we are two or three months old, we begin to respond to the emotional expressions of our primary caregiver. We play with our parents by making faces and exchanging excited noises with each other. By five months of age, we can tell that there is a difference among different emotional expressions of others. By the time we are one year old, we can tell that facial expressions or changes of voice intonation have particular emotional meanings. We then know that other people have feelings distinct from our own. If you have been around one-year-olds, you may have seen them checking out other people's reactions to figure out how they themselves should respond to a situation. Parents often take advantage of this habit to prevent a child from getting upset over a minor tumble. If a child falls down, she will look to her parent to see how that parent is reacting. If the parent stays calm, it is likely that the child will also. Empathy development continues at a rapid clip throughout the second year. By 15 to 18 months of age, we share, cooperate, and give care, as long as the situation is not too stressful. Think of the

16-month-old who tries to pat someone who is crying. By two years of age, we are very empathic people. We try to comfort people in distress. We express sympathy. We make suggestions. We bring a tissue to someone who is crying.

Learning to Be Responsible

But more than empathy is developing. By age two, we begin to show some grasp of justice, responsibility, and blame. We have all heard children as young as three or four respond to real or imagined injustice with an emphatic, "That's not fair!" Many of us begin at an early age to do things we know will be upsetting to others. Being negative is an important part of learning to be moral. If we didn't do bad things once in a while, it would be difficult to understand the difference between right and wrong behavior. Think of the earliest time you can remember doing something wrong. How old were you? What did you do? How did you know it was the wrong thing to do? Most of us can recall getting in trouble with our parents for some early childhood infraction. They used those incidents to teach us some version of the golden rule—treat others as you would want to be treated. *Think of others. Don't take something that belongs to someone else. Tell the truth.* We learn to be moral, not just from being scolded for bad behavior, but by being loved unconditionally for who we are. We grow morally through the interplay between our biological disposition to be empathetic and through our loving relationship with our parents. Because they love us, we love them, and because we love them, we work to please them. Eventually, we adopt our parents' values because we want to be like them. Throughout our preschool years, we grow in empathy and in our moral sense. By the time we are six or seven years of age, we can tell right from wrong and feel guilty if we do something we know we shouldn't.[11]

When Things Go Wrong

We tend to take the natural process of moral development for granted until we see a situation in which it doesn't happen. It can't happen, for instance, if we are born with certain neurological problems. Moral development also goes off course if our caregivers are not willing or able to provide the right kind of early nurturing. Our parents don't need to be perfect. They do need to be "good enough" to treat us well most of the time.[12] They need to be consistently affectionate and dependable. They must show us how to be empathetic, and they must help us develop positive beliefs about ourselves.

If our parents don't provide that kind of support, we won't develop into those amazingly empathetic two-year-olds and, later on, into morally competent adults. Again, moral development is much like language development. If you happened to be raised by wolves for the first five years of your life (as a rare number of people have been), you'll learn how to howl, but you'll probably never learn to speak normally. No amount of inborn ability to develop language can help you if you weren't also exposed to the right set of experiences at the right time.

Inside Your (Moral) Brain

In the previous section, we looked at our moral development from the outside in. We saw that our moral development, like language development, depends on both biology and learning. We saw that our relationship with our parents is key to our growing moral understanding. But we can't learn positive values and altruistic motivation before we are neurologically ready to acquire them.

Let's recall once again the crying babies in the hospital nursery. The empathic response of newborns happens so immediately that it is most likely genetically based rather than learned.[13] Think about the biological priorities involved: Before we can crawl or speak, we can respond empathically to our peers. Empathy must be incredibly important. We also learn that by age two; those of us who have been exposed to "good enough" parenting spontaneously demonstrate helping behavior. What is going on in our brains at age two? The brain of a normal two-year-old who has had "good enough" parenting also happens to have a normal limbic system—the part of the brain involved in emotional processing. But if we haven't had good-enough parenting, our brains do not grow normally. When a child has been abused or neglected, the cortical and subcortical areas of the brain are *roughly 20 to 30% smaller* than normal. In addition, the brain "wiring" isn't as dense or complex so that abused or neglected children are lacking some brain organization that would enable them to make strong connections to other human beings.[14] Without those connections, no empathy is realized, and without empathy, you have impaired morality.

It's All in Your Head

Scientists who study the relationship between brain function and behavior are beginning to chart the *moral anatomy* of the brain. They've learned how the brain affects moral behavior by studying both normal and brain-injured individuals. Perhaps the most famous case of moral impairment caused by brain damage happened more than 150 years ago. Phineas Gage headed up a group of men who were laying track for a new rail route across Vermont. Admired by family and friends, Gage also had a great reputation as a strong, intelligent, and efficient worker. But something went wrong one hot summer day in 1848, when the group was preparing to blast through rock to pave the way for the new track. The explosive went off prematurely, propelling a 13-pound iron rod through the prefrontal cortex of Gage's brain. Miraculously, Gage survived with his faculties intact—or so the doctors thought. He remained conscious, was able to speak and walk immediately after the injury, and survived a serious infection around the wound. Within two months, the doctors considered him cured. Gage looked the same as he always had, but his personality was completely altered, and his family and friends soon realized that the man they had known was gone. No longer able to work as a railway foreman, Gage began a downward spiral of impulsive, aggressive, and socially disconnected behavior that ended with his death from severe epileptic seizures in 1861.

Gage's chroniclers don't tell us whether his value system was destroyed by his prefrontal injury or whether he was simply unable to act on a value system that survived his injury. For practical purposes, it did not matter—either way, Gage could no longer function as a moral being. But there is a big practical distinction between *moral intelligence* (our internal moral compass) and *moral competence* (our ability to act in alignment with what we know is right). Most of us know what's right. Sometimes, though, it's a struggle to do what we know is right—when we lack the moral competence to act in alignment with our moral compass. Researchers have discovered that our brain makes the same distinction. When neuroscientists compared the behavior of two adults who had suffered prefrontal brain injuries as infants with patients who had suffered similar injuries as adults, they found a striking difference in their post-injury capacities.[15] One patient, a woman, was run over by a car when she was 15-months-old. Although she recovered from her physical injuries, her parents were dismayed to discover that by the time she was three-years-old, she simply did not respond to verbal instructions or even physical punishment. Although her intelligence was normal, her behavior became increasingly disruptive, and she could not function in a regular school. As a teenager, she shoplifted, stole, lied, and was verbally and physically abusive. She showed no remorse for her behavior, blamed her misdeeds on others, and seemed incapable of empathy. The second patient, a man, had surgery for a brain tumor when he was three-months-old. He seemed to recover fully from his surgery, and his parents were relieved that his physical development was normal, given that he began to walk and talk on a typical timetable. He seemed a little behind academically in early elementary school, and by age nine, his overall behavior was becoming cause for concern. He was generally unmotivated, had few social contacts with peers, and lacked normal expressiveness, although occasionally he would lose his temper. He got through high school, but after graduation, his behavior deteriorated. He sat around watching TV or listening to music, ate his way into obesity, and neglected his personal hygiene. He could not keep a job and committed numerous petty crimes. Like the first patient, he showed no guilt or remorse for his bad behavior and seemed incapable of empathy for others.

What actually caused the behavioral problems of the two brain-injured individuals? Both came from middle-class homes with attentive, college-educated parents, so we can assume they had "good enough" parenting. Neurological testing showed that both were normal on tests of basic mental ability. But when they were tested on tasks that required them to use reasoning to guide social behavior, they had trouble. Their moral capabilities were severely impaired. On moral reasoning tasks, they could think about moral situations only from the perspective of avoiding punishment, much like that of children before nine years of age. They lacked any capacity for moral reasoning based on the golden rule or any ability to consider what is fair from an empathetic perspective.

Because the two suffered their brain injuries so early in life, their moral capabilities were more severely affected than those of people who suffer brain injuries later in life. People whose brains are injured as adults show different levels of moral impairment. People with adult-onset injuries have already acquired their moral reasoning ability as part of normal childhood development. They may have had years of experience in applying moral judgments in actual life situations before becoming injured. If you ask people who have suffered an adult-onset brain injury to respond to a hypothetical moral reasoning scenario, for example, *should someone steal a drug to save someone's life*, they are quite able to tell you what the morally correct decision should be. In real life, however, they don't seem able to put their abstract moral sense into practice. Researchers speculate that the part of the brain that holds emotionally related knowledge essential for good, moral decision making has been disabled or disconnected by the adult-onset brain injury, even though the individual retains factual knowledge of moral rules. Young children who suffer a prefrontal brain injury apparently never get the chance to learn the moral rules because the part of their brains that would have allowed them to develop moral reasoning has been unalterably damaged. The impact of the time of injury is considerable. Adult-onset brain injury patients suffer impairments in their social and moral behavior but generally do not display the kind of antisocial or criminal behavior characteristic of people who suffered prefrontal brain damage in infancy.[16]

The Moral Map of Your Brain

Studies of brain-damaged individuals tell us what general area of the brain is involved in moral reasoning and decision making. They don't tell us exactly how our brains typically function when confronted with a moral decision. To find out, scientists have been studying the brains of normal individuals (if you can call college students who are the most common research subjects "normal") using a technique called *functional magnetic resonance imaging (fMRI)*. fMRIs resemble the MRI procedures that you might have undergone to diagnose an injury or illness. Regular MRIs produce "snapshots" of thin slices of body tissue, whereas functional MRIs use an advanced scanner that detects changes in blood flow to areas of the brain. When a particular part of the brain is involved in a certain activity, the fMRI image of that area "lights up." For example, if you were put under an fMRI scanner and you heard a loud noise, the area of your brain that processes sound would show a lot more activity. fMRI technology is now used to chart the unique parts of the brain involved in our moral intelligence. One study, for example, found that viewing pictures with moral content (such as physical assaults, poor children abandoned in the streets, and war scenes) *activated distinct areas of the brain that were not activated by any of the other types of pictures,* including those with strong emotional content.[17]

Why We're Good and Why We're Bad

It's clear we are programmed to be moral. But why? Though many philosophers and psychologists believe that truly moral emotions are uniquely human, anthropologists have found evidence of altruism, fairness, and empathy in other species. A whale, for instance, might go to the aid of a sick member of the pod, or a squirrel might risk its own safety by giving a warning call about a nearby predator. Perhaps the reason we are programmed to be moral comes not from our uniqueness as a species, but from what we have in common with other species such as whales, squirrels, or chimpanzees—we all live in social groups. As members of social societies, we need others to help us survive and prosper. Most of us are familiar with Charles Darwin's theory of natural selection, the idea of "survival of the fittest." Darwin believed that plants and animals with physical characteristics that help them survive are more likely to reproduce—carrying their survival-friendly genes forward into future generations. Similarly, it is likely that altruistic and cooperative behavior is part of basic human behavior today because it was crucial to the survival of our early human ancestors.[18] People who banded together were better able to master the elements, fight off predators, and acquire food. Individuals who cooperated and helped others tended to live longer. They were more likely to procreate and thereby get their traits into the gene pool. As an example, the tendency to provide care for helpless infants would be an advantage to our species, protecting us from extinction. Because early humans lived in small groups of related individuals, we would expect to see in our own behavior today a tendency to care for our relatives. Given the complexity of contemporary society, it's likely that evolution has favored the genes of those who extended their cooperation beyond their immediate kin. What would have guided those cooperative relationships of our earliest ancestors? It's not hard to see how the golden rule might have evolved—*treat others as you would like to be treated*—is a practical principle for living harmoniously and working for the common good.

So What Goes Wrong?

If it is true that we have been wired over eons to follow the golden rule, how then can we explain all its flagrant violations? We could try to write off crime and cruelty as mutations of normal human nature. Most of us, however, realize that there is a dark side to our own nature. There are times when selfishness prevails and when other needs overtake us, and we will not, or think we cannot, do what we know is right. According to Harvard Business School professors Paul Lawrence and Nitin Nohria, we all have four basic human drives created by evolution to improve survival.[19] Our drives can sometimes conflict. For example, the competitiveness generated by our drive to acquire will often act at odds with our desire to cooperate, driven by our desire to bond. We see the conflict play out in young children who want exclusive use of a new toy at the same time that they want to play with their friends. We see it in corporations where senior managers rake in salaries that are 100 or 1,000 times greater than that of some employees, while preaching to their employees—and honestly believing—that "we're all in this together." In the battle between competing drives, selfishness often wins out. We may want to live by the golden rule, but in some cases, the drive to acquire or defend overtakes our drive to bond. Lawrence and Nohria also point out that there is a "dark side" to each drive. Even the drive to bond, arguably the foundation of human morality, has a dark side, setting us up to define an "in group" and an "out group." We bond with our "in group." It is a series of short steps from connecting with our own group to demonizing an "out group." Early humans flourished by expanding their definitions of their "in group." At this time in history, our survival may depend on expanding our "in group" to include all the people on Earth. With the inevitable march of globalization, in which economic trouble in one country reverberates throughout the global economy, the need to recognize the importance of interdependence is even clearer. Radioactive material from nuclear warfare or HIV and H1N1 viruses do not recognize cultural or governmental boundaries. Balancing competing drives and managing the dark side of our human nature is the essence of moral intelligence. Choosing among competing desires is the essence of morality. There is no morality without choice. Making decisions between our sometimes competing drives requires us to make moral choices.

The Neuroscience of Moral Decision Making

The work of choosing between competing drives is complicated by the way our brains are wired. To understand how we make moral decisions, or decisions of any kind, we first need to understand how our brain operates. The brain is divided into three major sections (see Figure 2.1).

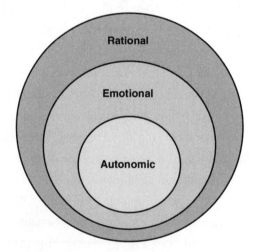

FIGURE 2.1   Simplified Model of the Brain

In the outer layer is the brain's rational center, which handles complicated cognitive processes such as objective thinking and rational decision making. The brain's rational center is largely composed of an anatomical section of the brain called the cerebral cortex. In the middle layer of the brain is its emotional center, which processes emotions, motivations, and drives. The major anatomical component of the brain's emotional center is called the limbic system. Within the limbic system is the amygdala, which translates outside stimulation into specific emotions such as fear or excitement. The inner part of the brain, the habit center, processes everything we do automatically without thinking. The major anatomical component of the brain's habit center is the basal ganglia. It includes not only habits, but also basic body functions such as breathing, circulation, movement, and sensation. These three parts of the brain—the rational center, the emotional center, and the habit center—work together. They are connected to one another by neural circuits, that is, pathways that use special chemicals to send information back and forth among different parts of the brain.[20]

Here's an example of how the three parts of the brain are connected: Imagine you are a junior executive in a meeting with the senior executive team. Prior to the meeting, you met with your fellow junior executives (who were also participating in the meeting). Based on the premeeting with your peers, you were aware of some sensitive information going to be brought up in the meeting with the senior executives (one of whom is your boss). The junior executives had chosen a spokesperson to present the information to the senior group. You knew that this information would not be well received by the senior executives, but that it was important for the group of junior executives to share. During the meeting with the senior executives, the junior executives' spokesperson raises the hot-button issue. Your boss explodes, looks directly at you and says, "Did you know this was going to happen?" In the heat of the moment, you blurt out, "No." As soon as you say that, you know you have made a mistake. Not only did you lie, but your lie made your peers more vulnerable to the senior team's anger and jeopardized your relationships with your fellow junior executives. So why did you lie? What happened to those connections between the three parts of your brain? The answer: Your emotions of fear and anxiety were so strong that they disabled the rational center of your brain—the part of your brain that you need the most to make effective moral decisions. It's not that you *weren't* thinking at all—or that you don't understand what's right and wrong—but that your strong feelings affected the *quality* of your thinking. The message that your brain's rational center received had already been "spun' by your brain's emotional center. Out of fear for yourself, you did the morally incorrect thing and in so doing threw your colleagues under the bus. Your lapse in moral judgment happened because the triggering event—your boss's anger—was *emotionally stimulating*. When we're in such an emotionally charged situation, our brain acts *reflexively*: We do things automatically, without thinking clearly. So you defaulted to a habit, in this case a habit of saying whatever you need to say to deflect others' negative emotions. You haven't yet established the habit to do the right thing instantaneously under pressure.

If our emotions are highly negative, they activate the brain's *loss avoidance* or *danger system,* a complex set of neural circuits that communicate across all three anatomical sections of the brain whenever we perceive threats or dangers in our environment.[21] If our emotions are highly positive, they activate the brain's *reward system*, a collection of neural circuits running across the three divisions of the brain that scans our environment in search of things we want.[22] When our reward system is highly activated (in the presence of highly positive emotions,) it turns off our danger system. When our danger system is activated, it neutralizes our reward system. As far as our brain is concerned, there are no shades of gray: We are either excited and pursuing rewards, or we are fearful and trying to avoid danger. Perhaps you've had the experience of feeling so worried about something that it was impossible to enjoy a normally pleasurable event. That's because in the presence of either highly exciting or anxiety-producing financial situations, our rational brains are MIA. In the example of the angry boss, for instance, anxiety and fear blocked the junior executive's ability to make a rational decision to tell the truth.

The Danger System

The danger system is the circuitry in the brain that gets activated when we feel threats to our survival. Neuroscientists have not yet definitively mapped the brain anatomy of the danger system. However, it is believed to largely involve structures in the limbic system, including the insula, which registers pain or disgust; the amygdala, which processes emotions; and the hippocampus, which processes long-term memory. The danger system also is thought to include the hypothalamus, which secretes hormones that send messages to other systems in our body, including the endocrine system. When our danger system is activated, the whole body is involved. Our adrenal gland produces two chemicals: cortisol (often referred to as the stress hormone) and epinephrine (AKA adrenaline), which are secreted into the bloodstream, preparing our body to fight or flee the danger we are facing. Cortisol gives us the energy to deal with physical threats by increasing our blood pressure and blood sugar. Epinephrine prepares the body for action in emergency situations. It boosts the supply of oxygen and glucose to the brain and muscles, while suppressing nonemergency bodily processes. Some signs that your danger system is in charge are shaking, sweating, breathing quickly, or feeling panicky. But just because you don't feel any of those symptoms doesn't mean that your danger system isn't active. When your brain's danger system is in charge, fear or anxiety may keep you from doing the right thing because your decision-making ability is impaired. Effective moral decisions almost invariably involve doing what's best for others, rather than optimizing your personal gain. But when your danger system is in charge, "survival of the fittest" is in full swing, and you automatically do what your emotions and existing habits dictate—not what your rational brain would have chosen to do, that is, act in the best long-term interest of you, your work colleagues, or the common good.

The Reward System

The reward system is the set of circuits in the brain that helps us identify and acquire things we want. It is made up of a bundle of neurons in the midbrain that send projections throughout the prefrontal cortex, affecting the rational processing ability of the brain. The neurons in the reward system communicate primarily by releasing a chemical called *dopamine.* When we see something potentially desirable (chocolate, an attractive person, or a higher-paying job), our reward system turns on, motivating us to want this thing that has come to our attention.[23] What's interesting is how dopamine helps motivate us to go after what we want by making us feel good. That's why dopamine is typically referred to as the pleasure chemical. Thanks to dopamine, we feel good when we anticipate getting what we want, and we feel good when we've gotten what we wanted. Just as with our danger system, when our reward system is running the show, our automatic response mechanisms take over because our rational decision making is impaired.

What's worse, our reward and danger systems tend to operate without our knowing it. As psychiatrist and neurofinance expert Dr. Richard Peterson explains,"When the reward system is turned on it disables the danger system, and when the danger system is turned on it disables the reward system."[24] That means we can be under the sway of emotions we're not consciously aware of, making decisions that we delude ourselves are moral—when what we're actually doing is simply avoiding personal danger or pursuing immediate gratification.

Can We Actually Change Our Brain?

Given the way our ancient brains are wired, how can we possibly make smart moral decisions under duress or in the thrall of an exciting opportunity? We *can* change the way our brains respond to the moral challenges life and leadership present us. Our brains have an amazing capacity to create new response patterns and new habits. And it is this ability to change our brains that allows us to live up to the promise of our innate moral intelligence. We are all disposed to be moral. But it takes practice to behave consistently in a moral way. A violin virtuoso is born with musical talent, just as we are born with a "talent" to be moral. But if the would-be violinist doesn't practice, she will never reach her potential to join the elite group of top violinists in the world. And if we don't practice moral decision making, we'll never reach our potential to be compassionate, responsible, forgiving, and trustworthy members of the human community. We'll also never reach our potential to be inspiring business and organizational leaders.

Fortunately, recent neuroscience research has revealed that the brain is "plastic." As Jeffrey Schwartz explains so powerfully in his book, *The Mind and the Brain: Neuroplasticity and the Power of Mental Force*,[25] neuroplasticity means that we *can* change our brains. We can create new habits so that when faced with morally challenging choices, we can respond in ways that optimize not just our own best interest, but also serve the best interests of family, friends, and the work colleagues whom we lead. With practice, we can develop control over our typical reactions to morally charged situations, and establish new, morally competent responses that involve the logical parts of our brain. And the first step to reprogramming our brain is to align our behaviors with the principles and values we would like our moral decisions to reflect.

Moral Software

By now, you should have a flavor for the compelling evidence that we are biologically wired to be moral. We have used the analogy that our innate moral disposition is our "moral hardware." We come into the world with rudimentary skills, such as empathy, which are the building blocks for our moral intelligence. Before we are two years of age, we seem naturally to help others in distress, and by the time we are four or five, we have a good idea of what our parents and caretakers think is right and wrong. Our moral hardware is preinstalled, and the upgrades come online surprisingly quickly. But we've also learned that there are physiological brain dynamics that can interfere with our ability to make wise, moral choices. Developing our moral skills in the face of a primitive brain requires two major ingredients. First, we need to be grounded in our "moral software," those moral principles and competencies that guide our actions and decisions as moral leaders and principled human beings. Second, we need a process for neutralizing the primitive brain mechanisms that can keep us from making decisions out of alignment with the fundamental moral principles we all hold dear. Chapters 3 through 7 focus both on our "moral software," that is, the contents of our moral compass that form the underpinnings of our moral decisions, and the moral competencies that make those principles come alive. Chapter 8, "Emotions," highlights the emotional competencies that work in tandem with our moral intelligence to help us stay aligned with our principles and values. Chapter 9, "Making Moral Decisions," lays out a simple and powerful process (The 4Rs) that successful leaders use to activate the logical parts of their brains required to make optimal moral decisions. Throughout the book, you will see that it is the leaders' commitment to moral principles, and their willingness to do the hard work of developing their moral competencies, that account for the enduring success of their organizations.

Endnotes

1. Joseph Badaracco, Jr. *Leading Quietly*, Boston: Harvard Business School Press, 2002.

2. Jim Collins. *Good to Great: Why Some Companies Make the Leap...and Others Don't*, New York: Harper Collins, 2001.

3. Dan Goleman, Richard Boyatzis, and Annie McKee. *Primal Leadership: Realizing the Power of Emotional Intelligence*, Boston: Harvard Business School Press, 2002.

4. Peter Drucker. "What Makes an Effective Executive," *Harvard Business Review*, June 2004.

5. Donald E. Brown. *Human Universals*, Philadelphia: Temple University Press, 1991.

6. Reported in Damon W. "The Moral Development of Children," *Scientific American*, August 1999.

7. R.T. Kinnier, J.L. Kernes, and T.M. Dautheribes. "A Short List of Universal Moral Principles," *Counseling and Values*, October 1, 2000.

8. Covey SR. "Universal Principles," *Executive Excellence,* May 1, 2000.

9 Christopher Peterson and Martin E.P. Seligman. *Character Strengths and Virtues: A Handbook and Classification*, Oxford, UK: Oxford University Press, 2004.

10. Personal interview with Doug Lennick. April 2009.

11. Jerome Kagan and Sharon Lamb (eds.). *The Emergence of Morality in Young Children*, Chicago: University of Chicago Press, 1987.

12. English Pediatrician D.W. Winnicott's concept of "good enough" parenting as described in Robert Cole's *The Moral Intelligence of Children*, New York: Random House, 1997.

13. Interpretation of Martin Hoffman's work on empathy by author William A. Rottschaefer in *The Biology and Psychology of Moral Agency*, Cambridge, UK: Cambridge University Press, 1998.

14. Bruce Perry and Ronnie Pollard. "Altered brain development following global neglect in early childhood," *Society for Neuroscience: Proceedings from Annual Meeting*, New Orleans, 1997.

15. Steven W. Anderson, Antoine Bechara, Hanna Damasio, Daniel Tranel, and Antonio R. Damasio. "Impairment of Social and Moral Behavior Related to Early Damage in Human Prefrontal Cortex," *Nature Neuroscience*, Vol. 2 No. 11, November 1999.

16. Ibid.

17. Fabio Sala. "Do Programs Designed to Increase Emotional Intelligence at Work-Work?" *Research Report*, Hay/McBer Group and Consortium for Resarch on Emotional Intelligence in Organizations (http://www.eiconsortium.org/research/do_ei_programs_work.htm).

18. E.O. Wilson, author of *Sociobiology: The New Synthesis*. Cambridge, MA: Belknap Press, 1975, a pioneer of sociobiological theory.

19. Paul Lawrence and Nitin Nohria. *Driven: How Human Nature Shapes our Choices*. San Francisco: Jossey-Bass, October 2001.

20. Adapted from Peterson, Richard L. 2007. *Inside the Investor's Brain: The Power of Mind Over Money*. Hoboken, New Jersey, John Wiley & Sons, pp. 23–25 and Zweig, Jason, 2007. *Your Money & Your Brain: How the New Science of Neuroeconomics Can Help Make You Rich*, New York, Simon & Schuster: pp. 14-18.

21. Peterson, Richard L., 2007. *Inside the Investor's Brain: The Power of Mind Over Money*, Hoboken, New Jersey, John Wiley & Sons: pp. 25.

22. Ibid.
23. Ibid.
24. Personal interview with Doug Lennick, May 2010.
25. Harper Collins, 2003.

3

Your Moral Compass

As we've just seen, nearly all of us have an inborn "talent" to be moral. But talent is never enough. Think of the major league baseball teams who spend fortunes on rookies and then send them off to farm teams for a few years to hone their skills. Professional ball players begin with *baseball intelligence*, but they must train hard to turn their baseball intelligence into on-the-field *baseball competence*. So they practice technical skills such as batting or pitching, along with nontechnical skills such strategy, judgment, and emotional composure. Why do they work so hard? Because they want to satisfy their goals and desires. Maybe they like winning, or money, or adulation, or they love playing the game. Successful ball players know that getting what they want means doing whatever it takes to reach their goals. In other words, the best ball players make sure that their talents, skills, and actions are *aligned* with their goals.

Reaching our own personal goals also requires alignment. When we decide to start a daily exercise program but never get on the treadmill, we feel uneasy because our actions are inconsistent with our goals. If we want to go on vacation, we feel good when we book the flight because we're doing something to reach our goal. Similarly, most of us want to be moral because we crave that experience of consistency between our moral values, our goals, and our actions. We call that state of moral consistency *living in alignment.*

As important and satisfying as it is to make decisions based on values, aligning your decisions with values doesn't come easy. There are lots of landmines: emotions, such as fear or excitement, mental biases, such as overconfidence in our leadership smarts, and a brain that was built for hunting woolly mammoths, not riding the roller coasters of life and leadership in today's complex organizations. In the following chapters, you learn skills to deal with all those obstacles to moral decision making. But first, you need to understand what living in alignment means because that is the foundation for becoming a true leader.

Think of living in alignment as the interconnection of three frames, as shown in Figure 3.1.

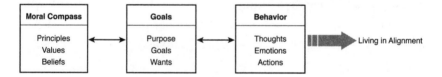

FIGURE 3.1   Living in Alignment

The first frame contains your moral compass—basic moral principles, personal values, and beliefs. The second frame holds your goals. Your goals range from the lofty (your life's purpose) to the ordinary (a new house). The third frame contains your behavior, including thoughts, emotions, and actions. Living in alignment means that your behavior is consistent with your goals and that your goals are consistent with your moral compass. Living in alignment keeps you on course to accomplish your life purpose and achieve the best possible performance in all your life roles.

Mark Phillips, SVP Distribution, Ovations (a United Health Group company), discovered that living in alignment can be difficult, especially when you're bucking a popular business trend. When Mark was SVP of Sales for Schwab Bank, he would frequently have to turn away business that he knew Schwab's competitors would grab in a heartbeat:

> **I was the front line, where issues escalated to me, and I would sometimes have to say, "We're not doing that kind of business because it's wrong for the customers and it's wrong for us." We had to turn away business we knew others would do because we focused on doing the right thing. People were coming to us for loans when they had no way to demonstrate their ability to pay us back. When we said, "We can't give you this credit," it was a tough conversation, but we did it. We turned them down, and some of them were clients who would say they would take their other business away from us, and some of them did. This upset our brokers. But I could already see the problems coming by 2006. Eighteen months later things imploded. There were companies that had been writing credit at all costs. Now we know what happened to them.**

Despite the challenges of living in alignment, smart leaders recognize that acting consistently with values ultimately pays off. Spenser Segal is CEO of Actifi, which makes innovative software supporting the financial services industry. As Spenser tells it, living in alignment was key to helping his company navigate the 2008 economic downturn.

> **I really used the alignment model well in being really transparent with my people. Because of that, we haven't lost any people. The senior management team and I bore the brunt of the financial implications. 2007 had been our best year ever, but then revenues dropped precipitously in 2008. Top line improved slightly in 2009 and the bottom line got much better, and now in 2010 we're back. The congruency with**

values and goals that is the heart of living in alignment carried us through. Having weathered this makes us know we can get through anything.

Living in alignment is an approach to life, not just an approach to leadership. New Jersey mathematics professor Dr. Rich Bastian is passionate about teaching the next generation the skills needed to help the United States remain competitive in engineering and the sciences. Rich also is deeply devoted to his family and deliberately lives near his daughter and her three children. When he accepted a position at a local college, he made sure his schedule would enable him to align his actions with both of his passions. Four days a week he teaches classes and meets with students. Each Friday he spends time with one of his three grandchildren. He rotates their schedule so that at least once a month, each grandchild gets quality time with their granddad. In addition, Rich and his partner Louise host a weekly dinner for the kids, along with their mom and dad, Rich's daughter Jessica, and her husband Erik.

Living in alignment may sometimes be difficult, but it doesn't require superhuman acts. It is about the day-to-day steps we take to do what we need to do to reach our goals. One of our colleagues used to avoid speaking engagements before large audiences, preferring to work with people one on one or in small groups. Eventually, he realized that he could not effectively communicate his values and beliefs if he limited himself to small group presentations. So he joined Toastmasters, the worldwide organization that helps people develop their public-speaking abilities. Our friend's desire to have a positive impact on the world led him to work on overcoming the anxiety of large group presentations.

Living in alignment is also not accidental. It requires doing things on purpose and for a purpose. Living in alignment is a two-part process: First, you build your own personal alignment model, by understanding what is inside each of these three frames:

- **Moral Compass**—What do you value, and what are your most important beliefs?

- **Goals**—What do you want to accomplish personally and professionally?

- **Behavior**—What actions will allow you to achieve your goals?

Then, after you build your own alignment model and know what should be in each frame, you work consciously and consistently to maintain alignment among your frames—simple, but as you might already suspect, far from easy.

Frame 1: Moral Compass

This frame contains the core moral principles and values that are the foundation of who we would ideally like to be as productive and fulfilled human beings. Principles and values overlap. They key difference is that principles are virtually universal: People everywhere tend to believe in their importance. As noted in Chapter 2, "Born to Be Moral," these fundamental beliefs have been embedded in human society for so long that they are now widely recognized as universal. Four primary principles held in common globally are especially significant for effective leadership:

- Integrity

- Responsibility

- Compassion

- Forgiveness

It's no coincidence that successful leaders, no matter what their style or personality, all seem to follow the beat of the same drum. They listen carefully to the call of moral principles that already lie within all of us. The leaders studied and interviewed for this book consistently demonstrated the importance of these principles. They were at their most effective when acting in alignment with principles. When they ignored them, business results suffered. Integrity and responsibility are essential minimum requirements for effective leadership. Lynn Sontag is President of Menttium Corporation, which helps companies nationwide coordinate mentoring programs for high potential emerging leaders. As Lynn points out, "Leaders who don't step up and do the right thing will be left behind, because in today's world with new technologies and social and business networking, there is no place to hide." *Compassion* and *forgiveness* are equally important. They make the difference between a good leader and a great one. Consider the following example of the business value of compassion. Don Froude, president of Ameriprise Financial's The Personal Advisor Group (TPAG) tells this story:

> **A year ago I became aware of a situation involving an advisor who was new to the firm and was behind his requirements to keep pace. When I talked to the advisor, I learned that his family responsibilities in the wake of his father's recent death had made it impossible for him to dedicate enough time to his work. His leaders thought they had to follow the rules about dealing with every advisor, [no] matter what their situation. I told his leaders, "I can get a robot to just follow the rules. I need you to demonstrate some leadership judgment. That's what I'm paying you for." I've always believed that if someone doesn't succeed, it's because we have failed as their leaders. In this case, the leaders made an exception for this advisor, and that judgment paid off. The advisor is still with us and is now successful and meeting all of his performance requirements.**

Values

Values differ from principles in that values are more personal beliefs about what is important to us as individuals. They are usually consistent with principles, and they enable us to put our own stamp on the meaning of the principles. For example, responsibility is a key principle, but our values help us choose how we individually express the principle of responsibility. We may value competence, challenge, or creativity. In each case, we can align our life choices both with those values *and* with the principle of responsibility. Will I be responsible by using my competence, by taking on challenges, or by finding creative solutions to areas such as work or family needs?

As we grew up, we learned a set of values, those qualities or standards that parents or caregivers considered important to our well-being and that of others. Over time, we came to adopt those values as guides to our own behavior. Families vary in the weight they place on certain values. Families often emphasize a variety of values, such as helping others, creativity, knowledge, financial security, or wealth accumulation. Early in our lives, we typically adopt our families' values, and as we mature, we often add our own. By selecting, interweaving, and prioritizing our values, we define who we are—or at least who we want to be. Just as we recognize people by their physical characteristics such as hair color, height, or the way they laugh, we also come to know people by the values they embody. As we get to know friends or people with whom we work, we begin to recognize what means the most to them. Do they crave excitement, care about the environment, or seek status? We evaluate others based on how well our values mesh with theirs. You might value personal time for creative work more than social activities, while I might value relationships and family time more than professional recognition. We feel comfortable around people who share our most important values and often avoid those who don't. If you value loyalty, for example, you may not like working with people who are self-serving.

Discovering Your Values

What is the set of values that anchors you? How would you want others to think of you? It's no coincidence that successful leaders consistently make decisions aligned with their values. To act in alignment with our values, we must deeply understand what they are.

Try this: In the next 30 seconds, say out loud your five most important values. If you're like most, you may be stuttering, or struggling to think. "Uh... family...financial security. Umm...." Our values are typically not top of mind. It's so hard to figure out our values, that most values clarification exercises provide a "cheat sheet" list of common values. Steve Pavilla, a noted personal-development blogger, offers a list of 374 values on his web site. Author Doug's company, the Lennick Aberman Group, created a pack of values cards, akin to trading cards, each of which names and explains a value. The following exercise, designed to help you become more aware of your values, is based on the Lennick Aberman Group values cards.

Exercise: What Are Your Top Five Values?

Review this checklist of values and select the five that are most important to you. If you have an important value not on the list, use the blank spaces below to record other values. Don't rush through this exercise. Take some time to reflect on what really matters most to you.

☐ Adventure	☐ Autonomy	☐ Challenges	☐ Change
☐ Community	☐ Competence	☐ Competition	☐ Cooperation
☐ Creativity	☐ Decisiveness	☐ Diversity	☐ Environment
☐ Education	☐ Ethics	☐ Excellence	☐ Excitement
☐ Fairness	☐ Fame	☐ Family	☐ Flexibility
☐ Freedom	☐ Friendship	☐ Happiness	☐ Health
☐ Helping Others	☐ Honesty	☐ Independence	☐ Integrity
☐ Leadership	☐ Loyalty	☐ Meaningful Work	☐ Money
☐ Order	☐ Philanthropy	☐ Play	☐ Pleasure
☐ Power	☐ Privacy	☐ Recognition	☐ Relationships

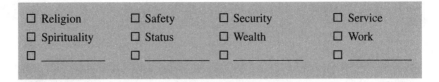

☐ Religion	☐ Safety	☐ Security	☐ Service
☐ Spirituality	☐ Status	☐ Wealth	☐ Work
☐ _____	☐ _____	☐ _____	☐ _____

The Morality of Values

Not all values are created equal, as in the previous example. Without some context, values are neither moral nor immoral. It is only when we need to make decisions that have moral consequences that values take on moral significance. In the wake of the recent economic crisis, examples of values misalignment are plentiful. For example, what were heads of many United States banks and some other financial services companies thinking when in 2009 they accepted federal TARP funds but refused to use the cash infusion to ease lending for responsible businesses and qualified individuals?

When we make a decision that does not have any particular moral significance, as in deciding where to go on vacation, we might indulge our desire for adventure without a second thought. But when we make a decision that involves others, as is the case when considering a career move that would affect family members, the priorities we assign to our values must be consistent with universal principles. In that instance, we must honor the principle of responsibility. We may realize that our desire for adventure, growth, or more money would come at the cost of our responsibility to family.

What Your Decisions Reveal About Your Values

Sometimes, we don't actually value what we say we do. If, over time, you find yourself behaving inconsistently with your espoused values, you have a choice. You can learn to better align your behavior with your values by developing your moral and emotional competencies, or you may simply accept that you value some things that you did not realize were important to you. Either path is fine, as long as your actions don't violate the universal principles.

Exercise: What Your Decisions Tell You About Your Values

To find out what your outward behavior can tell you about your values, keep a running log of all your decisions over the course of a few weeks. For each decision:

- Write down the values that influenced your decision.

- Ask yourself, "If people who did not know my inner motivations saw the outcome of this decision, what value or values would they think this decision reflected?"

Sample Decision and Values Log

Problem and Decision	What Values Drove Your Decision	What Values Others Might Think Drove the Decision
Example: Financial shortfall in division led to laying off the three newest employees.	Responsibility to preserve jobs for the most by stabilizing the division. Loyalty to longer-term employees.	Power—being seen as a take-charge leader. Financial gain—for company and for manager's bonus.
Example: A senior employee with many years of loyal service but a mixed reputation for competence is promoted to a new position.	Responsibility to reward and promote loyalty to organization. Compassion.	Friendship—in this case was more important than merit in promotion decisions. Order—making promotions predictable.

This exercise can give you some insight into personal motivations that you might not have admitted to yourself before. Consider whether the values others might attribute to your decision may actually have some bearing on your choices.

Uncovering Values Conflicts

After you identify what you value, ideally and actually—look at your list of values and compare it with the universal principles. To ensure that your values are consistent with principles, ponder questions like these:

- Is my desire to achieve financial results so strong that I behave as if the end justifies the means?

- Does my desire for high achievement lead me to lack compassion for an employee whose family crisis takes him away from work at a critical time?

- Does my need for economic security discourage me from speaking out with integrity about an unethical corporate practice?

If you accept the importance of universal principles, you must—as a morally intelligent leader—reprioritize your values in line with the principles. We are not saying that you should not value what you value. But in some cases, it will be important to find a way to honor your values while upholding principles. You can honor both principles and personal values when you look for answers to questions such as, *"How can I arrange my financial affairs so that I am protected if my ethical position gets me fired?"* Or *"How can I creatively allocate resources to preserve or improve group productivity while an employee is out on leave?"*

It should be clear by now that values can be applied in a morally negative, neutral, or positive way. Consider, for example, power, which is a value important to many leaders, but many leaders often don't want to admit that power motivates them. That's because a desire for power often gets a bad rap. Power has the potential to be seductive, intoxicating, or lead to abuse. When power is abused, individuals and organization suffer. But like most other values, power can be leveraged for good or ill. Power used to promote universal principles is a tremendous force

for organizational success and global advancement. As the late Robert
F. Kennedy said

> **The problem of power is how to achieve its responsible use
> rather than its irresponsible and indulgent use—of how to
> get men of power to live for the public rather than off the
> public.**[1]

Beliefs

Beliefs are the third component of our guidance system. For each of us,
our beliefs are the "executive summary" of our individual world view.
Beliefs represent our self-understanding about what we think is important and how we think of ourselves in relation to the outer world. They
are the condensed version of our moral compass. Beliefs capture our
larger list of principles and values in a streamlined form that is easier to
communicate. Beliefs are the language we use to describe our values
and our understanding of principles to ourselves and others. They connect our understanding of principles with our choice of values. You
can't actually know what your values are unless you can make a statement about what you believe.

Identifying Your Beliefs. You probably have 10,000 beliefs about
yourself, your world, and human nature. But most people have a relatively short list of beliefs that they hold as their "convictions"—beliefs
they use to guide decision making when the going gets rough. Many of
these might even operate at an unconscious level most of the time, but
with a little thought, most people can bring them up to the surface.
What do you believe? You can use the following exercise to reflect on
your top-ten beliefs.

Exercise: My Top-Ten Beliefs

Take a few minutes to record your top-ten beliefs here.
Remember...try to focus on your beliefs about yourself, your
world, and human nature.

1. _____

2. _____

3. _____

4. _____

5. _____

6. _____

7. _____

8. _____

9. _____

10. _____

By this point, you have identified the key elements of your moral compass. You have chosen the universal principles you embrace, you have
articulated your values, and you have summarized your beliefs.
Understanding your moral compass is essential for effective decision
making. Living in alignment means that you hold yourself accountable
for decisions consistent with your moral compass. But before you take
action, you need to understand your goals and wants.

Frame 2: Goals

Goals:
Purpose
Goals
Wants

Scientists who study behavior tell us that humans have an innate need to make sense out of their lives. We constantly develop theories to explain why events happen as they do. We have an even deeper need to understand the meaning of our lives. How do our day-to-day events combine to create a coherent whole? What is the point of doing what we do? If we can begin to answer those questions, we have the beginning of our highest goal—our life's purpose. Not everyone develops and follows a life purpose. People who were seriously brain-injured or severely neglected or abused might lack the capacity to formulate a meaningful purpose. But most of us are hungry to make sense out of our lives, so we create goals. Everyone's life purpose is distinctively theirs, but each must be consistent with universal values, compassion, and forgiveness. Albert Schweitzer once said, "I don't know what your destiny will be, but one thing I do know: The only ones among you who will be really happy are those who have sought and found how to serve." Oprah Winfrey, who created one of the wealthiest entertainment empires in the United States, says this about purpose: "I've come to believe that each of us has a personal calling that's as unique as a fingerprint—and that the best way to succeed is to discover what you love and then find a way to offer it to others in the form of service, working hard, and also allowing the energy of the universe to lead you."[2] Perhaps you already know your life's purpose. Many of us have only a vague sense of it. Discovering your life's purpose usually takes a period of reflection. One of the best resources for clarifying your life purpose can be found in Richard Leider's book *Repacking Your Bags: Lighten Your Load for the Rest of Your Life.*[3] Use the following purpose exercise to help provide you more insight about your life's purpose.

Exercise: What Is My Life's Purpose?[4]

Take some quiet time to reflect on the following questions. Answering these questions can help you clarify the high-level meaning and direction that you would like your life to take. You may also find it useful to discuss your responses with a family member or friend. Sharing your ideas with those closest to you can give you more confidence about what you are truly meant to do with your life.

1. What are my talents?

2. What am I passionate about?

3. What do I obsess about, daydream about?

4. What do I wish I had more time to put energy into?

5. What needs doing in the world that I'd like to put my talents to work on?

6. What are the main areas in which I'd like to invest my talents?

7. What environments or settings feel most natural to me?

8. In what work and life situations am I most comfortable expressing my talents?

Setting Purpose-Driven Goals

For each of us, our purpose is the major thing we want to accomplish in life. Our goals are more concrete things we'd like to accomplish to fulfill our purpose. The more aligned our goals are with our life purpose, the more effective we'll be as a person and as a leader. An easy and powerful way to decide on your life goals is to use the Widdy Wiffy process Roy Geer developed and which he and Doug Lennick detailed in their book *How to Get What You Want and Remain True to Yourself.*[5] Widdy Wiffy is the phonetic pronunciation of the acronym WDYWFY which stands for "What Do You Want for Yourself?" The title contains a bias: Getting what we want is good. Our goals can be at the same time "selfish" and morally aligned. Getting what one wants for oneself is a rightfully selfish process provided that what one wants is in alignment with our moral compass—our principles, values, and beliefs.

The WDYWFY process involves five profoundly simple steps:

- Have a goal (and write it down)

- Have a plan (and write it down)

- Implement the plan

- Control direction (keep score and when necessary redirect)

- Throw off discouragement (stay on track despite setbacks)

The importance of having specific goals is to ensure that what we actually do helps us create meaning out of our actions. Without goals, our ability to fulfill our life's purpose would be a matter of chance. Setting deliberate goals allows us to satisfy our wants in a way that is aligned with our moral compass.

Not only does your goal frame help you satisfy your personal desires within a moral framework, paying attention to your goals also increases the odds that you will actually accomplish what you desire. If you don't work on your goal frame, there is a random occurrence of achieving your goals. Career expert David Campbell made that point famously in his book *If You Don't Know Where You're Going, You'll Probably End Up Somewhere Else.*[6] Apparently, it's not enough to have a set of goals in your head. You will boost your ability to achieve your goals when you write down your goals and your plans to achieve them. Why do written goals have such a positive impact? The most basic reason is that we tend to forget things. The physical process of writing helps our brain retain and recall the things we want to accomplish.

When we write down goals, we have an opportunity to reflect carefully on what we actually want and consider the best ways to accomplish them. When we record our goals, we can use our list as a reminder to stay on track. The process of writing down goals enhances our commitment and capacity to be responsible for the choices we make. We have all known of highly intelligent individuals who never lived up to their potential. Goal setting can help you leverage the power of your moral intelligence to have a positive impact on your organization and the world.

Why Leaders Love Goals

Every effective leader we know has crystal clear goals. Goals are crucial to effective leadership because they move you beyond awareness or good intentions to specific actions. Effective leaders accept responsibility for their choices by "getting on the record" with their goals. Effective leaders have goals that they truly care about. They also encourage their followers to develop personally satisfying goals. One of the most powerful motivational tools of a good leader is to show that you care about the wants and goals of the people who work with you. Employees with that rare boss who shows genuine interest in their goals—and who spends time helping them chart a course to reach those goals—respond with loyalty and commitment.

Actifi's Spenser Segal is one such leader. "I take the WDYWFY thing seriously, and I really know what my people want. I use the alignment model to learn what people value and what their goals are. Money is never most important to my people, but meaningful work and making a difference is." Spenser's focus on his people's goals contributed greatly to the company's capability to weather the economic downturn. Although Actifi restructured and deferred compensation, it did not lose any employees during the downturn, and the company has emerged stronger than ever.

Your Goals

What exactly do you want for yourself? What are your goals? The majority of us want to play the roles we have in life well. Most people who are parents want to be good at it. Even terrible parents want to be good at it. There are few of us who don't care about how we perform. How many of you want to be part of a family that you are proud of? How many of you want to be part of an organization that you are proud of? What do you have to do to accomplish that?

Put It in Writing

Whether you are developing new goals or reinforcing long-standing goals, writing your goals down here can make them more real. Keep in mind that there are two kinds of goals. Some goals are a *state of being goal*, such as "I have three children. I want to be a good father now." Another type of goal is a *future-based goal*, for example, "I want to retire within five years" or "I want to lose weight." We recommend that you include goals of both types. We also recommend that you be clear with yourself about goals in three different areas: professional, personal, and self-development.

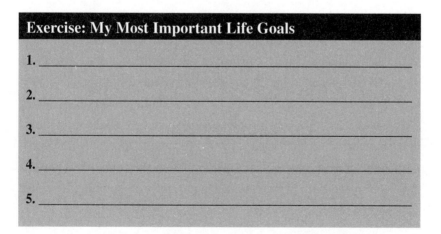

Exercise: My Most Important Life Goals

1. _____

2. _____

3. _____

4. _____

5. _____

Exercise: Goal Alignment Test

Think about your top long-term goals. How well do your goals fit with your principles, values, and beliefs?

Sample:
My goal: Buying a family vacation home.

My values and beliefs: I have a responsibility to care for others who are in need. I believe that it is important to do things to increase my family's happiness.

Potential goal alignment: Buying a vacation home would support my commitment to my family's happiness.

Potential goal misalignment: Spending money on a vacation home could reduce the amount of money I have to support charitable causes.

You don't need to abandon any goal that would make you wildly happy. But you will find that your overall happiness and effectiveness will be enhanced if each of your goals is strongly aligned with your moral compass.

Frame 3: Behavior

Behavior:
Thoughts
Emotions
Actions

The *behavior frame* puts the "living" in "living in alignment." Your behavior frame represents what you actually do, including your thoughts, emotions, and outward actions. Your behavior frame takes your values and beliefs from frame 1, and your goals from frame 2, and makes them real. We cannot be successful leaders—or human beings—unless we embrace principles and values, set clear goals, and act accordingly. Although we don't get to choose our emotions, we do get to choose our thoughts and actions. And wonderfully, we discover the thoughts and actions we choose actually do influence the emotions we experience. When we make choices that are not in alignment, we may give ourselves the benefit of the doubt, but our families, our colleagues, and our financial institutions do not. So keeping our behavior in alignment with our moral compass and goals is an essential task of a good leader.

Thoughts

What makes thoughts part of our behavior frame? Psychologists recognize thoughts as a form of *cognitive behavior*. Thoughts profoundly affect our emotions and our outward behavior. And the trouble with thoughts is that they often mask as facts. Even when we think we are being logical and objective, often that's not the case. Most of us are biased about many things, and some of those biases get baked into our logic. For example, if I'm an avid fan of my local football team that just made it into the Super Bowl, I might find it easy to justify spending a few thousands of dollars to travel across the country to see the big game. I may unwittingly "underestimate" the cost of the trip, because I really want to go. And I might justify the expense even if it will add to my credit card debt or cause me to miss my daughter's birthday.

We also tend to rely on rules of thumb, or mental shortcuts for making decisions. One of my rules of thumb might be "only hire people who graduated from Ivy League colleges." But how effective is my rule of thumb? What are the consequences of taking a mental shortcut when making hiring decisions? My rule of thumb might help me shrink the pile of resumes sitting on my desk. But by routinely ignoring potential employees who didn't attend certain schools, I probably lost the opportunity to hire some talented people who could have made significant contributions to my organization.

So always question your logic. It's important to think through your choices relative to your moral compass and your goals. Even careful questioning won't mean you will always be right. There is no silver bullet for making optimal leadership choices. But challenging your logic can make it more likely that you make the most of all your cognitive and technical abilities in support of your organization.

Emotions

Everyone has them, even the most rational and composed of us. Emotions have a strong influence on our view of financial situations and our response to them. That's because your brain is hard-wired to encourage emotional decision making. When we're in the presence of a strong external event—say a looming merger or downsizing—the part of our brain that processes emotions gets the message first. In other words, the triggering event stimulates our emotional intelligence before it stimulates our cognitive intelligence. Our emotional intelligence sacrifices accuracy for speed. We act on a flood of emotions—fear or excitement before the logical part of our brains gets a chance to evaluate the situation objectively. Why does our brain do something that can make it so difficult to apply our moral intelligence? As we learned in Chapter 2, our brain evolved to promote our physical survival, to keep us out of danger, and to encourage us to nourish ourselves. When we sense danger, our brain's "danger system" activates. It immediately sets off a whole host of physiological changes that help us get away from the source of the danger. Our danger system turns our analytical centers off, as if to say, "You don't have time to figure out the nuances of this situation. Just get out of here!" But even when we're not in physical danger, our automatic danger response still kicks in with a flood of emotions that are better suited for escaping from a bear than dealing with a business crisis. When we truly are in a life-threatening situation, we need a speedy response. It saves us. But business challenges, although often emotionally painful, are not life threatening. So sacrificing the accuracy of our thinking brain for the speed of our emotional brain begins to work against us.

Now take the case of a business opportunity that seems promising, not scary. As soon as we feel stimulated by such a positive opportunity, our brain's reward system turns on. It secretes a chemical called *dopamine,* which gives us a sense of security and confidence that enables us to pursue opportunities. But when our reward system is turned on, our danger system is turned off. So we can't notice the risk that may be involved.

Keep in mind that emotions, in and of themselves, are neither good nor bad. They are simply emotions. But because strong emotions, whether positive or painful, can get in the way of effective decisions, emotions must be managed. The most effective leaders know how to regulate their own and others' emotional responses in a way that promotes a positive and high-performing work environment. If leaders lack emotional control or insight into the emotional needs of their followers, the work environment suffers.

Earlier in her career, when Menttium President Lynn Sontag was a senior leader in executive development at a Fortune 100 company, she once made the mistake of transferring a call from an irate executive spouse to her boss. The caller, who had considerable clout, was having a temper tantrum about something that the organization wouldn't as a matter of policy give her. Lynn realized too late that she should have prepared her boss for the call so that he wouldn't get stuck in a political bind. She still has vivid memories of his reaction and the impact on her subsequent performance:

> **I can visualize the whole thing. My office was kitty corner from the executive director, and I could see his expressions as he talked to her, and it was pretty visual. His door was closed, but I could see him through his window, and I knew where he was heading as soon as he opened the door. He**

blew up in front of me and everyone else around. The next day he calmed down, and we walked through it and processed it so that it wouldn't happen again. We got through it, but I was derailed on a personal level for a long time. I still had to work with the woman for another year and a half. It took me more than a couple months to let go. It hit me right where my confidence was. I didn't trust my own judgment, and I became unwilling to make decisions without checking with a lot of people first.

Actions

We all know that actions speak louder than words. Having a moral compass and admirable goals is worthless unless we do what it takes to make them real. Failure to act in concert with our values and goals is worse than worthless. It is a failure of the core principle of responsibility. It does harm to everyone and everything we care about—family, co-workers, and community. And it does us harm. Often we lose something extremely precious—other people's trust and respect.

In Search of Alignment

Now that you see the canvas inside each of your frames, how do you keep your frames aligned? Most people agree that the notion of living in alignment makes sense. If that's true, then why is living in alignment so hard? Why is it so difficult to use our inborn moral intelligence to make smart choices that support our values and goals? In the next chapter, you begin to discover the obstacles to living in alignment—and the secrets for overcoming them.

Endnotes

1. Robert F. Kennedy (1925–1968), "I Remember, I Believe," *The Pursuit of Justice*, 1964.

2. Oprah Winfrey, *O The Oprah Magazine*, September 2002.

3. Richard J. Leider. *Repacking Your Bags: Lighten Your Load for the Rest of Your Life,* San Francisco: Berrett-Koehler Publishers, 1995.

4. Based on an exercise in Richard J. Leider. *Repacking Your Bags: Lighten Your Load for the Rest of Your Life,* San Francisco: Berrett-Koehler Publishers, 1995.

5. Doug Lennick and Roy Geer. *How to Get What You Want and Remain True to Yourself*, Minneapolis, Minnesota: Lerner Publications Company, 1989.

6. David Campbell. *If You Don't Know Where You're Going, You'll Probably End Up Somewhere Else*, Notre Dame, Indiana: Ave Maria Press, 1990.

4

Staying True to Your Moral Compass

Knowing who you want to be—an honest, responsible, and compassionate leader—is one thing. Knowing *how* to become your best self is another. Actually *doing* what you know you should is still another matter. That is the essence of *alignment,* a shorthand term that means "your goals and your behaviors are consistent with your moral compass." We need three qualities to help us keep us in alignment:

- **Moral intelligence**—Part of us that shapes our moral compass and ensures that our goals are consistent with our moral compass

- **Moral competence**—Ability to act on our moral principles

- **Emotional competence**—Ability to manage our and others' emotions in morally charged situations

Moral intelligence. Can you interpret this formula?

$$\frac{d}{dx} \int_a^x f(s)ds = f(x)$$

Here's a hint: The equation here represents the "fundamental theorem of calculus." It expresses that differentiation and integration are inverse operations of each other. Now do you understand? If you're like most people, that explanation helps a little, but not much. You can tell that the diagram is a mathematical equation, and you've heard of calculus, but you might not understand or remember the distinction between differentiation and integration. For people who are mathematically inclined, the fundamental theorem of calculus probably looks as simple to them as $2 + 2 = 4$ does to the rest of us. A complicated equation makes sense to the mathematician because she has two qualities—mathematical intelligence (basic aptitude) and mathematical competence (learned skills). Mathematical intelligence isn't sufficient to be good at math, but no amount of practice can make you a good mathematician if you don't have an underlying aptitude. Moral intelligence is another kind of aptitude. Without it, no amount of training can turn us into moral leaders. Recall the brain-injured toddlers. No matter how hard their parents tried to instill positive values, they simply lacked the basic neurological equipment to distinguish between right and wrong.

Moral intelligence is our basic aptitude for moral thought and action. We call on it to make sense out of moral principles (the "fundamental theorems" of morality). Moral intelligence enables us to develop moral values and beliefs and to integrate those values and beliefs into a coherent moral compass. Because it's the part of us that knows what's right, we use it to ensure that our goals and behavior are in alignment with our moral compass. Like a smoke detector, our moral intelligence sounds the alarms when our goals or actions move out of synch with our moral compass.

When Charlie Zelle was a young New York investment banker, his family's Midwestern transportation and real-estate business went into a financial tailspin. After he returned home to help save the business, company lawyers called a meeting of management and key family shareholders to decide the firm's fate. When lawyers and family members began to talk, Charlie was astonished at how glib they all seemed. It was clear that they had already decided to throw in the towel and no one seemed all that upset about it. Charlie got angry—his moral intelligence alarms were deafening. He thought shutting down the company was unfair and a selfish move on the part of his family. If the company folded, 500 employees would lose their jobs, and people in the community would lose access to the public transportation they provided.

Moral competence. Although moral intelligence involves *knowing* what to do, moral competence is the skill of actually *doing* the right thing. How do we do what we know is right? How do we do the right thing even when we are scared or pressured? For that, we need moral competence. We need it to understand what goals will enable us to be true to our principles, and we need moral competence to act in alignment with our values and beliefs. Charlie Zelle's moral intelligence told him that it was selfish for his family to simply cut their losses at the cost of fairness to employees and the community. But it took moral competence for Charlie to act on that awareness. He was just a kid, but fueled by his anger and encouraged by a mentor, Charlie found his voice. He found some investors, formed a new company, bought the buses back from bankruptcy court, and rehired all the employees from his family's old company. The odds of success were low, but with the help of a senior vice president who knew and loved the business, they survived. Fifteen years later, Charlie's company, Jefferson Bus Lines, is a thriving regional bus operator.

Emotional competence. To live in alignment, we also need to be emotionally competent. Emotional competence helps us manage our emotions and the emotional quality of our relationships with others. It's almost impossible to be morally competent without being emotionally competent as well. For example, most of us value honesty and most of us have the moral competence to be truthful. After all, we've told the truth countless times. But if we're such experts at telling the truth, why then do many of us lie so often? A UK women's magazine survey, for instance, found that 94% of women admitted that they tell lies, half of them lying on a daily basis. Emotional competence helps us answer questions like these:

- What makes it hard to tell the truth in a particular situation?

- How will others act if I tell the truth or fail to tell the truth?

- How can I tell the truth in a way that will preserve my relationships with others?

Emotional competence enables us to understand our own emotions, especially those that can get in the way of doing the right thing. Emotional competence also helps us understand and respond intelligently to the emotions of others. That ability to respond to others' emotional needs in turn creates a positive work environment in which people feel safe enough to do what is morally right—and not incidentally, perform at their best.

When leaders lack emotional competence, they create a negative climate that encourages self-protection rather than integrity. Lori Kaiser, Pacific Northwest Managing Partner at Tatum LLC, ran into an emotionally incompetent manager at a previous company where she had worked early in her career. He was a foul-mouthed senior manager who routinely harassed his juniors. Everyone knew he was obnoxious, but no one called him on it. Lori tolerated it for years. Then while on maternity leave, she realized how great it felt to be away from him. When she returned from leave, she took advantage of her newfound status as the company's most senior woman to draw a line in the sand. Lori told her superiors she would return only if she did not have to work with the obnoxious manager. Her superiors agreed but did nothing to correct his behavior. Other employees, in part weary of dealing with him, began to leave the company. Only then did management begin to pay attention to his behavior, but by then, they had lost some valuable people—largely because of the negative environment created by one emotionally incompetent leader.

Lori faults herself for failing to act sooner. She tolerated his negative behavior for a long time because the company paid her well to do the kind of work she wanted to do. Though she was not the source of a negative environment, she believes she was partially responsible for allowing it to continue. "Even though I may be able to tolerate difficult people," says Lori, "the people who follow me need someone who can speak up. If I condone bad behavior in front of junior men or women, it's unacceptable. Now I speak up for all of the people who are junior to me and can't speak up, even if it makes me look like I'm not one of the gang."

Staying aligned. When you consistently use your moral intelligence, moral competence, and emotional competence, you will find that you are spending more and more time living in alignment with your moral compass. When your three frames are in synch, you feel as though you are "in the zone," and your creativity and performance are at their best. When you are in a leadership role, your state of alignment is palpable and appealing to followers. Your state of alignment contributes to an emotionally positive and high-performing work environment for others.

Think of the leaders who have inspired you the most. They are almost invariably those who consistently demonstrate their commitment to principles that you also believe in. Lynn Fantom, CEO of ID Media, says of her former boss, David Bell, now Chairman Emeritus of parent company Interpublic, "I would do anything for him because he shows respect to me and everyone in the company by doing simple things like sending short email messages of appreciation."

Moral misalignment. The most successful leaders spend the majority of their time in alignment. But all of us experience times when it is hard to stay in alignment, times when our moral intelligence doesn't seem to be having an impact on what we want or what we actually do.

Instead of being connected to our ideal selves—who we would like to be at our best—we disconnect from our moral compass. Misalignments don't usually happen because we lack moral or emotional skills. Typically, they occur because **moral viruses** or **destructive emotions** are interfering with our ability to use moral and emotional competencies that we have successfully used in the past.

Moral viruses are disabling and inaccurate negative beliefs that interfere with alignment (see Figure 4.1). Moral viruses infect our moral compass and lead us to adopt goals that are inconsistent with our moral compass.

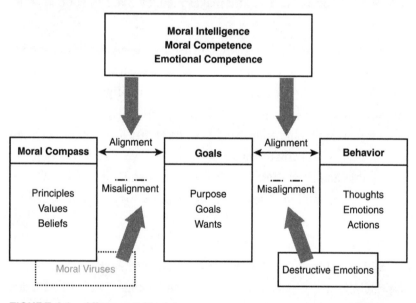

FIGURE 4.1   Alignment Model

Diagnosing a moral virus. Moral viruses are unfounded negative beliefs that are in conflict with universal principles. Like computer viruses that infect a computer's operating system, moral viruses invade your moral compass and often lead to breakdown. Moral viruses remind us of computer "adware," the insidious advertising software programs that are installed on your computer via the Internet without your consent. Suddenly, your computer desktop is overwhelmed by pop-up ads, and when you try to find and delete the adware program, you find it's difficult. Your antivirus software probably will not work. The unwanted program has the capability to hide its files and to resist attempts to remove it. Like adware, moral viruses sneak into your moral operating system. They hide themselves well: At a conscious level, you may articulate a set of principles, values, and beliefs that are admirable, without realizing that you are secretly harboring an unsavory belief that affects the quality of your goals. Your "official" goals are in alignment with your moral compass. But without your awareness, you have adopted some "unofficial" goals that are at odds with your moral compass. The end result is that you do things that are inconsistent with your moral compass, and you are probably pretty confused about the reasons why.

Consider the experience of John Simmons (pseudonym), founding partner in a growing professional services firm. He was attending a partner's meeting for his firm. Compensation was on the agenda, and during the discussion, John found himself insisting that his fellow owners adopt a lot of legalistic provisions that he thought necessary to ensure he would be compensated fairly for all his efforts. During the discussion, John became increasingly rigid, frustrating his partners. Finally, they told him he was acting as if they were his enemies rather than people who shared his goals. John knew instantly they were right, but it took a few hours of reflection to figure out why he had behaved with such suspicion.

John explains, "When I was about four years old, I got into an argument with my older brother and I bit him! My father insisted that I apologize. I refused. Before I realized the stakes of the game I was playing, my father said, "If you don't apologize, you can't be a part of this family." He proceeded to take me about a half a mile away from our farmhouse and dump me off in the pasture. I recall running back home, crying as I ran. My false conclusion was that when it comes to basic needs like personal safety you really can't trust anyone, even those close to you. Even people who have never actually taken advantage of you might still turn on you in unpredictable ways. Always be on guard!"

When John uncovered his "moral virus," he went back to his fellow owners to own up to the negative beliefs that had infected his moral compass and disrupted their meeting.

Common Moral Viruses

- Most people can't be trusted.

- I'm not worth much.

- I'm better than most other people.

- Might makes right.

- If it feels good, do it.

- My needs are more important than anyone else's.

- Most people care more about themselves than anyone else.

- People of other (races, religions, and nationalities) are not as good as people of my (race, religion, and nationality).

Dealing with moral viruses. A good way to manage moral viruses is to scan for them in your thoughts. To figure out what you are thinking, tune in to your "self talk"—the continuous internal conversation that you have with yourself. Like computer antivirus software that periodically scans for new viruses, you should regularly scan your self talk to stay aware of the internal beliefs that are influencing your daily actions. In addition to regular moral virus scans, we recommend that you scan your self-talk for possible moral viruses whenever you experience strong emotion, either positive or negative. Because thoughts and emotions mutually influence each other, it is especially important to understand the beliefs that may be the root cause of uncomfortable emotions.

Disabling a moral virus. When you have detected a moral virus in your thoughts, you have the opportunity to replace it with a thought or belief consistent with your moral compass. Countering a moral virus is effective in the moment, but it is not a permanent fix. Moral viruses sometimes act like certain biological viruses that lurk indefinitely within us. For example, the virus that causes shingles, a relative of the chicken pox virus, is a chronic virus. After an outbreak of shingles, the virus doesn't die. It retreats to the base of a bundle of nerves, where it lies dormant unless the affected person's immune system is weakened by another illness, allowing the old virus' symptoms to reappear. Similarly, when we are under stress, the symptoms of a moral virus can once again resurface. In the example just described, John Simmons figured out how he had been infected by a moral virus, but he knows he may run into the same virus in the future. John is not "cured," but his awareness can help him to recognize moral virus symptoms and move quickly to minimize its negative affects in the future.

Because none of us had a perfect upbringing, most of us will have at least one moral virus lying in wait to overtake us in a difficult moment. That is why it is important to scan our thoughts regularly and why it is necessary to actively remind ourselves of our more desirable Frame 1 beliefs. A good rule of thumb is this: When you find yourself doing something that is puzzling to you when you say to yourself, "I don't know *why* I behaved that way...," you are likely dealing with some sort of moral virus. That is a good signal to talk it out with a good friend or trusted advisor. Like a virus that thrives in the dark, moral viruses brought out into the light often wither and die.

Destructive emotions. Destructive emotions are the most common culprits in keeping us from acting consistently with our goals. Emotions such as greed, hate, or jealousy are powerful and can overwhelm our normal ability to act in a morally and emotionally competent manner. It is human nature to experience periodic emotional "breakdowns"—not usually the kind that sends us off for a long rest cure, but the more commonplace stresses that can lead us to become emotionally overwhelmed. Our moral compass is intact, and our goals are clear, but in the heat of the moment, we act in a way completely inconsistent with what we say we want. We lose control and allow destructive emotions to take hold. Greed is an especially destructive emotion, one that likely lies at the heart of the corporate accounting scandals of the early 2000s and the more recent economic crisis of the late 2000s. It's hard to imagine that any of the executives implicated for accounting or securities fraud in the last decade needed more money than they already had. For an executive in the throes of greed, however, enough is never enough. We're all too familiar with the impact of greed-driven schemes—employees deprived of jobs and retirement funds, shareholders betrayed, homeowners being evicted, and companies going out of business.

Managing destructive emotions. There will always be occasions when you feel negative emotions. Your goal should not be to eliminate all traces of negative feelings from your experience, but rather to develop the emotional control to manage destructive emotions so they don't derail you. Managing destructive emotions is vital to a successful leadership career because left unchecked, they are a frequent cause of career derailment among executives. A senior manufacturing executive interviewed for this book notes the importance of managing potentially destructive emotions: "Someone will renege on something or not do something they promised, or they'll misrepresent things and I just want to get even. I've had to develop a lot of self-control. I don't often lose my temper and if I do, I try to do it behind closed doors with my team. So the challenge is treating people the way I'd like to be treated versus the way I'd like to treat them because they screwed me. I don't feel like I've had to be extremely sensitive so much as I've needed to control my revenge motive and be professional."

A powerful antidote to negative emotions is the deliberate cultivation of a positive emotional state. Controlling emotions must come from within. No one having a temper tantrum—child or adult—wants to be told by others to "calm down." Fortunately, we can learn how to short-circuit highly charged negative emotions. Deep breathing exercises, deep muscle relaxation exercises, and meditation, are just a few of the scientifically documented ways to produce more positive emotional states.[1] Depending on your personal preferences, activities as varied as hobbies, community service, spending time in nature or with family members, even washing the dishes can trigger a positive mental state. They work because you cannot have two incompatible physiological states at the same time. You cannot be angry when you are happy. You cannot be anxious when you are calm. Regular practice of your preferred technique is key to your ability to manage your emotions. Through practice, you can create a calm and peaceful internal state that automatically kicks in when you need it. When you deliberately cultivate a positive and relaxed emotional state, you can call upon that positive state whenever a destructive emotion is beginning to take hold.

The experiential triangle. We each operate within an *experiential triangle* of *thoughts, emotions*, and *behavior,* all of which mutually influence one another. Although we discussed moral viruses and destructive emotions as though they were separate phenomena, in reality, they are typically found together and often reinforce the negative effects of each. Emotions are usually the product of our thoughts. When we admire someone, for example, our happiness in seeing that person stems not from their physical existence, but because of the *ideas* we have about them. Similarly, when we are in the throes of a destructive emotion, we have a reason. Our negative feeling is prompted by some thoughts or beliefs we have about the situation we are in. You think, "I knew I couldn't trust them," or "I should have gotten more," and you feel terrible. The worse you feel, the more likely it is that a moral virus has invaded your belief system. Destructive emotions such as anger and jealousy are the "fever" that often accompanies a moral virus. But emotions also stimulate thought processes. When a destructive emotion overcomes you, it can negatively influence the way you think about yourself or others, thereby causing a moral virus. Finally, our thoughts and emotions affect our behavior. The behavioral impact of moral viruses and destructive emotions is widespread and obvious. For a leader, the effects of moral viruses and destructive emotions can be career-ending. At the very least, your performance suffers along with that of your co-workers.

Consider these contrasting experiential triangles.

A Case of Alignment

The situation: My boss is hiding the extent of a new product line's manufacturing problems from the senior management group until performance reviews are completed.

Thought: I know that my boss's actions are violating the principle of integrity and I have a responsibility to get involved.

Emotions: Some apprehension about challenging my boss's decision, mixed with confidence and determination.

Behavior: I confront my boss about her actions and urge her to provide accurate information about production problems.

Suppose, on the other hand, that you found yourself unable to confront your boss. Would it be because you were unaware that what she was doing was wrong, or because you did not know how to raise the issue? Probably not. More likely, your failure to act would be the result of your beliefs about the situation. Your beliefs create a context, or framework, for deciding how to respond to your boss's actions. You might then be operating in an experiential triangle that operates something like this:

A Case of Misalignment

Thoughts: What other people do is none of my business. Human nature being what it is, I will probably be punished for standing up for what is right. If I do get involved, my boss might retaliate and I could lose my bonus or even my job.

Emotions: Fear and anxiety.

Behaviors: I look the other way, or I help my boss conceal the extent of the production line problems.

In this example, we can detect a moral virus in the belief that one should "mind one's own business," coupled with the belief that others will do you harm if you challenge their negative behavior. This moral virus is likely contaminating more positive beliefs about human nature and our responsibility to do what is right. But a moral virus can deactivate positive beliefs in a difficult moment, replacing them with negative beliefs about other's motives and our own responsibility. In this example, we can also see the destructive power of emotions such as fear and anxiety that further reinforce negative beliefs and the misguided actions that result.

Preventive maintenance. Staying in alignment requires regular tune-ups to monitor and prevent damaging effects of moral viruses and destructive emotions. But most important, alignment depends on continuously developing our moral and emotional competence. But how? What are the practical day-to-day actions we must take to stay in alignment? For that, we need to be proficient in a group of specific moral and emotional skills—as you see in the next several chapters of this book.

Endnote

1. Many techniques for inducing positive emotional states can be found in Herbert Benson, M.D. and William Proctor's *The Break-Out Principle*, New York: Scribner, 2003.

PART II

DEVELOPING MORAL SKILLS

5

Integrity

Every individual, like a statue, develops in his life the laws of harmony, integrity, and freedom; or those of deformity, immorality, and bondage. Whether we wish to or not, we are all drawing our own pictures in the lives we are living....

—Harriot K. Hunt (1805–1875), U.S. Physician and Feminist

*To starve to death is a small thing,
but to lose one's integrity is a great one.*

—Chinese Proverb

The Integrity Competencies	• Acting consistently with principles, values, and beliefs • Telling the truth • Standing up for what is right • Keeping promises

Acting Consistently with Principles, Values, and Beliefs

This is the primary moral competency that encompasses the others. Acting consistently with principles, values, and beliefs means being purposeful in everything you do and say. Integrity is authenticity. It is saying what you stand for and standing for what you say. Awareness is the first step to acting with consistent integrity. That's why it's so important to be clear about what's in your moral compass. Acting consistently with your moral compass also means letting others know the principles that are most important to you, and holding yourself accountable for decisions and behaviors consistent with that. Before becoming an advisor with financial services company Thrivent Financial for Lutherans, Walt Bradley spent 20 years selling cars. One day, a young woman came on the used car lot to buy her first car. The only car she could afford had a lot of miles, a few dents, and a leaky exhaust. Walt told her that if she bought the car, they would check out the leak and fix it. "When we inspected it, the pipe was shot," says Walt. "My boss said to just patch it. I argued with him, but he said, 'I don't give a shit. Just get it out of the building. There's no warranty.' Right in front of my boss, I told the mechanic not to do that—to fix the car right. My boss and I got into a shouting match about it, but the mechanic fixed it." Asked how hard was it to stand up to his boss, Walt replies, "I hate confrontation, but the woman trusted me, and I know that if my word isn't any good, then my product isn't any good."

The high cost of inconsistency. Leaders who blatantly ignore universal principles do great harm to their constituencies and ultimately to their bottom line. But just as bad are leaders who pay lip service to integrity while ignoring it in practice. Take this example of Kevin Reynolds (pseudonym), CEO of a $400 million dollar consumer products company. Kevin talked a lot about integrity in his speeches to shareholders, employees, and his board. But Kevin's direct reports didn't trust him at all, and each could cite numerous examples of betrayal or deception on Kevin's part. None of Kevin's direct reports was willing to go out on a limb for their company in the environment that he had created. Some of them spent a lot of time planning how to protect themselves from his treachery, while a few braver souls openly threatened to leave if the board did not fire him. The final straw came when, at the end of a financially troubled year, Kevin manipulated the bonus pool to get his maximum year-end bonus, leaving his team with unfairly low payouts. For a time, Kevin managed to conceal his bonus scheme by withholding information and presenting confusing data, but eventually, his mishandling of the bonus money leaked out. The board asked for his resignation. No one mourned Kevin's departure. His reputation for dishonesty dogged him in the industry, barring him from landing a top executive post anywhere else.

In corporate settings, a lack of integrity usually signals a lack of moral competence, as was the case with Kevin. But at times, a lack of integrity stems from a deeper lack of moral intelligence. There are some people whose moral compass is badly dented, like Jeff Walsh (pseudonym), who applied for a job as regional sales manager for a large Fortune 500 company. On paper, Jeff had a great track record in sales and management and an MBA from a prestigious university. The vice president of Sales was so impressed after interviewing Jeff that he was ready to hire him on the spot. "Don't let that one get out the door," he told the recruiter. But when the recruiter checked his credentials, he discovered that Jeff had no undergraduate college degree, let alone an MBA; he had never taken a single college course. When the recruiter confronted him, Jeff broke into a sweat and admitted that he had faked his resume. You might think that the sweat on Jeff's forehead was evidence that he knew right from wrong. But Jeff recovered his composure quickly and promptly talked his way back into the VP of Sales' office to try to convince him that it really wouldn't matter that he did not have his MBA. Without a functioning moral compass, Jeff completely missed the notion that lying about his credentials was a big deal. He might sweat because he was caught—but not because he had a guilty conscience.

Telling the Truth

Susan Desimone (fictitious name) was chief financial officer for a major division of a huge financial services firm. Her CEO, a demanding and explosive character (in actuality a high-profile top executive), was determined to meet Wall Street's expectations for the quarter's profits— no matter what it took. The financial analysts who worked for Susan were stressed. "The CEO is badgering us to make these numbers work," they complained. "If we show him the results we have right now, he will blow his fuse." Susan knew they weren't exaggerating, but she also knew she could handle her CEO's tantrum without letting it unhinge her. "What is the worst thing he can do to us?" she replied. "He'll yell at us for sure, but he's yelled at us before, and we are going to tell the truth." Susan's moral stance did more than keep her company out of the scandal section of *The Wall Street Journal.* She provided "cover" for the people in her finance unit and by her actions made it safer for them to do what they knew was right. Her truthful response to the CEO's pressure was both morally skilled and fiscally smart. She motivated her people to keep working for the company during an economic boom when their skills were highly marketable and corporate attrition was at record high levels.

Leading with the Truth

Imagine that you are captain on a sailboat cruising through the Caribbean. When you left dock a few hours ago, it was warm and sunny with a gentle breeze pushing the boat forward. Then the weather turns suddenly ugly. Before long, the wind is fierce, the waves are pounding, and your passengers are afraid. What should you do? You tell them the truth. You say, "This is a dangerous storm. Something bad could happen. You need to keep your life jackets on and stay below deck while I get us through this. I have been through storms like this before, and I am very optimistic that we are going to weather the storm."

In organizational settings, telling the truth often means defining reality under challenging circumstances. When times are tough, leaders need to tell the truth while providing people with real reasons for hope and optimism.

Sally Jewell, CEO of outdoor gear retailer REI, agrees: "Over the past two years we have learned some tremendous lessons, and one is about the importance of consistently telling people the truth about what's going on." Sally continues

Shortly before things started falling apart in the fall of 2008, we started sending weekly messages to employees about the storm clouds on the horizon and what we were doing about it. At the time we felt that perhaps we were even over-communicating. But we've discovered that trust in senior management went up during that period. The confidence in the company went to an all time high. It fell a bit this year and we realized that we haven't been communicating as consistently this past year as we did during that period. We weren't over-communicating at all—this is what we need to do all the time!

We also had a layoff during 2009. We were upfront about this as well, and gave the business reasons why we needed to do this. We worked really hard to train managers and to role play with them how to answer questions. Afterward, multiple people who had been laid off sent me messages about this. Some said they obviously didn't like being laid off but they understood why it had to happen. Many said they'd come back to work for us in a heartbeat.

So, what did we learn? Taking the mystery out of the situation and speaking the truth right up front was the lesson we learned. The more we communicated the more we were reinforced for communicating. And people expressed their

**appreciation. Several said things like, "Thank you for being
on top of these things." It was a great opportunity for our
leaders to reduce the uncertainty that people were feeling.**

Larson Doors' Dale Larson is another advocate of the need for leaders
to tell the truth:

**We had a period of time when we lost a big account—
Home Depot. We had to tell everyone that their jobs might
be in jeopardy. I guess we could have held off that information for a while, but we felt that we needed to be honest
with our employees about what was happening. And
because we did, we came bouncing back and are a lot better for it today. We did have to lay off a lot of the factory
workers for three or four months but many of them came
back. And at least we were able to give them as much time
as possible to prepare for tough times.**

Lon Dolber, president and CEO of American Portfolios Financial
Services. doesn't shrink from telling unpleasant truths either. He's discovered it's the only way to secure the trust of employees and customers. Until a few years ago, American Portfolios used two firms to
clear financial transactions. Then Lon realized that it would be best for
the business to merge into one clearing firm. But there was a catch: The
clearing firm's charges would result in financial gains for Lon's business, while lowering brokers' compensation. As Lon relates:

**I could have said we had to consolidate, that we had no
choice. The truth was I decided that we needed to do this to
be competitive. I didn't hide the fact that the brokers would
make less and the efficiencies we gained would actually
mean more profit for us. I pointed out that we need to do
this to grow and sustain ourselves during the economic
downturn. I explained why I did it. I could constantly**

blame the government and regulators, but I never do that. I'm always honest about it. I say, "We are doing it and these are the reasons." So I've developed more trust with the brokers. If you're truthful, you'll develop trust. You'll develop loyal customers [the brokers] with trust. I believe that truth leads to trust and trust leads to loyalty and loyal customers are the best customers. Our customers recognize and feel very comfortable with that.

Telling the Truth About Performance

Many of us are afraid to discuss poor performance with a subordinate. We imagine that people will be upset, and we don't want to be responsible for causing them pain.

Paul Clayton, former president of Burger King North America, and former CEO of Jamba Juice, is not known for pulling his punches. The only time he can recall when he has withheld the truth was when he had to sit down with someone and talk about his or her performance. "I have made mistakes in not being direct enough. I had to give a negative performance review and circled around the issues, and I've had that happen to me as well. I've always been critical of my communication skills, but for a long time, no one said a word to me. I knew that if someone had the courage to tell me sooner that I needed work, it would have helped me."

We have all heard horror stories about co-workers who got a glowing performance review coupled with a bonus, only to be fired a month later. When that happens, it is usually because the manager has not been honest about the employee's performance problems over some period of time. Some managers are so nonassertive that employees who are being given negative feedback have no idea that they are being criticized. We know of several extreme examples when an employee who was fired on a Friday showed up for work as usual on Monday because she didn't realize she had been terminated.

Exceptions to the rule of honesty. A seemingly contradictory aspect of the competency of telling the truth is that it includes knowing when *not to* tell the truth. Consider an example posed by 18th century philosopher, Immanuel Kant. Imagine that a murderer comes to your door, wanting to know where your friend is—so that he can kill her. Your friend is hiding in your bedroom closet. Most people would probably agree that your obligation to your friend overrides your general obligation to tell the truth. For some brave World War II Europeans, this scenario was not hypothetical—they risked their lives sheltering Jews from the Nazis. *The Diary of Anne Frank* is a famous telling of the story of a Dutch Jewish family hidden by a former employee of Anne Frank's father. When the Nazis made their regular sweeps of their Amsterdam neighborhood in search of Jews, the family protecting the Franks would have failed in moral competence if they had told the truth about what they were doing.

Honesty is often complicated for business leaders as well. At times, a leader has information that cannot be divulged. This is common in situations involving downsizings, initial public offerings, and mergers and acquisitions. When planning workforce reductions, for example, leaders know that employees would find it helpful to get advance warning that their job could be at risk. On the other hand, leaders have a responsibility to owners not to divulge information that could be harmful to the market value of their companies. To tell the truth prematurely would be a disservice to the business, yet to say when asked that no reorganization is looming would be dishonest. If there are legal requirements to withhold information, the leader should simply acknowledge that. A leader can still be truthful by saying something like, "We do have plans but we cannot discuss them at this time. Please know that we will implement the plan with high regard for our employees, our customers, and the people who own the company."

Withholding information is also justified to protect the privacy of employees. Consider computer programmer, Jeanetta Shaw (pseudonym) who discovered that her husband and his family were all involved in criminal activity that was about to hit the newspaper headlines. Her distress was obvious to her co-workers, and they began to ask their manager what was going on. The manager decided to tell the truth, but not the whole truth. He told Jeanetta's colleagues that there were personal circumstances beyond her control that were causing her a great deal of stress. He expressed his commitment to help her get through a rough time and asked others to do the same.

The painful truth? Telling the truth and tact are not incompatible. Some of us pride ourselves on being honest to a fault. We might say things others would be afraid to say, but it doesn't necessarily add up to more truth. Some of us use "honesty" as an excuse to vent our hostility. We might make cruel, competitive, or aggressive comments under the guise of "calling it like you see it" and then excuse ourselves by claiming, "I'm only being truthful." According to Jefferson Bus Line's CEO, Charlie Zelle, the disclaimer "'I'm just being honest' is a classic Minnesota passive-aggressive way of being hurtful." When we go out of our way to communicate a hurtful truth, we are usually not being honest with ourselves. So, when we feel obligated to tell another something "for his own good," we need first to examine our own motivations. Are we competitive? Are we jealous? Are we trying to even up an old score? And we might be wise to add one more question: Is there a way we can be compassionately honest versus brutally honest?

Good intentions. Truth telling works best when paired with the emotional competency of self-awareness. We need self-awareness to understand how our own goals and desires influence what we say to others. Leaders who limit information about pending changes should rigorously examine their motivations. Although it is important to protect their companies, leaders who withhold information because they put personal stock option considerations over employee well being, clearly violate principle of integrity.

We also need emotional competencies to understand other's emotions and discuss the truth in ways that people can accept and use productively. Employees sense when their leaders make self-serving decisions or shade the truth about pending changes. The resulting negative impact on morale and performance can undermine the implementation of any change effort.

How truth fuels performance. Truth telling has a huge impact on leadership effectiveness and workforce engagement. When people work for a dishonest leader, they censor information to protect themselves from a negative or unpredictable reaction. The dishonest boss creates a climate dominated by political intrigue. Instead of working productively, people who work for dishonest superiors spend a lot of time wondering about their manager's agenda, trying to gather information, trying to jockey for power, and doing only those things they think will keep them out of harm's way. In contrast, leaders who are known for being honest generate a powerful climate of trust. People who work for honest superiors relax because they know there will be no hidden surprises coming out of the organizational woodwork. People accomplish more and can work with great creativity when they don't have to waste energy watching their back.

Standing Up for What Is Right

Leaders who live the principle of integrity inevitably must take principled stands.

Ben Smith began his career as an attorney and has extensive executive experience in the banking industry as a former Co-CEO of American Partners Bank, former EVP of Wells Fargo and former EVP at GMAC. Ben relays this story about taking a stand when it was difficult to do so:

> **One of our top loan officers was a great guy and well liked by everyone at the bank. It came to my attention he would do more than one loan per year to quite a few of his customers to both keep them from default and to generate new**

business for himself and the bank. What he was doing wasn't illegal, but it wasn't right. Sometimes he would give three loans to the same customer in one year. I knew this wasn't good for those customers because it enabled them to stay current on loans they couldn't really afford, and it wasn't good for the bank long term even though it generated income for the bank in the short term. It also generated commissions for the loan officer. I chose to terminate him, and that was hard to do because I liked him personally and because people liked him at the bank, but that was the right thing to do.

Ben's leadership approach also highlights how often the principles of integrity, responsibility, and compassion are interrelated. On one occasion, American Partners Bank had a job candidate for an underwriting position. Ben really wanted to hire her. But she had a young child and wanted the flexibility to work from home, so Ben agreed. She quickly became one of the banks' best underwriters. When American Partners Bank was sold, Ben made sure that the new owners retained all but two of their employees. After the acquisition, the new owners planned to lay off a woman who had just had a baby. Ben knew she really needed the income, so he persuaded the new owners to retain her in a contracting role for another year. Was Ben demonstrating integrity? Responsibility? Compassion? Clearly his behavior demonstrated he was aligned with all three principles.

American Portfolio's Lon Dolber is another role model for standing up for what is right. When clients are unhappy about the results of an investment, it's tempting to heed the lawyers' advice to "Make it go away." It's one thing if a broker does something that's not good for the client. In that case, Lon believes the firm should stand by the client and make it right. But most investment losses are not the fault of the brokers who sold them. So there are instances when Lon believes he must stand up and fight. One time, for example, his firm had a sophisticated client who bought an investment that he wanted through a broker and the investment went bad, so the client took the firm to arbitration. As Lon recalls:

> **[He was] an accredited investor and knew the risk, but [he] got an aggressive lawyer who was looking to pin it on us. It was absolutely not a case of an uninformed investor or a broker misleading an investor. Well, we won the case. If I hadn't won, it would have made me rethink the business I'm in. If we could be taken to arbitration for everyone who loses money, it would be a loser of a business. So, in fighting this, we gained more trust from our brokers and we stood up for what's right, and the employees and the customers all see that. It's smart both ways.**

University of Washington e-commerce professor David Risher recalls this incident of standing up for an employee during his tenure as a Microsoft executive:

> **One day, we were in the middle of a meeting, and my strong-willed boss started to beat up on a young, new employee of mine, asking her questions she couldn't possibly have answered because she was so new. My boss was a hard person to stand up to, but in this case, I did. I remember that it caused a bit of a commotion in the room because people couldn't believe I was standing up to her—she was just that strong. When I later went to Amazon.com, my former boss ended up working for me. She ended up being a supporter of mine, and I think it was because she respected me for having been willing to stand up for people.**

Gary Kessler, senior vice president of Human Resources, Administration and Corporate Affairs with American Honda Motor Company recalls a time when he took a quiet but vital stand. He discovered that a member of his team who was also a personal friend had fabricated his academic background. Gary knew that he could forgive his friend, and he knew he could keep anyone else from finding out what his friend had done. But Gary believed that to ignore his friend's deception would be deceptive on his part. It would devalue the efforts of others who were expected to have a certain level of academic training. So he steeled his courage and fired his friend.

Unlike Gary's admirable private stand, most principled stands must be taken in the face of stiff resistance. Don Hall, Jr., is the president and CEO of Hallmark Cards. Early in his career, Don headed product development. Don had a fine-tuned sense of what customers expected from Hallmark. He steadfastly resisted proposals to save on production costs by cheapening their product. To maintain customer loyalty, Don insisted that quality, rather than cost, be the company's primary focus.

Defying conventional wisdom to make a principled stand can be challenging. In most organizations, there is a lot of pressure to agree with popular positions. People who take unpopular stands can put their career advancement or their livelihoods at risk. Acting with integrity means that you accept the risks that come with taking a principled stand because the moral consequences of looking the other way are unacceptable. Think of the hazards that have resulted when no one stood up for what was right—buildings that collapse because of poor construction, lives lost because a bridge's need for repair was ignored, bankruptcies caused by predatory lending practices in low-income neighborhoods, and the explosion of the space shuttle *Challenger* after NASA executives ignored engineers' concerns about faulty O-rings.

Keeping Promises

Keeping promises is a hallmark of integrity because it demonstrates that we can be trusted to do what we say we will do. Keeping promises is a competency highly valued in organizational settings, but in our wired

24/7 world, it's a competency many of us have a hard time practicing consistently. We have good intentions but may let our ever-expanding to-do list overtake our earlier promises. This was the case with Kari Wang (pseudonym), a senior executive in a professional services firm, whose career was in jeopardy and whose team was delivering inferior results. Kari had lost the respect of her colleagues because of her poor track record in keeping her commitments to them. When a high-profile project came her way, Kari dug in and took over all the detailed work herself, saddling herself with more work than even an overachiever like Kari could handle. Kari resisted delegating, rationalizing that she'd be happy to delegate if only she could find someone who could do a good enough job. When Kari did reluctantly delegate, she routinely forgot to provide all the information needed for the work to be done successfully. She changed her mind about priorities seemingly every hour and then failed to communicate those changes to her staff. Kari was incapable of saying "no"—she agreed to do so many things that she inevitably dropped the ball on some important commitments.

People who knew Kari well did their best to work around her bad habits, believing that though her execution was poor, her motives were good. People who did not know Kari personally saw only her lapses. They mistrusted her and labeled her a liar. Her harshest critics viewed her missteps as deliberate efforts to advance her own career by sabotaging others. Fortunately, Kari's boss proposed that she use a leadership coach to help her make the transition from high-powered individual performer to leader of others. As a result, Kari came to recognize the costs of her actions and developed the disciplined work habits that would eventually enable her to rebuild her credibility with her team.

Keeping promises usually requires assistance from a few emotional competencies–the self-awareness to recognize the inconsistency between our intentions and actions and the self-control to adopt disciplined work habits that enable us to keep our promises.

Honoring confidences. One of the most frequent promises leaders are asked to keep is to preserve the privacy of others. A common complaint about low-integrity leaders is that they have failed to keep confidences. Some leaders betray confidences with good intentions because they believe that sharing the information with someone else will help the person who revealed private information. Others wrongly believe that it is acceptable to share confidential information about a third party that they trust will not pass the confidential information on to others. It's ironic that some of us expect a third party to keep a confidence that we ourselves have betrayed. When you discuss private information about another person with anyone, you can assume that it will become public—*and* that the person whose confidence you betrayed will know that you were the source.

When leaders betray confidences, they lose more than the respect of their work associates. They also dry up valuable sources of information because their employees and colleagues learn to withhold sensitive information from a loose-lipped leader.

Leaders who pass on confidential personal information do not suffer as much career damage as those who lack other dimensions of integrity. If the leader has an otherwise good reputation, people may try to compensate by emphasizing forcefully to the leader that certain information *must* be held in confidence. When a well-intentioned leader hears the urgency of the request, he will usually get the message.

Acting on Confidences Without Betraying Them

If you hear something in confidence that you strongly believe needs to be shared with others, ask for permission to share the confidence, or work with the person who disclosed the information to find a way to communicate about the issue in a protective way. Finally, if you hear something in confidence that you have a legal requirement to disclose, inform those who provided the information that you have that obligation.

6 Responsibility

*I think of a hero as someone who understands the degree
of responsibility that comes with his freedom.*

—Bob Dylan

*We've gotten to the point where everybody's got a right
and nobody's got a responsibility.*

—Newton Minow, former chairman of the FCC

The Responsibility Competencies	• Taking responsibility for personal choices
	• Admitting mistakes and failures
	• Embracing responsibility for serving others

The Buck Stops Here. That was the saying on the plaque on President Harry Truman's desk in the Oval Office. He referred to it on several occasions to underscore the idea that an American president didn't have the luxury of passing off accountability for decisions to anyone else. That the expression has survived for over half a century is testament to the importance of the responsibility principle. Needing the reminder is an indication of how difficult it can be to live in alignment with the responsibility principle.

Irresponsibility is nothing new. In biblical lore, the first human excuse followed close on the heels of God's creation of the species: When God caught Adam eating the forbidden fruit, Adam promptly claimed, "Eve made me do it." We live in a culture that tolerates a high degree of daily responsibility-dodging, but when it gets to the level of, say, widespread corporate scandals, it's the failures of responsibility that upset us most. As one example, until the day he died, Enron CEO Ken Lay never admitted that he had any idea former CFO Andrew Fastow was manipulating the accounting ledger. Fast forward to the economic crisis of the late 2000s. As *The Wall Street Journal* reported in December 2008:

> **For the U.S. securities industry to unravel as spectacularly as it did in September, many parities had to pull on many threads. Mortgage bankers gave loans to Americans for homes they couldn't afford. Investment houses packaged these loans into complex instruments whose risk they didn't always understand. Ratings agencies often gave their seal of approval, investors borrowed heavily to buy, regulators missed the warning signs.[1]**

Despite this seemingly obvious and widespread irresponsibility on the part of financial services companies, regulators, politicians, and even consumers, no one seems to accept responsibility for the part they played in the worst economic crisis since the Great Depression. No one has admitted that they or their organizations were at fault in any way.

And so far, no one has gone to jail. It seems that no one involved in the corporate accounting scandals or the subprime mortgage debacle ever heard about the sign on Truman's desk. Leaders are responsible. It comes with the job. We can shirk it, and we can make excuses when things get tough, but we do so at our peril. We suffer and so does our business. But as challenging as it may be to accept responsibility, the rewards of accepting responsibly are great. As with every other moral competency, we do it because it's morally right and then discover that it's right for our business as well.

Taking Responsibility for Personal Choices

The hallmark of personal responsibility is our willingness to accept that we are accountable for the results of the choices we make. Everything we do follows the law of cause and effect. When we cause something to happen, there is an effect, usually more than one effect. Some of the consequences of our actions are planned; other consequences come as a surprise. Owning personal choice entails that we take responsibility for all consequences of our behavior, both anticipated effects and unintended consequences.

Middle managers frequently struggle with the responsibility competency because they often feel caught between their responsibility for the people they lead and the demands of their senior managers. Frustrated middle managers often complain that they have all the responsibility and none of the authority. That complaint may be code for "I am not really responsible for my actions because my boss made me do it."

Responsibility is a radical competency because it requires that we accept personal responsibility for everything that we do, even though we each live in a complicated world where bosses, family members, and friends all exert pressure on us to act in certain ways. Responsibility means no excuses, even though none of us is perfect and all of us have good explanations for failing to do what we know is right.

No excuses. Mike Manning (pseudonym) loves golf. Ironically, his passion for golf led him to a moral crossroads early in his career. Mike's goals at one time were to be successful in business, be a great golfer, and be a good father. Mike was clear about what he needed to do to be successful in his work. He knew what he had to do to become a better golfer—he had to get in a certain number of rounds per week to improve his game. "The trouble is," Mike said, "I don't have time to be a good father if I want to do well in business and excel in golf." Someone suggested he kill two birds with one stone by golfing with his kids. Mike was scornful. "That wouldn't work at all," he complained. "It wouldn't be fun, and it certainly wouldn't help my game." But on reflection, Mike came to this realization: "Saying I don't have time to be a good father makes it sound like it's not my responsibility, as though time is at fault. Being a good father is a more important goal than being a good golfer. If I want to be a good father, I have to make choices about how I spend my time." At first, Mike thought he would have to give up golf, and then he realized that the idea about golfing with his kids was a good one. He could enjoy playing golf and let go of the need to aggressively improve his game. Mike admitted responsibility for his choice to put other goals above his desire to be a good parent. Only when he realized that the choice was his could he take steps to be a more responsible father.

Accepting responsibility for personal choice does not mean mindlessly holding to decisions no matter how unproductive they turn out to be. But neither does it mean that we have to be sure we have made the perfect choice. Responsibility is not about making the perfect choice. Instead, it is about making the choice you have made the perfect choice for you. Some leaders make it a priority to find work consistent with their moral compass, even if it involves declining promotions or passing up tempting external job offers. Jim Thomsen, senior vice president of Member Services with Thrivent Financial for Lutherans, says,

What has kept me with this organization is that I can make a difference while honoring my values. I've had opportunities to make more money, and I've had opportunities that would give me more prestige. But values have played a central role in my decision to work where I work.

Other leaders who have been seduced by jobs, with attractive compensation and perks, come to feel trapped in roles that might not reflect their most deeply held values. They may sense a need for change, but out of a misguided notion of responsibility cling to their current position. "I took this job, so I need to see it through." A leader who senses he or she is in the wrong job can demonstrate responsibility in one of two ways—help reshape the organization so it is worth remaining or have the courage to make a values-driven career change.

Admitting Mistakes and Failures

Another important aspect of responsibility includes the willingness to take responsibility when things go wrong. Many of us grew up naively assuming that when we turned 21, graduated from college, got married, or got our first job, we would then be perfect finished products. Others have found that career success has enabled them the illusion that they are indeed perfect. The higher you go in an organization, the less likely it is that people around you will give you accurate feedback, so it becomes easy to forget that you are as flawed as the most junior staffer. What's more, the higher you go in an organization, the easier it is for you to confuse power with perfection. So, the best advice to senior managers is, "Don't believe your PR." The more elevated your organizational status, the more important it is for you to actively solicit feedback on your weaknesses.

Even if you know you are not perfect and even if you realize that you make mistakes, it may be frightening to admit it. Some organizational cultures are punitive, and the cost of failure can be high. You may worry about losing a raise, a promotion, or even a job if your mistake is discovered. The irony is that punishing mistakes dampens the risk-taking and experimentation so crucial to sustainable business performance.

If you work in an organization that does not tolerate mistakes, our advice is to get out as soon as you can.

Fortunately, most of us work in organizations that tolerate our mistakes, even if they aren't happy about them. Even more fortunately, admitting mistakes and failures can enhance our leadership reputation more often than it damages it. Caroline Stockdale, senior vice president and chief talent officer for medical technology company Medtronic, can attest to that. As Caroline recalls:

> **Earlier in my career, I was two weeks into a new senior job with a company. I'm a bit of a data geek and I started looking under the covers right away to see what was going on. I discovered we had an issue with our own benefits plan for our people. The people working on the program were good people but were inexperienced, and I discovered a major and potentially very expensive mistake. I went to the CEO and shared with him the problem and suggested he had two possible courses of action: one, eat a several million dollar mistake without passing on the cost of the mistake to the employees; two, go back to the employees and tell them you aren't going to be able to honor the commitment you had given them just a couple weeks before. He knew and I knew that trust is hard to build and easy to break. He chose to eat the expense, and that was the right choice. He kept his promise. He did what was right.**

Don MacPherson of Modern Survey can also attest to the positive effects of admitting mistakes. "One time, we had prepared a report for the SVPs of a Fortune 500 company. We made a mistake in some top line data. We inadvertently didn't include all the survey responses in the results, and it seriously distorted the picture. Of course, we realized that if we didn't tell them about our mistake, they would have no way of knowing that the report was inaccurate. But we didn't want them to make decisions based on faulty data, so we never debated whether or not to tell them, only how we should go about it. I called my client contact, let her know the extent of the problem, and shared what I thought we should do to fix the problem. Her reputation was important to her and to us, and it was essential that we take 100% of the responsibility for the error. We redid the report—of course, at no cost—and we submitted a signed memo taking the blame. They are now our best client, and our client contact is the same woman, and she is fiercely loyal to us."

Admitting personal mistakes helps an organization be healthier in several ways. First, admitting that you have screwed up prevents someone else from being blamed for your mistake. It's common in organizational hierarchies for junior staff to take the fall for their senior managers, and few things are more demoralizing to employees than unfair criticism. Second, admitting mistakes creates a bond with other employees who feel that you are more approachable by virtue of your admission of fallibility. Finally, admitting mistakes communicates a strong message of tolerance to the organization at large. It says, "We all make mistakes. We know that mistakes and failures are a part of the road to success. We want you to learn from your mistakes, and we hope in the future you will make new mistakes and not repeat old ones." By admitting mistakes and failures, you can help create a more risk-tolerant climate that leads to innovation and financial success.

Rick Clevette, now corporate vice president, Human Resources at the Carlson Companies, tells a story from his days as an executive in a large Fortune 500 company. One of the firm's top business heads was a pillar of a leader, long on integrity but a bit short on patience. He had a reputation for being hard on people. The training department had brought in Ken Blanchard of "The One Minute Manager" fame to talk to hundreds of top and mid-level managers. Ken gave his usual entertaining and enlightening stump speech about the importance of looking for opportunities to give employees "one minute" of praise. Not long after, this leader blew up at a junior manager who was making a presentation. The leader soon realized his mistake. He apologized—in writing. He sent a memo to the manager and a copy to the training people, asking them to contact Ken Blanchard about adding another principle to the "One Minute Manager,"—suggesting the need for a "one minute apology." By apologizing in such a public way, this leader not only admitted his own error, but modeled the value of admitting mistakes to his whole organization.

Admitting mistakes makes sense, not only as a moral imperative, but also as a practical one. Covering up mistakes takes a lot of time and energy and often makes a situation far worse than it need be. Martha Stewart's conviction and prison sentence is a famous example. Stewart was not convicted of insider trading but of obstructing justice. When the FBI interviewed her in connection with their investigation of insider trading, they concluded she lied about why she had sold her ImClone stock. Had she admitted that she sold her stock when she heard that ImClone's CEO was dumping his, she would probably never have been charged with a serious crime.

As important as it is to admit mistakes, it is not a "free pass." It does not absolve you of responsibility for the situation you created or magically undo the harm you may have caused. Though most people would understandably prefer to avoid mistakes that hurt others, there are times when admitting a mistake creates opportunities that would not have existed otherwise. Consider this example of a mistake that transformed a contentious work relationship. Faith Shanley (pseudonym) was a bright, up-and-coming executive who was frequently on the opposite side of issues from her colleague Louis Draper (pseudonym), a seasoned executive who had been with their company since its inception. At a management meeting both attended, Faith decided she needed to make a stand about a proposal she viewed as unethical. She made her point forcefully and, in the process, became sarcastic and confrontational with Louis. Faith felt great after the meeting, proud that she had said something important and confident that her views were well founded. Shortly after, Louis walked into Faith's office and told her he was upset about what she had done in the meeting. In a flash, Faith realized that she had been so caught up in standing up for what she thought was right, that she was oblivious to the impact of her confrontational style on Louis and the rest of the group. Faith promptly apologized to Louis. She admitted that she should have come to him privately before the meeting to explain her point of view because she knew in advance that there would be a conflict with his ideas. Faith was grateful that Louis came directly to her to discuss her behavior instead of gossiping behind her back. Louis was impressed with Faith's willingness to admit her mistake. Instead of avoiding each other as they had done in the past, Faith and Louis began to meet regularly on the issues that affected them, and over time, their once-distant relationship became closer and more productive.

Embracing Responsibility for Serving Others

We are all responsible for contributing to the well-being of others. Why is serving others an essential moral competence? Think back to the biological origins of morality. We come into the world programmed to be interdependent. We wouldn't be around today if our earliest human ancestors hadn't huddled together to help their fellow tribes people survive. If we do not work to serve others, we fail to act as morally intelligent leaders. Serving others is a great way to show integrity and to encourage others to model it—in other words, to lead by example.

Ken Krei, president of the Wealth Management Group of M&I Bank, is a strong advocate of the principle of responsibility:

We all have personal accountability. At M&I we focus on customers, shareholders, and community. We have responsibility to our employees in terms of their safety and their families. From the shareholders perspective, we have to realize that they expect and deserve a return. And with the community we have to give back to the community's welfare, to culture and arts, etc. That's an awesome responsibility and I personally take it seriously. Responsibility is a pretty awesome part of running a successful business. The customer is most important. If we don't provide good value and products and services we're not doing the job that will win their loyalty and attract new customers.

When Charlie Zelle bought out his family's troubled transportation business, much of his motivation was to be of service to his employees and the community. Explaining his distress at the family's plans to close up shop, he added, "I just felt that some kind of moral boundary was being violated—perhaps it is the idea that you should consider everyone, not just yourself, in any decision."

Suppose you don't buy the idea that interdependence is innate. It still makes sense to actively care about the well-being of others. Here's why: We all value personal happiness. We want to be happy even though we know it is a self-centered motivation. For most of us, the happiness we seek doesn't happen in a vacuum. Happiness is hard to come by without help from others. Most of us need others to help us be happy.

Gary O'Hagan agrees that service is important, but he thinks that serving others serves himself at least as much. "Every time I've done something for others, it's given me a better feeling about myself. When I help family or friends or even charities, I actually have stopped and asked myself if I'm really serving others or if I'm just being selfish."

Ignoring the needs of others keeps us from experiencing the genuine pleasure that Gary experienced in helping others. The mentality expressed by the 1990s bumper sticker, "Whoever dies with the most toys wins," describes fleeting pleasure but not true happiness. For most people, lasting happiness comes from activities that give us a sense of meaning and purpose—such as serving others. Recent studies on longevity have found that serving as a volunteer with some worthwhile organization adds years to our lives (not to mention life to our years).

Accepting responsibility for serving others is also a secret weapon for leaders who want to promote high performance among their workforce. To make their businesses successful, leaders need committed employees. One of the best ways to encourage people to unleash their creative energy in service to their company is for their leaders to serve *them*. Employees don't need to be coerced into doing their best work for your organization. People have an inherent and insatiable appetite for personal growth. Left to their own devices, employees will spontaneously contribute to your organization as their way of growing and succeeding in life. That is why leaders don't need to impose goals from on high. Much of the time and effort companies devote to complicated performance management systems is unnecessary. The most efficient way to elicit strong financial results is for leaders to serve their employees. When we serve our employees, we send them this message:

I know that what you are capable of producing is far greater than what our company needs to succeed. So my opportunity as your leader is to serve you as you do what you want to do, which I already know goes beyond what I need from you. My goal is to serve your needs and help each of you be as successful as you want to be and help you get out of life what you want. If I can help you accomplish what you want to do, then I know our company will do very well. I don't have to focus on the numbers. I have to focus on you and all our people. Then the numbers will be fine.

Because together our people will perform better than our financial targets require. I know that serving you serves the bottom line.

The retention value of servant leadership. Imagine how your employees will respond if you consistently demonstrate that your primary leadership job is to help employees accomplish their own goals. They will stay. Because most businesses yield more value from experienced employees than new recruits, your decision to serve employees will translate into higher levels of knowledge and performance. Because you respect your employees' goals, they will be highly motivated to give their best efforts to you and your organization.

At Ameriprise Financial, managers are encouraged to spend considerable time helping financial advisors to develop life goals that include business goals *and* important personal goals. Managers are also expected to find ways to support their advisors as they reach for their goals. This approach has resulted in excellent retention and bottom-line performance. Because the company can keep a high percentage of financial advisors, it generates revenue it would have otherwise lost—while at the same time lowering expenses through reduced turnover costs.

Endnote

1. Susanne Craig, Jeffrey McCracken, Aaron Lucchette, and Kate Kelly, "The Weekend that Wall Street Died—Ties that Long United Strongest Firms Unraveled as Lehman Sank Toward Failure," *Wall Street Journal*, December 29, 2008.

7

Compassion and Forgiveness

If you want others to be happy, practice compassion.
If you want to be happy, practice compassion.

—The Dalai Lama

Forgiveness is almost a selfish act because of its
immense benefits to the one who forgives.

—Lawana Blackwell, **The Dowry of Miss Lydia Clark**

The Compassion Competency	• Actively caring about others

Actively Caring About Others

When you are a leader, embracing your responsibility to serve others flows into compassion. Actively caring about others means that you do things that actively support the personal choices of others. Sometimes, it means you care about others' goals as much as they do. At times, you might find yourself taking others' goals more seriously than they feel able to. Mike Woodward, former SVP of Amerprise Financial and now a senior advisor at Ducks Unlimited, is a conscientious and productive leader but also a private person who, early in his career, was reluctant to share his personal goals with his manager. After some nudging from his boss, Mike confided, "I really want to spend more time with my daughters. I have done a lot of hunting and fishing with my sons, but I haven't spent as much time with my girls, and I'm missing that." Then, soccer season rolled around for one of his daughters who was a strong athlete. Mike had arranged his schedule to attend her soccer games. Then, Mike was called to a meeting of the top national sales managers to be held in Minneapolis. The meeting was running late, and Mike's boss realized Mike would need to leave before the meeting ended if he wanted to see his daughter's soccer game. But Mike wasn't moving. Mike's boss interrupted the meeting. "Mike, don't you have a flight to catch?" he asked. "Yeah," Mike answered, "but the meeting is going long." His boss then demonstrated his support for Mike's personal goals, saying, "Leave now. Go to the airport. Go home and see your daughter's game."

Former president of Ameriprise Financial's Personal Advisor group Brian Heath, a body-builder with a bouncer's physique, doesn't look like a compassionate type. Appearances to the contrary, he is deeply compassionate. In Brian's mind, compassion isn't just about taking pity on the helpless. It is about taking people's hopes and dreams seriously and doing what he can to help them achieve their aspirations. He sets ambitious goals, but only after he is sure he understands what his people hope to accomplish.

IMG Coaches' division president Gary O'Hagan also subscribes to the notion that compassion means challenging people to do their best, believing that they can accomplish their goals, and providing the tools they need to succeed. There was a time right after Gary was cut by the New York Jets when he coached junior varsity high-school football. There were only 25 teens on his team, and 4 of them were handicapped. He wasn't sure what to do. He was afraid his handicapped players would get hurt, but they wanted to play badly, so he decided that they were going to play. Gary explains, "The handicapped kids were offside all the time, but we decided to work on that. With the help of the non-handicapped kids—who were phenomenal—we instituted a special series of concentration drills—that by the way had nothing specifically to do with football. We put in some penalties for not doing the drills right. We were very nurturing, and the coaching staff and the whole team were very compassionate, and we converted the handicapped kids' weakness into a strength. We never went offside during a game that whole season. Their progress was incredible. The solution was unique, and it allowed everyone to contribute."

Jefferson Bus Line's CEO, Charlie Zelle, points out that compassion doesn't mean ignoring bad behavior—that sometimes the most compassionate thing a leader can do is hold an employee accountable for unacceptable behavior. A number of years ago, Charlie had a senior manager who began to act like a loose cannon. It was a stressful time because the company had to close down a division. In a misguided attempt to show compassion for an employee he was letting go, the manager started badmouthing the company's decision during his termination discussion with her. Every employee he laid off got a different explanation for the layoff. Then, the manager began an affair with someone in the corporate office. Other people tried to ignore the manager's missteps, but Charlie knew he had to let him go. If Charlie ignored the manager's bad behavior, it would wreak havoc with the trust other employees had in him and the company.

Three years later, the manager he had fired came back and asked for a half hour with Charlie. Turns out, he came to thank Charlie. He had been drinking heavily during those last few months with Charlie's company and getting fired had been the wake-up call that prompted his entry into a treatment program. If Charlie had kept the manager on board out of misplaced compassion, it might have taken a lot longer for him to get the help he needed. Charlie's reaction? "This said to me, you've got to do the right thing even if at the moment it feels like the person will really hate you."

ID Media's Lynn Fantom has an unusual appreciation for compassion. She considers it central to her leadership approach. "I take my model for management from my mother. To me, the behavioral model of a mother is perfect for management. A mother is compassionate and encouraging and forgiving. Think about how a mother behaves when she is helping a young child learn to walk. When I became a mother, I became a much better manager."

Forgiveness

The Forgiveness Competencies	• Letting go of one's own mistakes • Letting go of others' mistakes

The two forgiveness competencies are frequently considered "mirror competencies," clearly closely related. It is hard to talk about one without the other, but they are not the same skill. Some of us are much better at forgiving ourselves than others and vice versa. Many of us are hard on ourselves because of perfectionism. We can let go of other's mistakes but hold on to our own. Sometimes, we are our own worst critics. Others of us have an easier time forgiving ourselves because we know our own underlying good intentions, whereas we may resist forgiving others because we distrust their motives. Effective leaders know that letting go of mistakes—their own and others—clears the way for better future performance.

Letting Go of Your Own Mistakes

The founders of Modern Survey were riding high. They knew they had developed a unique technology for providing survey-based business information. Right out of the gate, they landed a big contract with a Fortune 500 client and had several projects going on at the same time, each with a different contact person. They worked hard on the various projects and were sure the results had impressed their clients. They geared up to bid on another project for this company. Then co-founder Don MacPherson got an unwelcome call from a key contact in the company. They were taking all their business to a competitor and wouldn't even let Modern Survey submit a bid. The problem? Don and his partners had assumed that their superior technology was the only thing they needed to be successful. Don was responsible for managing the account, and he hadn't spent any time cultivating high-quality relationships with his client contacts. They wanted more attentive service, and when they didn't get it from Modern Survey, they went elsewhere. Don says, "My mistake was not taking good care of that relationship. We expected the business. We felt entitled to the business rather than understanding we have to continually work for the business. We've never gotten the client back."

Don's partners were upset about the situation, but they didn't blame Don. Don, however, blamed himself. He dwelled on his mistake for almost six months. Several years later, he still thinks about it occasionally and gets upset. But only by letting go were Don and his partners able to think more clearly about how to change their business practices, and those changes have helped the company with their other clients. "Now," says Don, "I make sure I give all my clients the kind of service and nurturing that I failed to give the one we lost."

Letting go of our mistakes doesn't mean we have to excuse or explain away unacceptable behavior. It is important, after all, to accept responsibility for what you did and commit to do better going forward. But we do have to give up the negative self-talk that can crowd our brain when we have disappointed ourselves. Why? When we are busy talking to ourselves about our frustration, anxiety, and guilt, there is no mental space for learning the lessons of our mistakes. If we can't forgive ourselves, we stay stuck; we hold ourselves back from fresh experiences and opportunities.

Brian Heath discovered that the hardest part of letting go of a mistake is first to admit that you have made one (the responsibility competency of admitting mistakes). When Brian was promoted from a regional VP to the newly created Group VP job, he had a stellar track record for developing high-performing sales teams. Several months into his new role, his group's performance had slid below the national average. For someone who had never been in that territory, the experience was shocking and debilitating. It took him a while to figure out what was going wrong. He was frustrated in his job and missed the direct contact he used to have with his field sales force. Now, instead of concentrating on developing his field team, he was spending a lot of energy developing a new piece of the bureaucracy—a mandated coordinating team intended to link him to the regional market groups. Finally, Brian had an epiphany, "I was focusing more on a method than an outcome. The evidence was there for several months, but I couldn't or wouldn't see it. It was hard to let go because I was vested in my own decision how to go about my new job. Finally, I realized I needed to be more courageous at helping advisors and helping clients."

In some professions, constant self-forgiveness is the only way to survive. When Gary O'Hagan was a young bond trader with Solomon Brothers, he found that if he didn't quickly let go of trading mistakes, he would be immobilized. When he made a mistake, he had to let it go, so he'd have the courage to trade another day. Gary reminisces, "I recall one day when I was managing the municipal bonds trading desk. For some reason, the municipal market was lagging in spite of other bond markets doing pretty well. I decided to take more risk and add to our position. I didn't find out until the day was over that Congress was considering removing tax exempt status from municipal bonds. I could have and should have paused and dug in to find out why the municipals' prices were dropping. Another bond house had done its homework, but I didn't, and it cost the firm a lot of money." Asked what happened after that, Gary responds, "Although we lost a lot of money that day because of my mistake, I was able to let it go the next day, and we went on to have a very good year!"

Letting Go of Others' Mistakes

There is an apocryphal story about legendary IBM CEO, Thomas Watson. A high-potential junior manager reputedly made a mistake that cost IBM $5 million dollars. Devastated by his error, the junior executive offered his resignation, but Watson would not accept it. The young man was confused. "I don't understand," he told Watson, "I made a terrible mistake. Why on earth would you want to keep me?" Watson replied, "I just invested $5 million on your learning curve. Why would I want to waste that kind of money?"

Forgiving others is not only the compassionate thing to do but it's also essential to keep valuable employees engaged and productive. Medtronic's Chief Talent Officer Caroline Stockdale has applied this lesson well:

> **Just last week one of my teams was preparing material for a board meeting and had made a huge mistake. We had already sent the preliminary material to the board with the mistake in it. The head of compensation called me and told me about it when he discovered it. I have always fostered**

an environment where people can do that. We sent out a correction sheet prior to the meeting. I personally called the woman who made the mistake and told her " I've got your back." I said, "I have made mistakes, too." I knew she felt panicked, but I told her "We're going to move on. You've been your own harshest critic, and you don't need me to pile [it] on. You will learn from this, and you will not make this mistake again."

ID Media's Lynn Fantom also recognizes the business benefits of forgiving others:

Just yesterday I was sitting with a senior employee of mine. We were discussing a project where she had failed to supervise effectively. We talked about the dynamics of her relationship with people on the project. If I had accused her of failing, I'm pretty sure she would have become defensive. But on the spot I could see that and forgave her and was able to help her think about the relationship she had with others. I offered the hypothesis that she was maybe too directive and not collaborative enough. I immediately expressed my forgiveness for the result and asked her to give that some thought. She knew I cared about her. She trusted my input. We all make mistakes, and when we admit it we don't have to accuse and defend. We will move on. She will move on. I already know she will handle things differently next time.

The forgiving leader's perspective. Imagine that I have made a mistake that affects you or causes you harm. Forgiving you does not mean that I endorse what you have done. In the case of serious harm, it does not mean giving up my claim for justice. You are still accountable for what you did. When I forgive you, what remains is a belief in your probable good intentions (unless you are a *very* bad person). But when

I forgive you, I allow my resentment and anger to recede, along with my negative judgments about you that would prevent me from considering you as a potential resource. When I forgive you, I continue to recognize that you have flaws, but I do not define you completely in terms of your flaws. I allow for the possibility that you have strengths that I can draw on in the future.

Without forgiveness, human life is virtually impossible. Intimate relationships with friends, family, and co-workers cannot exist without forgiveness. Without forgiveness, a leader's organizational performance is artificially capped. The effective leader forms a relationship with followers with forgiveness at its core. The forgiving leader's message to followers is essentially this:

You might as well know in advance that I will make mistakes, and so will you. As your boss, there are times when I won't be doing my best work. There will be days when you're not in top form, either. If you can't forgive me for not always being your perfect boss, our relationship will be ineffective. It will be not only emotionally hurtful, but also neither of us will perform as well as we should. If we can forgive each other for not being perfect, we will both be able to use each other as a valuable resource. We will be able to help each other be happy and perform at our best.

In the previous three chapters, we have talked about the specific moral competencies we need to live in alignment with our principles. Taken together, our moral competencies are the behavioral glue that binds together all the frames of the alignment model. Though we've considered them one by one, it's rare to find moral competencies in isolation. The moral competencies overlap because the universal principles themselves overlap. It's hard to imagine someone who has integrity but lacks responsibility or someone who has compassion but lacks forgiveness. Our moral competencies act synergistically to keep our day-to-day actions lined up with who we want to become and what we hope to achieve. We each have relative strengths and weaknesses in our moral competencies. The more competent we become across the full spectrum of moral competencies, the more we will live in alignment. The more aligned we are, the happier we will be, and the more productive and successful our organizations will be.

8

Emotions

Usually, we know the right thing to do (using our moral compass), and frequently, we know how to do the right thing (using our moral competencies). What then stops us from doing what we know is right? Moral challenges usually provoke highly charged emotions. How can we manage our emotions in a positive way? This chapter explores how our emotional intelligence competencies can help us reinforce our moral intelligence. By acting together, our emotional and moral competencies can enable us to conform more deeply to universal human principles and gain greater moral intelligence.

Recall the potential obstacles to staying in alignment. When destructive emotions and moral viruses threaten, our emotional skills help us stay connected with our values. There is nothing necessarily moral about emotional competencies. But emotional competencies are essential tools for the morally smart leader.

Keith Reinhard, Chairman Emeritus of DDB Worldwide tells this story:

> **I can remember being excited when my boss decided that he wanted me to be his successor. But there was a hitch. Charlie, the guy everyone thought would get the job, figured he had it all wrapped up. So my boss decided that he would create a new job for Charlie and sell it to him as a promotion, thereby getting him out of the way so I could have [a] clear shot for my boss's job. Then after I got my new job, my boss would find a way to get Charlie out of the company. I wouldn't accept it. I told my boss that Charlie had always been straight with me and I couldn't do this to him. I thought it would be better for my boss to be straight with Charlie. I even quoted him some of his own public statements about integrity. So he was honest with Charlie after all, and things worked out fine.**

How tempting it would have been for Keith to let his promotion play out the way his boss originally planned. Keith could have stood by quietly while his boss cleared the playing field by offering a bogus job to the heir apparent. Keith wanted that job, and he knew he could get it without being personally responsible for sidelining Charlie. All he had to do was keep his mouth shut. But as much as he wanted the job, Keith knew that his personal integrity was at stake. So he told his boss that he wouldn't take the job if it meant treating Charlie badly. Some executive power players may not have taken that message kindly. But Keith was no fool. He gave his boss a way to deal with Charlie that was aligned with values—both his and his boss's. Keith's goal of advancement could have easily overcome his values had he not tapped into his moral and emotional skills to find a morally acceptable way to get promoted. Keith needed the moral competencies of acting consistently with values and telling the truth. But he also needed the emotional skill of self-awareness to recognize two conflicting emotions—both his strong desire for the job and his discomfort about how Charlie might be treated. He needed the confidence that he could handle a negative reaction from his boss if he challenged him about his treatment of Charlie. He needed the interpersonal savvy to convince his boss to deal with Charlie in a morally competent manner.

Self-Awareness

Every waking moment, we face the world from within an **experiential triangle** of thoughts, emotions, and actions. No matter what is going on, we are always *thinking*, *feeling*, and *doing*, and we are doing all those things simultaneously. As leaders and decision makers, many of us are more comfortable operating in one of those three domains. Some of us are thinking types who tend to rely on logic and ideas; others are feeling types who tend to make decisions based on emotion, or some are physical types who want to *do*, to take action, as a way to respond to a problem. Research on work styles shows that American business leaders tend to be thinking and doing types, rather than feeling types. It's not that business people don't know they have feelings. It's just that many feel uncomfortable expressing them. Why the discomfort? English-speaking cultures place a high value on the products of the cognitive mind. No doubt thoughts *are* powerful. What we think certainly affects how we feel and what we do. But emotions are equally powerful. How we feel strongly affects what we think and what we do. Fear may paralyze us into inaction; anger may prompt us to strike out; optimistic beliefs may give us courage. Life's experiential triangle is an endless loop in which thoughts, feelings, and actions are continuously and mutually influencing one another.

Whether you are aware of your own experiential triangle, people around you see the outward behavior that results. What your colleagues notice about you and how they interpret what they see have an enormous impact on your work relationships, for good or ill. Because those around you can't read your (thinking and feeling) mind, it is easy for them to misunderstand your actions. If you want to be an effective leader, you need your colleagues to accurately understand what you mean and why you do what you do. Without self-awareness, you will remain a mystery to yourself, and you'll be in the dark about how you come across to your colleagues. If you are unaware of your feelings, you are at their mercy. Without self-awareness, your capacity for self-correction is extremely limited. In Chapter 9, "Making Moral Decisions," you learn a systematic method for accessing self-awareness to make optimal moral choices.

Modern Survey's Don MacPherson is seething. Earlier today, he was presenting a software demonstration to a new client, and the demo didn't work. "I can be very hard on my partners. They are the ones who create what I sell. If something goes wrong with the technology, it upsets me. And I'm the one who has to deal with the fallout. I handle it professionally with the client, but then I go back to my partners and get angry with them." Don pauses, leans back in his chair, and then continues, "I haven't told my partners yet about the problem today, and now that I'm talking about it I'm sure I will handle it better and not blame them. I know they'll get it fixed, and the fact that the demo didn't work won't be a big deal. Sometimes, the software is complicated and mistakes happen."

Don's story illustrates the power of self-awareness. He recognized that his typical pattern when angry about technical problems was to haul off and blame his partners. But this time, he reflected on the situation. He became aware of his frustration. He had time to put some distance between how he felt and what he would do about it. That self-conscious pause—between reaction and action—made a big difference. It enabled

Don to plan how to talk constructively with his partners about the failed demo. He was even able to change his attitude about it: Instead of thinking "woe is me" because he had to deal with clients when things go wrong, Don could now see technical problems in a way that was both realistic and optimistic. That moment of self-awareness will pay dividends in reduced personal stress and a smoother relationship with his partners.

Recognizing feelings. When a moral choice is at stake, self-awareness is essential. Recall Keith and his promotion. Keith's awareness—of his excitement about a likely promotion *and* discomfort about the impact on a trusted colleague—was crucial to communicating with his mentor in a way that produced positive results. Without awareness, Keith's desire for advancement might have overridden any moral reservations he had. Without sensitivity to the pain his colleague would feel at being passed over in a manipulative way, Keith might have remained silent. If emotions—Keith's and Charlie's—had been factored out of the decision process, Keith's promotion would have played out in a way that was morally suspect and likely damaging to Keith's credibility in his new role. All business decisions have wide audiences. Keith and Charlie's colleagues would have known that Charlie had been manipulated. Charlie's closest colleagues probably would have resented Keith, even though he was not directly responsible for Charlie's bad fortune.

Inner feelings affect the outer world. Awareness of your feelings is also vital to your ability to create a positive work climate for your employees. Because emotions are contagious, you need to monitor your feelings so that the mood you project is a stable one. Leaders accomplish far more when they don't put their people in a position of wondering what kind of mood their leader is going to be in each day. If you can save your colleagues the trouble of having to navigate around your unexamined emotions, you will liberate more creative energy for performance that would otherwise be sapped by your employees' anxiety.

Understanding Your Thoughts

Tune in to your thoughts, and you can realize that you are in constant conversation with yourself. Listen in while you head to work: You pass a Lexus and think, "I'd love to have a car like that." You're stopped at an endless red light. When the light changes, you accelerate and someone cuts you off. "What a jerk!," you say to yourself. That constant internal dialogue is often called self-talk. Whether we are alone, our minds are full of ideas and attitudes that we express in the inner language of self-talk. That self-talk, in turn, has a major impact on our emotions *and* our physical state. Thoughts are powerful. We may shed tears when we think of a lost parent or smile when we think about our last vacation. We did not decide to cry or smile; our physical reaction happened spontaneously in response to our thoughts.

Effective leaders tend to be highly conscious of their internal thoughts. Ed Zore, Chairman Emeritus of Northwestern Mutual, is constantly aware of his feelings and reactions. "I sometimes have to sort them out from the objective facts because my feelings and the facts about a situation can be very different."

We need to understand our thoughts so that we can monitor and manage their emotional and physical effects. Our thoughts don't have to be random, and we are not at their mercy. As you'll discover in the next chapter, you can choose your thoughts. And when you change your thoughts, everything can change for the better.

Time Out to Tune In: A Self-Awareness Break

Pick a few times during each day to perform a mental check. Ask yourself:

- What am I thinking right now? What am I saying to myself?
- What am I feeling about that? Am I excited, frustrated, peaceful, annoyed?
- What am I doing physically at this moment? How is my breathing? Are my jaws clenched? Am I hungry or thirsty?

Personal Effectiveness

We don't cultivate self-awareness for its own sake, but because it provides us the data we need to manage ourselves and our emotions. Managing emotions, by the way, does *not* mean trying not to feel, denying hurt, or even necessarily concealing strong emotions. We are not meant to be unemotional automatons (like *Star Trek's* Mr. Spock). It is human to feel uncomfortable emotions. Personal effectiveness helps us channel our emotions so that we can spend more time living in alignment. The goal is not to increase our emotional awareness and emotional skills per se; it is to increase these competencies so we can achieve greater alignment and moral intelligence. Personal effectiveness encompasses all the skills we use to perform well in the face of strong emotions. These include

- Changing self-defeating beliefs that lead to upsetting emotions

- Deciding to behave well under trying circumstances

- Rolling with the punches when things don't go our way

- Taking care of ourselves so we can better handle stressful situations

Deciding What to Think

If your thoughts are self-critical, you will notice that your emotions are negative, your body is tight, and you cannot perform at your best. If you spend a few minutes to replace your critical thoughts with statements of realistic confidence in yourself, your mood lifts, your body relaxes, and your work performance improves. Negative self-talk is a program for failure, whereas positive self-talk frees you to do your best. A caveat: We are not advocating that you mindlessly allow only positive self-talk or that you ignore fears or failings. There are negative thoughts that are realistic and must be confronted seriously. But no matter how dire the situation at hand, realistically positive self-talk is the best way to get your mind and body ready to perform effectively. If we *think* we can't run a marathon, we won't even try. Now imagine replacing that belief with a different thought—"If I train hard, I'll bet I can finish the marathon." Our new thought makes it far more likely that we will ultimately reach the finish line. Why? Because now we have created the motivation we need to get ready for the race.

As you see in Chapter 9, when you are in a morally charged situation, it helps to remind yourself of your principles, values, and beliefs. Self-talk about your beliefs allows you to counteract disruptive emotions that can drive you out of alignment with your moral compass. When Tatums' Lori Kaiser is troubled or searching for direction, she thinks about the three principles that she tries to live by: "First, if I don't speak up, nobody will—don't assume it will be handled by someone else. Second, Winston Churchill said, 'Never, never, ever give up!' That kind of tenacity is important in business. Third is a quote from existentialist philosopher, Albert Camus, 'In the midst of the darkest day of winter, I find within myself the eternal day of summer.'"

Lori's practice of mentally recalling her principles is an example of the value of deliberately interrupting negative thought processes or feelings. When our minds are clear, we are ready to tackle the situation at hand. Then we can ask ourselves, "What do I need to think about to deliver what I need? There is a bonus that comes with changing our self-talk: When we alter our internal thoughts from negative to positive ones, any emotional and physical discomfort we may feel usually lessens or goes away entirely.

Self-Control

Effective leaders rely on self-control to maintain alignment with principles. Most successful leaders know from experience that losing emotional control is bad for their self-esteem, their reputations, and their

business performance. A healthcare executive we'll call Ellen understands the importance of emotional control. "I've blown up at someone
only twice in my career. In the heat of the moment, I felt there was such
an injustice, and I felt so 'in the right' that I justified my actions. But in
reality, I violated my moral code—I certainly didn't treat them the way
I'd like to be treated. Of course, they were treating me badly too, but
that's no excuse. In both cases, it damaged my relationships, and that
has had its costs." Asked what she learned, Ellen says, "When I get
really angry, I now know to say, 'I need some time to think about this;
let's talk tomorrow.' I've also learned when to consult with someone
who's not personally involved before I decide what to do."

An emotionally intelligent leader knows when *not* to trust gut reactions. A marketing executive says this about self-control: "I conscien-
tiously think about exercising self-control over my emotional responses.
A few months ago, I had a job opening and knew someone in another
department would be perfect for that spot. I started to recruit him but
then got a call from his boss telling me, 'No way.' My first thought was,
'Okay, fine—someday I'll do the same for you.' But then my self-
control kicks in. I know better than to retaliate."

Nurturing Emotional Health

Leaders need emotional reserves to deal effectively with moral challenges. It's hard to manage stressful situations without a baseline level
of emotional well-being. You can't expect yourself to deal with the
demands of leading morally if your emotional tank is empty. You can't
expect to influence others to be morally competent if they don't respect
the way you live your life. Dan Marvin (pseudonym), CEO of a large
retailing business, told us this story of a failed executive:

**Recently, I had to let go our chief operating officer. He was
probably the brightest and hardest working human being
I'd ever worked with. He is the first person I've ever told**

**that they worked too much—I've never been the poster
child for personal balance myself. He would come in at 9:00
a.m. and leave at 1 in the morning. When he got home, his
wife would get up and serve him dinner and talk to him for
an hour and then go back to bed. For the two years he was
here, he never got to a soccer game or baseball game of his
kid. He never did anything with his wife. He'd leave
early—at 11:00 at night—on birthdays and anniversaries.
People hated working for him. He'd call them at 10:00 at
night, and he did nothing to develop them. He lost three
VPs who worked for him. Though he worked a ton of
hours, he really didn't do a good job, and he put his entire
family and marriage at risk.**

Balance. One of the best emotional nutrients is a balanced life. Balance
means achieving equilibrium in the amount of time and energy you
spend on each of the many dimensions of your life. You establish emotional equilibrium by allocating personal resources—such as time,
energy, and money—to life areas in a way that makes sense to you.
There is no rule for creating balance. Only you can determine how
much time and energy you spend on which areas of your life. Only you
know the right mix of pursuits for each stage of your life.

Human resources expert Judy Skoglund was the first professional
to work part-time at the financial services company now known as
Ameriprise Financial. Judy was a role model for women who saw that
she was highly productive *because* of her decision to spend more time
with her family, not in spite of it. Today Judy works with nonprofits and
coaches women on managing their careers. "I don't call it work life balance anymore," Judy says, "I call it work life *happiness*. People don't
necessarily care about balance; they want to be happy."

Women are not the only folks who care about the quality of their
whole lives—men do, too. Consider the case of Frank, a successful
broker who makes more than $200,000 per year. Although Frank works
hard, he also values family time, taking one week off every seven weeks

to spend uninterrupted time with his family. His schedule was so personally rewarding that he started thinking about taking one week off every five weeks. But after planning to reduce his work hours, he then launched a new business partnership, a decision that would require he keep to his current work schedule. Frank was excited about his new business but wondered if he was copping out on his plan to spend even more time with his family. We don't think so. We think he made the decision he did because he had already achieved equilibrium. His work and family life were balanced in a way that worked both for him and his family.

Ecolab's Doug Baker works hard to keep his time expenditures aligned with his values. "Family, marriage, career, and community are all important to me. I barely have time for those four. So friends get the short end of the stick. I may only have three golf games a year that are just for fun with friends. Guys will call me and want to go golfing for two days—I'd love to but can't. I can golf or I can see my kids."

Despite the importance of creating balance, many managers, and executives in particular, do it poorly. Corporations may offer lip service about work/family balance, and some companies provide flexible work schedules or family-friendly services to enhance retention. But American business leaders rarely recognize the positive business benefits of encouraging employees to lead fulfilling and balanced lives. If they did, balance-enhancing strategies would be mandatory rather than tolerated.

Companies that support balanced lives among their employees soon discover the business benefits. They attract high-performing people who are happy and productive in multiple roles. Those content employees produce excellent business results independent of how many hours they spend at work. Consider American Express, which enjoys an enviable history of strong financial performance. The company employs approximately 80,000 people, some of whom are undoubtedly workaholics. But the American Express executive team doesn't believe it's reasonable to base a business model on an assumption that most of its employees are workaholics. The company bases its business model on the assumption that people care about other aspects of their lives beyond the office. The American Express workforce is energized because they know that the company they work for recognizes that they have lives and that the company's leaders truly want their total lives to be successful and joyful—and by the way—they do want their employees to "work their butts off" when they are at work.

Recharging your emotional batteries. You are your most precious asset. When you prioritize your activities, it's important to carve out time for yourself. Physical fitness, for instance, is a key contributor to emotional health. Aerobic exercise triggers the release of brain chemicals associated with feelings of pleasure and well-being. Evidence of the emotional importance of exercise is that medical research has found that regular aerobic exercise (such as brisk walking) is as effective as medication in reducing symptoms of moderate depression. Your emotional well-being will be enhanced if you choose activities that you enjoy, rather than activities that you do only because you think they are good for you. Daily relaxation activities also can contribute significantly to emotional and physical well-being. Medical research underscores the benefits of planned relaxation—from lowered blood pressure to faster healing and greater pain tolerance. Dr. Herbert Benson in his perennial best-selling book *The Relaxation Response*, provides an easy and efficient method for achieving a relaxed state.[1] Just as people need a unique balance in their life endeavors, each of us differs in the kind of activities that promote relaxation. Many people find deep breathing and meditation to be effective in calming their minds and bodies, whereas others may find it maddening to sit down and meditate, preferring a yoga class, a massage, or a relaxing after-dinner stroll. The important thing is to choose some daily practice that enables you to recharge your body, mind, and spirit.

Managing emotions for peak performance. The self-awareness competencies and personal effectiveness competencies discussed here are clearly synergistic. Taking charge of your emotions means mustering all your emotional resources to manage the competing demands of work and personal life. Most of us will never get to a state in which we perform at the absolute peak regardless of how we feel. However, the more we practice self-awareness and personal effectiveness skills, the more often we can outperform ourselves, and the more often we find ourselves conforming our behavior to universal moral principles. Rehearsing for emotional challenges is critical to effective performance. You cannot control what will happen to you in the course of a day. But you can imagine it. You can prepare for it. You can get ready to be successful. As the old saying goes, *"Good luck happens when preparation meets opportunity."* Coping effectively can keep you from being knocked off course by destructive emotions and ensure that your behavior stays in alignment with your goals and beliefs.

Interpersonal Effectiveness

Personal effectiveness skills such as *deciding what to think* and *self-control* are obvious aids to moral competence. We know we need emotional control to do the right thing. But why do we need people skills to be morally competent? To serve the needs of others, we have to understand them. To be compassionate or forgiving, we need to see the world through another's eyes. Interpersonal effectiveness is an indispensable leadership tool. Leaders get little done by themselves—they rely almost completely on the energy, strength, and commitment of the people who work with them. If we want to influence others, we must understand the complex emotional worlds of others and communicate to them in ways that satisfy their emotional needs.

Northwestern Mutual's Ed Zore knows this as well as anyone, "If you're oblivious about your impact on others you'll hurt people. So you have to make an appropriate response, and that means first being aware of the wake you're leaving."

Empathy

Empathy is a kind of "as if" mental state in which you experience a challenging situation through the eyes of another person. It is as though you put on a virtual-reality headset that instantly gives you the emotional mindset of another person. Empathy is critical to moral competence because it neutralizes destructive emotions that can interfere with living in alignment. Take college President James Norwell (pseudonym), for example. When James was the VP and Dean of another liberal arts college, he found himself in an awkward position. The college president at the time had been a highly popular appointment but turned out to lack the depth needed to meet the challenges the institution faced. Frustrated with his inadequacies, the board of trustees turned to James as a sounding board, problem solver, and potential presidential replacement. James recalls, "It would have been easy to let the board push the current president aside and put me in his job. But I knew how much he was struggling and wanted to do well. And because I was able to look at the situation from his point of view, I decided to take myself out of consideration so that I couldn't be used by the board in their attempt to resolve his limitations. I had to lay my own ambitions aside for him to be treated the way I would like to be treated in that situation."

Empathy as a conflict antidote. When we are at odds with others, often the last thing we want to do is to consider the situation from their point of view. Nevertheless, empathy is a powerful tool for managing conflict in a way that produces the best outcomes for you and your adversary. Recall the experiential triangle of emotions, thought, and action. If you have been clashing with a work associate, you are probably caught up in a high-energy negative emotional state that is clouding your thinking. Without empathy, you are limited by your own subjective view of reality. If you can see only your side of the conflict, you risk lashing out in anger. You may decide you have to win the battle at all costs; you may try to retaliate; you may make hurtful accusations—all actions that are inconsistent with your moral compass, actions that will also damage your reputation as a good leader.

After you experience a conflict from the perspective of another person, it is then possible for you to stay in alignment. With the expanded perspective that includes your feelings *and* the feelings of others, you can think more clearly, and the odds that you will make an aligned choice improve dramatically. Your ability to help your partner in conflict stay in alignment also improves because empathy activates both forgiveness and compassion. If you can imagine how someone else feels, you can understand why they acted as they did. With that understanding, you are more willing to let go of their mistakes and more disposed to help them accomplish their goals.

Misplaced Compassion

Empathy for another's life situation often inspires us to want to help them. It's important to distinguish between understanding another's world and being controlled by another's needs and preferences. It's possible to go too far in translating our empathy into unproductive caretaking. Pam Moret, senior vice president of Strategic Development at Thrivent Financial for Lutherans, demonstrates how to be empathetic without compromising your business. When two companies merged to form Thrivent, Pam decided to consolidate her dispersed workforce into a single location. Some employees were upset by the prospect of the move, and though Pam empathized with their feelings, she was convinced of the need to locate her group together. Though her empathy didn't change her business decision, it did cause her to engineer softer landings and lengthier transitions than many companies offer.

Listening. Leaders are generally rewarded for being decisive, for taking action, for being the experts, and for having something to say. That action orientation can make it difficult for leaders to value what may seem like the passive act of listening. Hearing may be passive, but listening attentively is an active skill requiring concentration and emotional intelligence. Thrivent's Pam Moret says, "Active listening is an unbelievably powerful personal skill. If you signal to someone that they're fourth priority on your list...for example, by canceling one-on-ones or doing email while you're meeting with them...it can really adversely affect them and the situation." To counteract her natural inclination to multitask when with others, Pam has established informal contracts with her direct reports that commit her to giving them her undivided attention. When she meets with them, she tries not to sit behind her desk, look out her window at her secretary, or take a quick glance at her computer. That, says Pam, keeps her from hurting someone or missing important information.

Listening attentively is essential to moral competence. Careful listening demonstrates respect for the values, beliefs, goals, and emotions of others. Listening skillfully also makes empathy possible because it provides the data on which compassion and forgiveness are based. Little of the meaning of what is said comes from the words themselves. What people really mean when they speak is found in their tone of voice and the physical movements ("body language") that accompany their spoken words. That is why active listening is so much more important than passively listening to words alone. You can get the message if you get the *whole* message. Suppose you get a call at work that your daughter is sick and needs to be picked up from school. As you rush out the office, your boss says, "Are you leaving again to pick up your daughter?" Stripped of your boss's tone of voice, the words themselves could represent a simple request for clarification. But you heard the way she made that statement. Embedded in the words was a point of view. Her tone suggests she thinks you are not getting your work done. Listening carefully allows you to form a useful hypothesis that your boss is not happy with you. But active listening goes a step further. Instead of simply assuming that you have correctly assessed your boss's attitude, you check with your boss about what she meant. If your boss was just asking for information, then you can let go of the anxiety that your interpretation of her message caused. If she really is annoyed with you, testing your assumption gives you and your boss an opportunity to resolve a problem and keep you both in alignment.

Listening to understand the contents of all three frames. Active listening is typically used to uncover underlying emotional messages. But listening well can provide information about all three frames. It is important to listen in a way that allows you to discover others' values and goals. If you listen only for emotional messages, you might be missing clues that can help you stay in alignment, and help you to help others to stay in alignment. If you simply listen to another's emotions without understanding their values and goals, you don't know whether they are in alignment.

Respecting Others

It's easy to work with people we like, or whose views match our own. But we all must work with some people we don't enjoy or who express opinions with which we disagree. Disrespect is a product of our inability to understand that each of us sees only part of what is true or real. We think we have all the facts, so when someone disagrees with us, we assume they are wrong. Respect comes when we understand that truth has many colors and we can't see all of them. Our view of the world is necessarily incomplete. None of us has perfect seats in the theater of life. When we realize that our sight lines are limited, we can then respect those who disagree with us—because we then appreciate that their opinion is based on seeing what we cannot see.

Respect is the glue that enables people of different backgrounds, perspectives, and habits to work together. Moral leaders know that they can only inspire people they respect. Respect is a tricky skill. It goes beyond the easy task of appreciating people whose ideas you like or the bogus politeness of "respectfully disagreeing" with someone. Respect comes from our deep appreciation of another's ideal self. When we say that we respect someone, what we are actually saying is that we connect with the best intentions of that other person. When we respect others, we establish a relationship with their ideal self, a positive relationship that is independent of our judgments about their current opinions and actions. Our respect for their positive intentions becomes the basis for our work together. When you respect a co-worker, you open yourself to the possibility that your co-worker—who you might not like and who sees the world differently—has something important to teach you that can help both of you succeed. When you genuinely respect another— when that other person feels respected by you—only then is that person open to the possibility that your perspective may also have merit.

It's not easy to stay connected to the ideal self of an obnoxious or seemingly wrong-headed co-worker. But you can keep the channel of respect open if you also call on your capacity for empathy and listening. To see what is ideal in another's mind, you have to listen. You need to observe. When you visit a co-worker's office, what do you see? What is there, and what is not there? What do those family pictures, trophies, or pieces of art tell you about what your co-worker cares about? You might not agree with their approach to a customer's problem, but your ability to connect with their ideal values allows you to negotiate from a position of respect.

Respecting differences. Imagine that you have hired a team that thinks a lot like you do. You like their ideas, and they like yours. Staff meetings are pleasant and convivial. Decisions are made quickly, and you are confident in those decisions because so many people agree. When you are right, things work out well. But because you share the same blind spots with your colleagues, before too long you make a big mistake that could have been prevented, or you lose a significant business opportunity that could have been identified with more diverse views on board.

Few leaders would deliberately hire their own clones, and most leaders intellectually understand the value of diversity. In an emotionally charged situation, however, it is tempting to over-rely on the opinions you trust the most—yours. That is why you must consciously cultivate an appreciation for others' ideas. You do that by ruthlessly challenging your own views, while aggressively looking for the wisdom in others' ideas.

By doing this, you can discover that the existence of differences creates great opportunities for synergy and gives people who work together the potential to accomplish far more than individuals can achieve on their own.

When financial planning was first coming into its own in the 1980s, most financial planners were paid for selling financial products, such as stocks or insurance policies. Industry critics had pointed out that commission-based financial advisors could be tempted to push certain profitable products, even if they were not in their clients' best interests. Martin Levy (pseudonym), division vice president of sales for a growing financial services company, vehemently objected to a proposal to charge clients for developing their financial plans. Martin thought the financial plan should be a free, relationship-building activity that would demonstrate the salesperson's competence and set the stage for subsequent sales of financial products. Only one thing disturbed Martin's argument. Jerry Masters (pseudonym), one of his sales managers, was as vocal an advocate of fee-based financial planning as Marty was an opponent. Over time, Martin decided, "If Jerry thinks it's a good idea, I have to find out what he sees that I don't see." Martin asked Jerry to convince him, and he did. Jerry laid out his rationale about the importance of charging for objective advice because of the integrity that brings to the equation and the increased confidence that customers have in the financial advice they get when they pay for objective information. Jerry also pointed out that other disciplines, including medicine, have emerged as respected professions because they acquired a body of knowledge and were then able to charge for what they knew. Martin was convinced. Because he respected Jerry and had learned to listen to divergent views, Martin let go of a strong personal bias and cleared the way for a new product that led to significant revenues increases in years to come.

Getting Along with Others

Because leaders need others to accomplish their goals, they have to get along with them. Empathy, listening ability, and respect are hallmarks of individuals who get along well with others. Leaders who get along exceptionally well with others share four additional qualities: They show genuine interest in other people's lives; they are open and approachable; they are flexible in accommodating other's preferences and needs; and they enjoy the differences among us. When people are skilled at getting along with us, we like them. And because we like them, we are more apt to view their ideas positively and more likely to cooperate with them. So personal likeability is an asset to moral competence because when we need to enlist others to help us do the right thing—especially when it's a hard thing to do—people who like us will be more motivated to join us.

Being approachable. Positive personal connections with your coworkers fuel highly committed and creative approaches to the work at hand. It might seem obvious that good leaders need to be approachable, but it is striking how often leaders make themselves inaccessible. Some maintain distance from their employees as a matter of personal style. Others may discourage contact unintentionally because of work overload. As managers are promoted to higher levels, there is a tendency for them to become invisible—they disappear to more remote offices or spend most of their time traveling or attending meetings with other senior managers. Even when you are in a high-pressure leadership job, it is vital to make time to deliberately cultivate warm and approachable relationships with others. We've all read books advocating the "open door policy" or "management by walking around." These are simple tools that are effective if actually applied.

Being an approachable leader begins with your willingness to share the contents of your moral compass—your principles, values, and beliefs. You add to your approachability by sharing your personal interests and human foibles. Do you play in a rock band on the weekends, sing in a church choir, or fix up vintage cars? Sharing your interests and asking about others' interests sets the stage for warm work relationships.

Being approachable does not mean "telling all." Each of us has a private zone of personal information that should not be shared indiscriminately. Neither does approachability require that you become a raving life-of-the-party extrovert. But you do need to actively help people feel comfortable around you because your approachability is an important element of a positive, highly productive work environment.

Being flexible. People who get along with others don't get stuck on doing things their way. Whether you are a work peer or leader, your success depends on your willingness to let others have a say about how work gets done. You also need to accept mid-course changes that affect how work gets done. What happens when your teammate who was slated to give a big presentation gets laryngitis and asks you to fill in at the eleventh hour? How do you handle an employee's request to work at home for the next few weeks? What if your boss asks you to head a project that you think the company doesn't care about? Rolling with the punches may not always get you exactly what you want in the moment, but over the long term it will cement important work relationships and help you cultivate inventive ways to solve inevitable problems.

Enjoying differences. People who are seen as getting along with others usually have a diverse network of people with whom they have positive relationships. It's easy to get along with people we like, but if our network is limited to people who are just like us, we will be seen, not as emotionally skilled, but as interpersonally biased.

Appreciating differences goes beyond respecting or valuing the diverse perspectives that others bring to the table. It is the capacity to savor those differences among us that makes us interesting. People who get along well with others don't merely tolerate differences; rather, they feel enriched by the unique personalities and perspectives that people of different backgrounds offer.

Endnote

1. Herbert Benson, M.D. with Miriam Z. Klipper, *The Relaxation Response,* HarperTorch, 1976.

9

Making Moral Decisions

Today, Roger Arnold is executive vice president and Chief Distribution Officer for Wealth Enhancement Group, a financial advisory firm based in Minneapolis that serves the Midwest. Roger recalls a dilemma he faced a few years back when he had the national responsibility for distribution for products for a large financial services company. His top-producing regional manager, whom we'll call Sam, was using a questionable sales technique to boost revenues. Sam's approach wasn't illegal. Roger wasn't even certain it was unethical. But deep down, Roger just knew that Sam's technique wasn't right. It wasn't in their clients' best interests. So Roger told Sam to stop using his technique. Roger thought he'd made it clear that he was serious: "If you do this again, Sam," Roger warned, "I'll fire you."

So Sam did it again. Roger thought briefly about how he should respond.

> **I could have kept it a secret and protected Sam, thereby protecting my own bonus. But I confronted him and gave him thirty days' notice. And my bonus was indeed negatively affected. It would have been easy to wink at Sam's behavior or turn the other way and act like I didn't know what he was doing. But I knew what the right thing to do was, so I did it. And because I was willing to let Sam go despite his impressive financial results, I sent a clear message to all the other sales leaders across the country that doing what's best for our clients really does matter.**

What allowed Roger to do the right thing—the hard thing—when he knew it would cost him personally, and when he could so easily have kept Sam's sales technique a secret? Roger practices the "4 Rs," a four-step decision-making method that overrides our natural tendency to make emotionally driven decisions that have moral implications when in the face of strong emotions such as fear or excitement. The 4 Rs consist of four steps (or skills): recognize, reflect, reframe, and respond.

Roger uses the 4Rs to keep his excitement about his group's financial performance, and the promise of a hefty bonus from driving a decision that was not consistent with his, or his company's, values.

In the following section, you see how Roger uses those critical skills, and as you proceed through the chapter, you learn how you can develop those same skills.

How Roger Used the 4 Rs

RECOGNIZE all the elements of the situation you are in. Stop whatever you are doing to take notice of everything you're thinking, feeling, and doing related to the situation you are in. Pay particular attention to what stimulates your thoughts and emotions.

Roger paid attention to everything he was thinking, feeling, and doing. He recognized how stimulated he was by his excitement about the financial results that Sam was producing. He also recognized that he was uncomfortable about the methods Sam was using to deliver those results. Finally, Roger recognized that he was tempted to look the other way and that he felt a conflict between his values and the potential for recognition and financial gain he and his group could obtain if he allowed Sam to continue doing what he was doing.

REFLECT on how you are interpreting your situation. What does the big picture look like for you? What values are important to you, and how should they influence your choices? What biases might influence your understanding of the situation you're considering?

Roger actively reflected on his situation. He thought about his values, including "Doing the right thing," and his company's value of doing what was best for the customer. He reflected on his potential short-term loss of some of his bonus if he were to let Sam go, and weighed that against the long-term opportunities that would come from doing the right thing for customers, and sending the right messages to other sales leaders about the right way to do business. Roger also recognized that he needed to stay clear about what "success" should mean to him and his team. Success didn't mean selling products at all costs, but about being financially successful by looking out for the best financial interests of their customers.

REFRAME your ideas about the situation by stating the most positive yet still realistic outcome for the decision you need to make.

Though Roger knew he would personally suffer financially in the short term if he terminated Sam, his reflection led him to reframe the situation as "Short-term pain. Long-term gain."

RESPOND by making a decision consistent with your values and goals and take the reality of your current situation into account.

Roger terminated Sam. He set an example about the kind of culture he expected in his organization. And he inspired other sales leaders to be responsible about their own groups' sales practices.

> ### The 4 Rs of Financial Intelligence
>
> - RECOGNIZE all the elements of your current situation and how you are interpreting (that is, framing) your situation.
>
> - REFLECT on the big picture and what matters most (your values and guiding principles).
>
> - REFRAME (modify) what you are thinking and how you are describing the situation to yourself.
>
> - RESPOND in a way consistent with your values, goals, and the big picture.

How the 4 Rs Work

Using the 4 Rs rewires our brains to make values-based decisions in the face of strong emotional responses that override rational thinking. Over time, these emotionally based responses to life situations become habits. These habits are encoded in the brain in the form of neural pathways that increase the likelihood that we will respond in the same emotionally driven manner time and time again. Fortunately, we've also learned that we have the power to change our response patterns in ways that allow us to make smarter decisions. The 4 Rs are designed to help us develop that power. By practicing the 4 Rs regularly, we create new neural pathways in the brain. By doing so, we establish new habits that, over time, replace our reflexive emotional responses with deliberate and reflective responses that take our values into account. The 4 Rs help retrain our brains in a number of ways.

The 4 Rs interrupt our brain's default responses to external situations.[1] When faced with highly stimulating events, our brain's emotional center typically disables our brain's rational center, thus provoking a fear or anger response that Daniel Goleman, author and emotional intelligence pioneer, labeled the "amygdala highjack"[2] Jeffrey Schwartz, noted psychiatrist and researcher in the field of neuroplasticity, has conducted research that explains the mechanisms underlying an amygdala highjack. According to Schwartz, in the process of shutting down our rational center, the amygdala leaves our habit center intact.[3] Our habit center, which activates primitive physiological behavior and habitual unthinking responses to events, is now in charge of complicated decisions such as those leaders face every day.

To prevent this chain of events, think of the 4 Rs as hitting the pause button on our brain's programmed responses to highly charged situations. We cannot always prevent our brains from kicking up an emotional storm in the face of a business challenge or opportunity, but we can, by practicing the 4 Rs, keep our emotional brain from hijacking our rational brain and setting our habit center free to run the show. And, because of the brain's capability to develop new neurons and new pathways (neuroplasticity), when we hit the play button again, whatever we did during the pause contributes to changing our brain's actions going forward.

The 4 Rs spur the development of new brain pathways that actually change the way we process information related to moral decisions. Extensive neuroscience research has left no doubt about the brain's capability to change. We can change our brains, but only if we deliberately try. As Jeffrey Schwartz explains, "Physical changes in the brain depend for their creation on a mental state in the mind—the state called attention."[4] That is why the 4 Rs are effective in changing our brains—because they force us to pay attention to what we are doing.

When we respond to a leadership challenge or face a key decision, we usually react emotionally to stimulation from the outside in. The 4 Rs give us the tools to respond to leadership challenges, such as the one Roger Arnold faced from the inside out. They change the power balance between the reflexive emotional center of our brain (which sacrifices accuracy for speed), and the reflective, rational center of our brain (which is more accurate, but not quite as fast). The 4 Rs give us better access to our rational, thinking brain. But they do more than that: The 4 Rs greatly improve the quality of the data upon which we make thoughtful decisions. The 4 Rs won't increase your IQ, but they can help you more effectively access the IQ you have, thereby enhancing your decision making effectiveness. The 4 Rs also ensure that you make decisions aligned with your most important personal values.

Practice Makes Permanent[5]

When practiced regularly, the 4 Rs create a strong foundation for making smart, responsible, values-based decisions about any aspect of our personal or professional lives. But changing habits requires commitment and persistence. Think about the last time you tried to change your behavior. Maybe you decided to lose a few pounds, or become more physically active. In each case, the process is simple: Maybe it's a matter of eating less, or eating more fruits and vegetables, or signing up for a yoga class, or getting up an hour earlier each day to take a walk. Maybe it's a decision to quit smoking. None of the things we need to do to make positive changes are complicated. But they can be hard to do. For example, nothing could be simpler—or harder—than not lighting up a cigarette. Why? Because our brains are wired to keep doing what we've already been doing. Similarly, the 4 Rs are both simple and hard. They are not complicated, but it can take some effort to make them part of how you live and think. You need to decide that you don't want to be at the mercy of your reflexive brain. You need to decide that living in alignment is worth the initial discomfort of developing new habits. You need to decide that you want to be someone who makes moral choices that benefit you, your company, your loved ones, and your community.

Practicing Recognition

To manage the emotions that affect your decisions, you must first *recognize* them. That's easier said than done. Most of us think we're self-aware. By the time we get to be adults, we think we know ourselves well. And most of us like to think that we're objective, even when we're not. But as we learned from Chapter 2, "Born to Be Moral," when it comes to making the best choices, we're simply not aware of how our physiological state may be clouding our thinking. So, the first step to greater moral competence is to recognize exactly what you are thinking, feeling, and doing when in the throes of a stimulating situation. And to recognize your cognitive, emotional, and physical states when you need to, you must train yourself in advance. You want to become so skilled at recognition that it becomes second nature for you. By practicing the skill of recognition, you can transform yourself from a *reflexive responder* to a *reflective recognizer.*

Recognition in the Moment: The Experiential Triangle

All our life experiences fall into one of three categories (see Figure 9.1):

- Cognitive (our thoughts)
- Emotional (our feelings)
- Physical (our physiology and our actions)

These are components of self-awareness.

FIGURE 9.1   The Experiential Triangle

Think of these three categories of experience as points on a triangle. Thoughts, feelings, and actions are interconnected and usually influence one another. For example, if I *think* about someone who punched me yesterday, I am likely to *feel* angry; my heart rate will go up (*physiology*) and I may clench my fists (*action*) at the thought of what happened. My feelings and actions may even set off a new cycle of the experiential triangle, perhaps causing me to think about exacting revenge, which in turn stimulates new feelings, and so on.

Try this to experience the powerful connections between thoughts, emotions, and physical responses:[6]

- First close your eyes and identify a memory of something that happened that made you angry.

- Focus your attention on what happened and who was involved, and think about that situation for two minutes.

- After two minutes, open your eyes and recognize what you just experienced relative to your thoughts, your emotions, and your physical being.

What you will notice if you are self-aware is that you thought about what made you angry. It usually was a person, and within two minutes you might have thought about how that person angered you more than one time, to other occurrences when that person angered you.

You may also have noticed that your emotional state changed. You might have become angry again; or you might have felt guilt or regret. Your focus on your initial response may change how you feel emotionally within the two minutes. You probably also noticed that you were beginning to feel physical tension in your shoulders, your heart rate picked up, and your breathing became shallower.

Everything that happened to you was a result of what you were thinking about. As neuroscientist Jeff Schwartz points out, "Focus is power. What you choose to focus your attention on has power over your emotional and physical state."[7]

Now, take the exercise to another step:

- Take a few deep breaths, close your eyes, and for the next two minutes, imagine that your brain is a radio receiver and that you have three channels permanently programmed into your automatic selections. One channel is the gratitude channel. The second channel is the love channel. The third channel is the beauty channel. For the next two minutes, turn on one of those channels. Depending on the channel you choose, focus completely on what you are grateful for, or whom you love deeply, or what beautiful aspects of life and your environment you most appreciate, for instance, mountains, ocean, desert, and so on.

- Now open your eyes and recognize what you have experienced.

If you're like most people, you notice that your emotional state became much more peaceful. You begin to feel love, relaxed, and calm. You might think about all the things you are grateful for; or you may discover that you have a deep appreciation for certain people or natural settings. What you surely notice is that your physiological state changed. Your heart rate and breathing are slower, and your face is relaxed. You might even notice a smile come across your face. Once again you discover the power of focus, and the surprising amount of control you have over what you think and feel.

These exercises help us understand the importance and power of recognizing our experiential triangle. Managing our thoughts, emotions, and physical state is central to our ability to make smart, responsible, values-based decisions. Therefore, cultivating the art of recognizing our thoughts, feelings, and emotions is a crucial skill of moral intelligence. Recognition helps us fully access our experiences so that we have information we need to *choose* our responses to events rather than automatically (and often unconsciously) *reacting* to them.

Freeze!

One of the simplest and most powerful ways to cultivate the skill of recognition is to practice the Freeze Game.[8] When you use the Freeze Game, you declare a short time out from whatever you happen to be doing in the moment. Imagine you've just hit the pause button on the DVD of your life. Then ask yourself these three questions:

- **What am I thinking right now?**

  For example, what am I saying to myself inside my head? Am I thinking about a problem at work? A relationship issue? The weather?

- **What am I feeling emotionally?**

  Emotions are words, not sentences; for example, I feel sad, excited, angry, or frustrated.

- **What am I doing and what is happening with me physically right now?**

  For example, am I sitting or standing? Am I smiling or frowning? What's the look on my face? Is my heart racing or calm? Is my breathing pattern normal or accelerated? Am I tense or relaxed?

As you probably noticed, each question is intended to help you become aware of one aspect of your experiential triangle of thoughts, feelings, and actions/physiological state. Why not try playing the Freeze Game right now?

When you played the Freeze Game, what did you become aware of that you hadn't noticed before? Your experiential triangle might not be too dramatic at this moment. But imagine now your experiential triangle when faced with a stimulating situation that could compromise your ability to make values-based decisions. Using the Freeze Game enables us to catch flaws in our thinking before they can cause us, or the people whom we lead, any harm.

Recognition *is* a powerful tool, but only if you use it. If you're not accustomed to taking time out for recognition, it probably won't occur to you to hit the pause button when in the throes of an emotionally charged situation. Your ability to call on recognition when you need it depends on your ability to make recognition second nature. That takes practice. The more you play the Freeze Game, the more natural it will become to check in with yourself to see what you're thinking and feeling and doing. After the Freeze Game is a habit, you are that much more likely to use it when you most need to stay in alignment. As you regularly play the Freeze Game, you'll probably begin to notice many other benefits in your life. You'll develop more self-awareness, and that deeper understanding of how you really think, feel, and act may translate into more positive relationships with family and friends, and even more productive behavior at work.

Recognizing Thinking Patterns

Our supposedly rational thought processes may not be as objective as we think. That's why it's useful to pay attention to the ways in which patterns of thought affect our actions. Our ability to make smart, responsible, values-based decisions is dependent on the way we *typically* think. One aspect of our thinking patterns is especially important to moral decision making: mental biases. Mental biases are a form of "self-spin" that fools us into thinking we are logical and objective when we actually aren't. Everyone has mental biases. And they're not necessarily bad. They are shorthand principles that the brain uses to manage the thousands of decisions and actions we must take in any given day. For instance, we may have a mental bias that "people are trustworthy." This principle enables us to deal with people in an efficient way. By assuming that most people can be trusted, we feel fine about answering the door, asking for directions, working on a project with a fellow employee, eating food prepared by others, and going to sleep at night next to our spouse. Imagine what your life would be like if, every time you came into contact with another person, you had to figure out whether that person could be trusted. Your daily life would probably collapse under the strain of gauging each person's trustworthiness from scratch. So, for the most part, our mental bias that "people are trustworthy" is highly functional—even though it's not completely true. Some people are not trustworthy. Some people could harm us, and everyone has had occasional negative experiences with untrustworthy people. Mental biases become a problem only when we forget that we have them. For example, assuming that people are trustworthy can blind us to the warning signs that a particular person may not have our best interests at heart. That's why we need to *recognize* our mental biases, not so that we can eliminate them (an impossible task) but so we can be aware of how they could influence the decisions we make. Some common mental biases include the following:

- **Overconfidence:** As opposed to appropriate self-confidence.

- **Excessive optimism:** The bias that can cause us to overestimate how frequently we will experience favorable outcomes and underestimate how often we will experience less than desirable results.

- **Confirmation bias:** A tendency to look for or interpret information in a way that confirms what we already think. Confirmation bias also involves ignoring information that would contradict what we already think.

- **Familiarity bias:** This is a tendency to apply too much weight to information with which we have had prior contact.

When it comes to moral decisions, mental biases operate in various ways; for example, they can cause us to ignore important data, attach too much importance to certain data, or encourage us to make decisions based on misguided beliefs about ourselves or the situation we're in. Imagine that you have a tendency to be trusting and are excessively optimistic and prone toward confirmation bias. If you have a colleague who behaves in an untrustworthy manner, your excessive optimism bias may lead you to believe that your colleague is basically a good person, and your confirmation bias may cause you to ignore data that your colleague should not be trusted. Therefore, you might continue to work with that person, exposing you and your organization to potential harm.

Recognizing Emotional Patterns

When you play the Freeze Game frequently and consistently, you may begin to notice similarities in how you react to everyday situations, positive and negative, at home and work. You may begin to see a pattern in your responses to situations as varied as being cut off by an aggressive driver, dealing with a difficult co-worker, tucking your kids in for the night, or facing a huge mound of laundry. Recognition of these patterns can further increase your self-awareness about common reactions that can trip you up in your decision making and behavior. We know that the emotions that cloud our judgment are those that are strongly positive or negative. So we can increase our recognition of emotional patterns by looking at past experiences that have prompted us to respond with strong emotions. You may, for instance, want to ask yourself the recognition questions such as *During what experiences in my past have I felt happy, excited, hopeful, angry, sad, or fearful?* Answering such questions can help you recognize some of your most important emotional patterns.

Practicing Reflection

Recognition increases your awareness of what you are experiencing in a particular moment and of your habitual responses to highly charged emotional events. Armed with that crucial information, you are in a much better position to practice reflection.

The primary purpose of reflection is to change the source of stimulation from the outside-in to the inside-out. Reflection begins the process of creating an internal source of stimulation, one based on your moral principles, personal values, and the big picture of your life. Following are three aspects to the practice of reflection:

- Preparing to be reflective. Like any habit, reflection often requires a "cueing mechanism" to help us get into the frame of mind required for reflective thought.

- Making reflection a daily habit. As with recognition, your ability to use reflection when you need it most requires routine practice. This means taking time to be reflective several times a day.

- Using your reflection skill in any moment when you are being actively stimulated by a personal or leadership challenge.

Preparing Your Mind for Reflection

Juggling the demands of family, work, and community obligations can leave us in a chronic physiological state in which our danger system is always operating at some level. That's why it's necessary to do something to help us break from our routines or detach from the emotions of the moment. Of course, practicing recognition is key to clearing the path to reflective thought. We stop action and observe what is going on in us. In addition to practicing recognition, a number of practices can calm the mind and body, paving the way for a more reflective and rational state of mind. Dr. Herbert Benson, founding president of the Mind/Body Medical Institute, calls these practices "triggers" because they change our physiology in ways that in turn trigger well-being and improved performance. Triggering activities include prayer or meditation, listening to your favorite music, biking or walking in nature, soaking in a hot tub, or even mundane tasks like yard work or dishes.

Making Reflection a Habit

When you're in the grip of a challenging situation, it's vital to reflect on your values, your big picture, and the realities of whatever situation you face. Developing the habit of reflection makes it much easier to be reflective when you need it most. When those exciting opportunities or scary crises do come along, we'll be programmed to use our values to make the best possible decisions. Cultivating the habit of reflection helps us align all our varied daily actions with our values and the realities of our lives and the world in which we live.

Reflecting on Values

In Chapter 3, "Your Moral Compass," you had an opportunity to identify your most important values. Reflecting daily on those values is a powerful way to set the stage for acting on challenging situations whenever they strike. Choose a regular time each day to reflect on your values and your life context. The more you practice reflection, the more easily you can call on it when you need it most.

Exercise: Daily Values Reflection

Use this technique daily to keep your values top of mind. For each of your top five or six values, say the following to yourself:

- Name the value. For example: " Family."
- Use verbs in front of your values to create an action orientation to each value. For example:
  - Love your family (directing yourself to put value into action).
  - I choose to love my family (making a choice to live out a value).

I love my family (reinforcing a desired state by visualizing it as already true).

Reflecting on the Big Picture

Understanding the big picture of your life creates a context in which you can make better decisions. Your big picture includes five major areas of life:

- Family
- Goals (business and personal)
- Finances (business and personal)
- Health
- Environment (business and personal)

Drawing a Picture of Your Big Picture

This activity can help you create a visual map of your big picture. After you completed your big picture, you can display it for a quick reminder of what to reflect on when you're reacting to a challenging situation.

Materials: A large piece of paper (newsprint or drawing paper) and colored markers or crayons.

Lay your paper on a table or floor. Draw a large circle, and divide the circle like a pie into five sections.

Label each section with the five parts of your big picture:

- Family
- Goals
- Finances
- Health
- Environment

In each section, jot down the most important facts—positive and negative—that apply to that part of your life. Repeat this exercise every four months or so to stay updated on the realities of your big picture.

Armed with the reflection skill, we are ready to be reflective in those highly charged moments or during those challenging times when a personal or leadership situation is causing us either anxiety or excitement.

Although all four of the Rs are important, reflection is probably the most central to our ability to make smart, values-based decisions. Reflection forces us to evaluate the reliability of our automatic outside-in responses to situations. Building our reflective skill is key to ensuring that the decisions we make are not impulsive but are aligned with what we want to accomplish in our lives. And as you may have already noticed, after you reflect on what's most important to you, and on the realities of the environment in which you live, it's almost inevitable that you will begin to think differently about the situations you face. Reflection can naturally lead to the third R—*reframing*—a new way to see yourself and interpret your reality. Reflection done well and consistently can dramatically alter your sense of what is and can be true for you.

Practicing Reframing

Our typical way to interpret reality is based on long-standing habit patterns burned into our brains. But because of our brain's plasticity, we can change the way we view situations we face. And that's what reframing is all about: taking the results of our reflections—about values, goals, and the big picture—and re-interpreting whatever situation we are in.

Every decision we face happens in the context of the attitudes and beliefs we have about our situation. That collection of attitudes constitutes our "frame" for that situation. And that frame, in turn, powerfully influences the actual decision we make. Often, our frames for leadership situations consist of attitudes that get in the way of our ability to make smart, responsible, values-based decisions. Say, for example, your boss has asked you to withhold information from senior management about a mistake your unit has made in manufacturing a product. What you say to yourself about this challenging event affects everything you do—or don't do—about it. The economy happens to be bad, and so you frame your situation like this: "If I don't go along with my boss, I'll lose my job, and I won't get another one." Of course, there is a chance that could happen, but by treating our beliefs about a situation as though they are objective facts, we limit our options for responding in a smart, values-based manner. And many of the frames we adopt may be unrealistically negative. When we reframe, we adopt a perspective about our situation that is realistically optimistic. For instance, we may adopt the following frame: "Our company's code of ethics calls for us to admit our unit's mistakes. There's a chance I can help my boss see that it's in our best interest to come clean about the manufacturing problem. Even if I can't convince him, he probably won't fire me. And even if he did fire me, I've got a good track record and should be able to get another job." Notice that this frame is optimistic but not unrealistic. We know there's no guarantee that our boss won't fire us if we don't go along with a deception, but our new perspective increases the odds that we will act in ways true to our values.

The way we reframe a situation virtually dictates how we respond to that situation. Reframing sets the stage for making a better decision than we would have made had we responded reflexively to our emotions. Dr. Rick Aberman of the Lennick Aberman Group came up with a simple way to understand and begin to practice reframing. He quotes Winnie the Pooh: "I was going to change my shirt but decided to change my mind instead." Once Winnie reframed, he no longer needed to change his shirt. As a leader, you might say to yourself, "I was going to scream at my assistant, but I decided to change my mind instead."

Responding

The first three Rs—recognize, reflect, and reframe—are meant to change a highly charged emotional state to a calm and productive emotional state that supports objective, unbiased thought. That is the state of mind that enables us to respond optimally to any challenging situation. Therefore, after we recognize our current state—reflected on our values, capabilities, and options—and reframed our situation, the next step is the fourth R—to *respond* with the best possible decisions. But it's not actually a "final" step. Although each of the 4 Rs is discussed separately, it's hard to separate them from one another in practice. Each R flows into the next—almost as soon as we recognize our thoughts, feelings, and physical state, we begin reflecting on what is going on in and around us. Almost as soon as we start reflecting on our values and the big picture, we begin to reframe our situation differently. And almost as soon as we reframe, we begin to think about how we want to respond. Many of us feel a strong desire to respond, that is, to act on those choices as soon as we've thought about them.

After we work through the first three Rs, it's tempting to assume that we are automatically ready to make an optimal decision. However, that's not necessarily true. When practiced regularly and thoroughly, the 4 Rs greatly increase the odds that we will be in the right cognitive and emotional frame of mind for smart decision making. But because we are not perfect, it's possible to use the 4 Rs in an imperfect way. There are two major reasons for putting on the brakes before *responding*:

First, the 4 Rs do not always produce the optimal *cognitive state* for making challenging decisions. The quality of our ultimate response depends of the quality we have brought to each of the previous three Rs: The quality of our response depends on the quality of our reframing, which depends on the quality of our reflecting, which depends on the quality of our recognizing. At each step of the way, it's possible for us to make cognitive mistakes. As you'll recall, when we stop to recognize, it's important to notice how mental biases may affect our thoughts. Unexamined biases affect the quality of our reflecting and therefore the value of the reframing we make in response to our reflecting. And if our reframing is not ideal, the options we act on when we respond might not be in our best interest or in the best interest of our organization.

Second, the 4 Rs do not always produce the optimal *emotional state* for making challenging decisions. The 4 Rs are meant to defuse emotions stimulated by outside events. However, each of the Rs can itself stimulate other emotions that occasionally get in the way of thinking at our best. For example, our collaborating writer Dr. Kathy Jordan lost a substantial number of clients in the economic downturn that began in the fall of 2008. Initially, she felt panicky about the drop in income. She had then reframed her situation as an opportunity to shift her career direction. She felt elated about this new opportunity, and in high spirits, responded by trying to market her new services, but without a lot of success. It took Kathy a few rounds of 4 Rs to recognize that she had become caught up in highly charged emotions that had been stimulated, not by outside events but as a result of her own reframing. She had unknowingly flipped her frame from excessive pessimism to excessive optimism. In effect, *Kathy had replaced one set of highly charged emotions with another, interfering with the quality of her response.* Had Kathy taken more time to reflect and spent more time analyzing the realities of the downturn, she would have recognized that it would be as difficult to find clients for her new services as it was to find clients for her original services. Economic conditions were a big picture reality that Kathy had to deal with no matter what kind of services she hoped to provide.

Recycling Before Responding

As tempting as it is to *respond*, after you've recognized, reflected, and reframed, there are times when it makes the most sense to postpone a response—postponing a response is frequently the best response. It's fine to consider how we want to respond, but before carrying out a decision, it's wise to repeat the first three Rs at least one more time. Responding naturally flows out of these other things, but the key is to keep cycling back among the other three Rs. As you prepare to respond, you have to continually keep recognizing what's going on in your mind. Before you act on your choices, it's essential to make sure you have done enough problem solving while reflecting. Look for aspect of your situation that you may have missed in your first go-around. For instance, ask yourself: "What haven't I noticed about my situation that I should consider?" or "What might be some unintended consequences of the response I am considering?"

As you reflect, it's also important to go back to recognition to confirm that reflecting actually *has* put you in a calm and productive state for decision making. For instance, how energized and how emotional are you as you reflect on your values? If you are excessively energized, you should recognize that you are still in a difficult situation to access your full faculties. As you think about your possible responses, use recognition once again to spot any mental biases. Are you looking for something to confirm your judgment? Are you choosing a course of action just because it's easy or familiar to you?

Finally, before responding, it's important to recheck your framing. Are you realistically positive or unrealistically optimistic in your view of your situation? The value of reframing is in seeing things clearly, with a slant toward optimism about your ability to deal with your situation. Looking at the situation through rose-colored glasses could lead you to consider responses that would be harmful to your organization or your personal well-being.

Now you have all the basic tools you need to be a morally intelligent leader: You understand how your brain works; you're in touch with your values; and you've learned the key moral and emotional competencies that make great leaders. And you have the 4 Rs to help you access those critical moral and emotional competencies. In Part III, "Moral Leadership," you discover how to put all these tools into action as you face the daily challenges of being a moral leader.

Endnotes

1. Neuroscientist Jeffrey Schwartz, author of *The Mind and the Brain: Neuroplasticity and the Power of Mental Force* (Harper Perennial, 2003), has confirmed the capability of the 4 Rs to disrupt habitual patterns to highly charged emotional events.

2. Daniel Goleman, *Working with Emotional Intelligence*. Bantam Books, 2000, p. 74–75.

3. Jeffrey Schwartz, *The Mind and the Brain: Neuroplasticity and the Power of Mental Force,* Harper Perennial, 2003.

4. Ongoing personal communications between Jeffrey Schwartz and Doug Lennick, 2008–2010.

5. Appreciation goes to Gilbert L. Hoffer, Ph.D., president of PsyCor and emotional intelligence expert, for the phrase "Practice Makes Permanent."

6. Doug Lennick learned this exercise from Fred Luskin, author of *Forgive for Good* and Rick Aberman, Ph.D., psychologist, and partner at the Lennick Aberman Group.

7. Interview with Jeffrey Schwartz.

8. The Freeze Game was introduced to Doug Lennick by psychologist Rick Amerman, Ph.D., a founding partner of the Lennick Aberman Group.

PART III

MORAL LEADERSHIP

10 ──────────────────────

The Moral Leader

Dick Harrington served as president and CEO of The Thomson Corporation, a global electronic information company, prior to its acquisition by Reuters in 2008. On September 11, 2001, Dick was in London for a meeting of The Thomson Corporation Board of Directors. He was talking on the phone with his Connecticut headquarters when he got word of the attack on the World Trade Center. Harrington, along with the other members of his executive team in London, was thunderstruck. More than 2,200 Thomson employees worked in the neighborhood of the World Trade Center, with offices of approximately 200 employees in the twin towers. It would be days, even weeks, before it knew for certain that 11 of its employees had been killed, including one who had been a passenger on the plane that struck the North Tower.

In the early hours following the terrorist attack, nothing was clear. But Dick and his team quickly shook off their shock and prioritized: people first, business second. They mobilized cell phones and Blackberries to track down missing employees. They commandeered limos from Connecticut to pick up employees who had escaped uptown or across the river to New Jersey. As they confirmed who was missing, they contacted family members, they sent cash and catered meals, and they arranged for transportation so that family members of victims could be together.

Beyond that, Dick and his team extended generous benefits to victims' families that they were too modest to publicize. What's more, even while they attended to the needs of victims' families, they didn't miss a beat when it came to serving their other constituencies—employees, shareholders, and customers across the globe. They communicated early and often. They comforted traumatized employees. They reassured investors and customers.

The moral leadership that Harrington exhibited was the norm for him and his fellow executives—and it was reciprocated with the same degree of loyalty from Thomson's employees. One employee's first act after escaping from the World Trade Center was to race to the back-up facility in New Jersey. Other employees talked their way back into condemned buildings near Ground Zero to rescue critical financial data. By September 13, Thomson announced that the financial information technology so crucial to Wall Street was up and running.

Other leaders demonstrated powerful moral leadership in the crucible of the 2001 attacks. Nine days after the World Trade Center towers collapsed, American Express CEO Ken Chenault gathered nearly 5,000 New York employees for a meeting at Madison Square Garden. Eleven American Express employees had died in one of the towers, and the company's headquarters across the street from the World Trade Center had been seriously damaged. Employees were shell-shocked and suffering from the loss of relatives, colleagues, and friends in the financial services community. Although business continuation was vital, Ken's first priority was his employees' well-being. The meeting wasn't about "busting butt" to keep the company on track. Instead, Ken expressed his grief about those who died in the attacks and invited his employees to share their own feelings of loss and remembrance. He encouraged people to reflect on all they were grateful for and to spend time attending to the parts of their lives that mean the most. Then he communicated his sense of hope and confidence in the face of tragedy. He told the gathering how the company was helping those who were affected—employees, customers, and the New York community—in their recovery. Ken's employees didn't need to be told to work hard. They needed to hear that their leaders cared about them. That is what enabled American Express employees to move forward in the aftermath of the attacks.

How did Ken Chenault manage to inspire and comfort his employees at a time when he was personally grieving and facing unprecedented threats to his business? Ken made hundreds of conscious decisions— and every one of them required not just business skills, but moral skills. Though we all need moral skills to be effective in our lives, as leaders we have a special responsibility to use our moral intelligence to ensure that the people and groups we lead act consistently with the principles of integrity, responsibility, compassion, and forgiveness. As leaders we have influence and power that we can use to communicate the importance of moral skills to the rest of our organizations.

Not all CEOs affected by 9/11 responded like Dick Harrington or Ken Chenault. Some had to consult professional handlers, PR firms, or legal experts before they did anything. Some took so long that when they finally did respond with compassion for victims' families, it came across as artificial and forced. Harrington and Chenault succeeded where others dropped the ball because they both operate from a set of principles, values, and beliefs that factor into every business decision they make. The result? Morale and job performance has remained consistently high in both companies. Thomson (now Thomson Reuters) employees say their company is a place they're proud to be part of. "No matter what my job level," said one information specialist not long after 9/11, "I know that Dick Harrington respects me enough to communicate about significant issues. I'm going to stay, and I'm going to recommend Thomson as a great place to work." With the kind of moral leadership that engages its workforce to do its best, Thomson Reuters has continued to produce enviable returns during both economic recession and recovery.

Leveraging the spotlight. When you are a leader, you are always on stage. Everything you do is scrutinized, analyzed, and interpreted by those around you. Celebrities and politicians recognize that visibility is a double-edged sword. On the one hand, you can use the spotlight to promote worthy causes. On the other hand, it's nearly impossible to hide bad behavior from the public eye. Sam Bronfman, former senior executive with Seagram Company, recalls a time when he eviscerated a marketing manager for presenting a merchandising plan that Sam thought was ridiculous. "Everyone was shocked. I eventually apologized for it—but people still remember the incident. I hope they remember the apology, but I think people remember the outburst more."

Sam's incident reminds us that a leader's high profile requires a particular sensitivity to those emotional states (in self and others) that have the strongest potential to stimulate either moral alignment or moral breakdown. Greed, jealously, envy, hate, and anger can all easily disrupt alignment, whereas emotions such as love, compassion, happiness, and joy have a tremendous capacity to enhance moral competence. Leaders who consistently display negative emotions tend to get involved in negative behavior, and by example encourage negative behavior in those around them. Leaders who act out of love, who demonstrate respect and regard for people, tend to encourage moral competence in others—like the CEO we know who spends $1,500 a month more on his commercial cleaning service than he could negotiate with another vendor because the woman who owns the cleaning business has been loyal and responsible, and he knows that their family relies on that income.

There is an upside to your visibility as a leader—you can capitalize on it by modeling moral skills for others in your organization. To communicate moral messages effectively, it might be necessary to stand up for what is right in an exaggerated way. In live theater, for instance, actors' makeup is plastered on thick so that their faces can be seen throughout the audience. You as a leader may need to "lay it on thick" to make your values clear to all of *your* audience. You may think that it should be obvious to others that certain business tactics are wrong and that you would never approve of them. But to avoid saying so is to miss an opportunity to underscore the importance of integrity to everyone's success. Harvey Golub, retired chairman of the Board and CEO of American Express agrees. "I made it a practice," Golub says, "to always model the behaviors I wanted others to show...I didn't just hope they observed well, but would point out behaviors to make sure they understood."

Leveraging power. Power is another leadership asset that you can use to influence your organization to adopt moral skills. Leadership and power are virtually synonymous, as evidenced in the characterization of leadership as "being in power." A common definition of power is that it is "possession of control, authority, or influence over others." Power, like visibility, is a double-edged sword. Certainly, you can use power to accomplish worthy goals through others that you could not reach on your own. But there is something about power that makes it potentially as dangerous as it can be helpful. Power is addictive. Using power activates brain chemicals called endorphins that create a highly enjoyable physiological state. Power can provide pleasure much like the satisfaction offered by food, sex, or vigorous physical exercise. Most people in formal leadership positions value power. But some leaders crave it. It is easy to get accustomed to the perks of the leadership role. It feels good to have people with less organizational power defer to our ideas and desires, so unlike our experience with family members who treat us like the fallible humans we actually are.

Leadership power is not just asserted by the leader—it is given to leaders by followers. Followers allow leaders to be powerful. Because leaders have power, followers are careful about how they present information to their leaders. Research has demonstrated that the higher one goes in an organization, the more distorted the information they receive. Followers provide information that they believe leaders want to hear and censor information that they fear would upset or anger leaders. The more heavy-handed leaders are in their use of power, the more distorted the information they are given. But even benevolent leaders who are careful in their use of power have trouble establishing accurate communication channels because of followers' strong tendency to defer to the leaders' position power, independent of the leaders' actual behavior.

Deference to power affects not only the quality of "hard" business data related to financial reports, product quality, and customer attitudes, but deference to power also limits the amount and quality of "soft data" available to the leader. When leaders make mistakes, it is difficult for followers to tell them so. Many organizational cultures discourage interpersonal feedback, even among peers, so imagine how reluctant most followers would be to openly criticize the actions of someone with greater power. This leaves most senior leaders operating in a feedback void. Their accomplishments might be praised, but their personal flaws are not brought to their attention. The absence of appropriate negative feedback about our leadership behavior can leave us with the mistaken notion that we are far better leaders than we actually are. Without accurate information about the business and about our own capacities, we are at risk to making a big mistake that can lead to a devastating business outcome. Workaholism can reflect a subtle abuse of power. When you insist on doing everything yourself rather than delegating work, you deprive others of opportunities for development and their own share of power.

So use power with caution. It's not a drug you can quit cold turkey. Like food, power can't be eliminated completely from your life. For a formal leader, power is inescapable; it comes with the territory. But power, like food, can be used carefully to promote health and well-being. You can leverage your power to accomplish morally positive goals that also produce higher business performance. As a moral leader, you can use power positively by modeling the moral skills that keep you in alignment. You also can use your power to encourage followers to live in alignment with their own moral compasses.

Higher standards. When you are highly skilled in all the moral competencies, you can use your leadership power and visibility to produce the best business results. We do know business leaders who are quite effective despite some gaps in their moral competencies. But we have never known a consistently successful business leader who was not highly skilled in the integrity and responsibility competencies. Many effective and honest senior executives are respected because they demonstrate integrity and responsibility, even though they lack notable compassion or forgiveness. But leaders who inspire their followers' best efforts are compassionate and forgiving as well. When followers see that such leaders actively care about them and are willing to let go of mistakes, they forge a bond with their leaders that just doesn't happen otherwise.

Why does emotional bonding between follower and leader matter? When leaders show compassion and forgiveness, they create a safe emotional environment. In this positive climate, followers feel free to be creative because they know their leaders will tolerate the inevitable mistakes that come from creative risk-taking. When followers believe their leaders care about them, they want to give their best efforts to the work at hand. It is as though the integrity and responsibility competencies come from the "head," while the compassion and forgiveness competencies come from the "heart." The most effective moral leaders are those who have both the head and the heart fully engaged.

It is interesting that moral competencies of the "head" are necessary and sufficient for a minimal level of leadership effectiveness, but moral competencies of the "heart" are not sufficient for effective leadership. Leaders could seem to actively care for others ("I feel your pain!"), could forgive themselves or others, and be open about mistakes, but if they do not tell the truth, don't keep promises, and don't act consistently with the values, beliefs, and principles of the organization, then they will not be effective leaders. Leaders who are known for their compassion and forgiveness, but who lack integrity and responsibility are often considered "nice people" but by virtue of their lack of integrity do not command the respect and trust required for high performance.

How moral leaders look at followers. So far, we have seen why moral leaders need to operate at the top of the moral competence scale. Because of their power and visibility, their behavior has a major impact on the behavior of those around them. In addition to high proficiency in moral and emotional competencies, the most effective leaders operate from a central organizing belief that informs their transactions with followers. Everything they do is inspired by a belief in the essential goodness of people. It can be summarized as follows: *Even though people are not perfect, and even though they make mistakes, most people have good intentions.* This belief is the moral leader's key to inspiring the best in others because your belief that people are essentially good has a profound impact on your leadership behavior. Knowing that the person with whom you are working has an *ideal self* (who he would like to be at his best)—and that the person would rather be his ideal self than his current flawed *real self*—allows you to practice compassion, forgiveness, and integrity. When you believe in a person's essential goodness, you cannot help but commit yourself to helping him become who he most wants to be.

Belief in the goodness of people is not a "technique." It is a potent frame of reference that, paradoxically, enables you to be as tough as nails in managing individual performance. Why? When followers sense your deep belief in their ideal selves—their potential to be their best— they are much more receptive to your feedback about their mistakes and failures. Similarly, when good performers recognize your belief in their ideal selves, they are inspired to give even more effort to your shared work.

Tom Perrine is senior vice president of Enterprise Systems IT with Cardinal Health, the largest health-care products distributor in the United States. Tom demonstrates his belief in the goodness of people when he says, "Helping others create who they want to be is a way of life for me." Tom adds, "Number-one value to me is *people matter most,* and they deserve to be treated with respect, consideration, understanding, and empathy. Do you brighten their light bulbs or dim their light bulbs? How are you managing the energy of your people? The greatest job of leadership is not personally doing things but helping others do things, and managing the energy of the workforce is what it's all about. If you do that well, you can accomplish great things as a company or in the world." Tom also notes the cost of temporarily losing touch with his positive beliefs about people. When Tom was chief development officer at Coca-Cola, he was forced to make a unilateral decision about an important issue because the team responsible was argumentative and uncooperative. Tom thought the resulting decision was not as good as it could have been if the team had focused on solving the problem instead of fighting with one another. So he convened the team and told them what he thought of them. "No one likes to be called on the carpet," recalls Tom, "and I called the group on the carpet. The manner in which I delivered the message was culturally unusual at Coca-Cola because people there weren't used to being reprimanded as a group. I didn't name names, but I was clearly angry and upset. After that, many of them decided they couldn't trust that wouldn't happen again, so for quite a while, they avoided coming to me with issues. My comments about their poor teamwork were factually true, but I delivered the message in the wrong spirit and mismanaged the energy of the group."

Developing employees. The moral leader's approach to performance management and development is guided by the leader's belief in the essential goodness of the people who report to him or her. It is an approach that encourages employees to live in alignment, releases their positive energy, and inspires their best efforts.

As a moral leader, you hold yourself responsible for helping others stay aligned with the ideals that are important to them. How? First, you do so by believing in employees' potential to do wonderful things for themselves and your organization. Second, you can use performance discussions to discuss the life goals that your employees care about— *not* just their business goals. Third, hold them accountable for meeting all their personal and professional goals.

When you acknowledge your employees' whole selves—ideal and real—they are energized by your support. Because you care about them and believe in them, employees are inspired to give you—and your company—their best efforts. Employees do not have to be coerced into performing—over the long term, you can't force people to produce. You cannot create good employees. You can only create conditions that spark their talents into a bonfire of innovative thought and action.

Developing employees is *the* central building block of moral leadership. Why? It's because people development is the way you create a workforce committed to the moral principles necessary for the sustained success of your organization. When moral leaders invest in employees' development, they goes beyond the typical focus on technical skills and behaviors that produce short-term corporate results. Development plans that lead to lasting business performance are comprehensive—they include actions that help employees realize not just business goals but also *all* their important personal and professional aspirations. An effective development plan is not the sole responsibility of your employees—it is a shared plan for the employees' growth to which both you and you employees are committed. You and your employees collaborate to achieve goals that are important to the employees and at the same time are intended to produce desirable organizational results.

Leaders who accept responsibility for helping employees achieve their development goals spend substantial amounts of time coaching employees. Leaders who are too busy meeting among themselves to spend time helping employees grow miss golden opportunities for better business results. Investing time in developing employees may seem daunting, but the payoff is exponential. Every hour we spend coaching employees translates into countless hours of enhanced performance.

Each element of a performance development discussion—communicating belief in the employee, reciprocal disclosure of beliefs and goals, contracting for mutual feedback, and mutual accountability—should be discussed and negotiated with every employee for whom you are responsible. If you are a leader responsible for a large organization, it is important to ask all supervisors in your organization to use this approach with their direct reports.

Communicating belief in the employee. Actions may speak louder than words, but communicating a belief in the goodness of the follower needs to be actively *spoken* as well. In reality, most of us are starved for affirmation. We appreciate any genuine communication of caring. The effective leader affirms employees most powerfully by acknowledging their strengths. Verbal references to the employees' accomplishments and abilities reinforce the notion that the leader believes in the employee's best self. Beyond acknowledgment of strengths, the leader should look for opportunities to state directly, "I believe in you. I know that you are capable of even more than you have already achieved." In our hard-nosed Western business culture, such a message may sound saccharine. When an employee makes a serious mistake, however, stating your belief in that employee's ideal self helps him or her deal more productively with the fallout of his or her real self failure. Even when employees under-perform, the wise moral leader concentrates primarily on how to improve performance by leveraging their strengths. Emphasizing an employee's weaknesses is rarely useful, as London Business School Professor Nigel Nicholson, reminds us:

> **... emotions can never be fully suppressed. That is why, for instance, even the most sensible employees cannot seem to receive feedback in the constructive vein in which it is often given. Because of the primacy of emotions, people hear bad news first and loudest.**
>
> **Managers should not assume they can balance positive and negative messages. The negatives have by far the greater**

power and can wipe out in one stroke all the build up-credit of positive messages. In fact, because of the primacy of emotions, perhaps the most discouraging and potentially dangerous thing you can do is to tell someone he or she failed. Be careful, then, of who you put in charge of appraisal systems in your organization. These managers must be sensitive to the emotional minefields that all negative messages must navigate.[1]

Reciprocal disclosure of the manager's and employee's respective moral compass and goals. Sharing your beliefs and goals and inviting your employee to do the same provides the basis for both to support the other's actions. You may want to introduce this idea to your employee by saying something like this:

> **To be a good manager, I need to know where I am and disclose that to you. I also need to know where you are at, and our shared knowledge of each other will give us the foundation for a trusting relationship.**

Begin by sharing the principles, values, and beliefs that form your moral compass because many employees will not have had a previous experience with a superior who asked for this kind of information. Your willingness to disclose personal beliefs will usually minimize any discomfort on the part of your employee. But you also should make it clear that your disclosure of beliefs and goals is not a formality. You are sharing your beliefs and goals because you also want help from your employee. You can tell your employee that you hope that together you can be enablers of each other. After you have discussed your own beliefs and goals, your dialogue as manager might sound something like this:

My job as your boss is to help you develop the necessary habits and routines that will help you achieve your goals while honoring your principles and beliefs. I start with a belief in you, but if we are going to work together closely, I need to do more than imagine greatness in you. I want to know what you really want your life to be about—the things that really matter to you. What roles do you play, and how good do you want to be at each of them?

Contracting for feedback. Managers often assume that they have a unilateral right to dispense feedback by virtue of their position. Unsolicited feedback is neither welcome nor effective. Managers are often frustrated to discover that negative feedback frequently results in further performance deterioration rather than improvement. This performance drop is caused by the negative emotions that uninvited feedback causes. Employees who receive unsolicited negative feedback feel unappreciated, misunderstood, and powerless. These are destructive emotions that cause further breakdown, not alignment. In contrast, critical feedback solicited in an environment in which the employee feels empowered is likely to enhance performance. The manager should seek permission to offer feedback and to solicit feedback from the employee about the manager's own performance. Seeking permission to give feedback and asking for feedback levels the emotional playing field for the employee. Because receiving feedback is part of a contract and because the employee has the opportunity to provide feedback to the manager, the employee feels empowered rather than ashamed. If the manager has been successful in communicating deep caring and belief in the employee, the employee can calibrate the negative aspect of the feedback in the context of feeling positively valued by the manager. Finally, if the manager can characterize the feedback as an opportunity to help the employee accomplish important personal or professional goals, the employee will see the feedback as a performance aid rather than an attack.

In contracting for mutual feedback, you might want to say something like this:

I know we will both make a bunch of mistakes. I want us to agree to help correct each other. I'm going to mess up. Would you be willing to let me know when you see me making a mistake?

Now who would not agree to that? When you have your employee's agreement, you may then ask this:

If there are times when your performance is not consistent with the goals you have shared with me, may I let you know about that?

Now you have set the stage for discussing performance problems in the context of goals that are important to your employee.

Mutual accountability. Contracting for feedback sets the stage for confronting performance gaps that will inevitably arise. Because you have invited your employees to call you on your own behavior, the way you respond to their first attempt will affect the quality of the relationships going forward. In short, you need to make it easy for your employees to offer feedback in the future, by responding well to their feedback. Responding well to employee feedback does not necessarily mean that you agree and instantly change your behavior. It does require at a minimum that you actively listen to their feedback, play it back to ensure that your employees know they have been heard, tell them how you plan to respond (even if you plan simply to think about it), and thank them for the respect they showed you by offering their feedback.

When you need to give negative feedback to your employees, it is important to reinforce the context of your belief in them. You might say something like this:

Based on everything you've shared with me, I know you want to be great at the work you do. I'm sure that you are aware that [your performance in this area] has not been good, and we need to focus on these few areas to help you reach the goals you agreed were important to you.

Performance Problems

Focusing on others' strengths and goodness does not mean that the moral leader ignores performance deficits. On the contrary, it is exactly that focus on others' ideal selves and the respect created by reciprocal disclosure of beliefs and mutual feedback that establishes an emotional bond between the manager and employees. That bond, in turn, enables a manager to be extremely tough in tackling performance issues.

When values collide. Caring for people and believing in their essential goodness does not necessarily make your leadership job easy. Perhaps the most daunting challenge moral leaders face is how to manage individual performance in a way that reconciles competing commitments to their people and their organizations. Jim Thomsen of Thrivent Financial for Lutherans understands the challenge well. Jim recalls how he dealt with the performance of a direct report who was also a close friend, "I should have decided to get him out of his job much earlier than I did. My personal relationships with the people I work with tend to be very strong. So it took me six months after I had made the decision to act on it. I tried to help him see that he was in the wrong job, but he never came to that conclusion. My decision to let him go damaged our friendship, but letting him stay would have had negative consequences for the organization. People who weren't close to this person thought it was about time we held an executive accountable for underperforming. For those loyal to him, I became the 'evil empire.' Emotionally, it was very hard. Out of integrity and responsibility I had to act, but I also had to be compassionate."

Moral leadership and management techniques. Believing in the goodness of people and managing employee performance consistent with that belief does not imply abandoning any of the leadership tools you may have found useful in the past. Most organizations provide leadership training and other resources that enhance their effectiveness in the day-to-day management of work and people. Other leadership techniques work best when you begin with your employees' ideal selves in mind, focus at least as much on their strengths as their weaknesses, and invite them to help you improve your personal performance just as you are trying to help them improve theirs. Any leadership technique will be that much more effective when you genuinely care about and believe in your employees and their potential. Leadership tools applied in the absence of caring and belief in others often backfire because employees may experience them as mechanistic or manipulative. On the other hand, leadership techniques infused with the spirit of caring tend to work very well, even when not perfectly applied.

Endnote

1. Nigel Nicholson. "How Hardwired Is Human Behavior," *Harvard Business Review*, July 1998.

11

Leading Large Organizations

The Fabric of Values

It was a blazing summer day outside the conference room in Sedona, where American Express executive Brenda Blake and her former colleague Dave Edwards gathered their two teams of international managers. Brenda stepped to the podium to roll out the company's two new corporate values. Amex had long espoused six values; now it had eight. For the past two weeks, Brenda had been pondering how to make the values memorable so that people would be more likely to practice them.

She decided to group the values into three categories—moral values, social values, and business values. Pushing aside her concerns about how her audience would react, she reminded them that success depends on a clear sense of what American Express stands for. She explained how values drive both business practices and business results.

Then, before launching into the new values, she put one more PowerPoint slide up on the screen. It said this:

If you don't subscribe to Amex's moral values, you probably shouldn't work here.

In making that claim, Brenda was out on a limb. It certainly wasn't a politically correct thing to say. No one had authorized her to say it. She hadn't even reviewed it with her superiors.

Indeed, it was only following the meeting in Sedona that Brenda emailed the presentation material to her boss. It would be two weeks before she found out his reaction. Over dinner, the night before she was to repeat her presentation to a group in London, he approvingly quoted the new mantra back to her: *"If you don't subscribe to Amex's moral values, you probably shouldn't work here."*

It turns out that Brenda, one of 25 designated "culture champions" at American Express, needn't have worried about her presentation. Employees at every level say that when she talks about the three sets of values—moral, social, and business—they immediately "get it." No one blinks an eye at the mention of moral values. The only question asked by some is how to reconcile conflicts between a new business value, "the will to win," and the longstanding value of "integrity." The Amex answer comes easily: Amex will win *with* integrity. It is not winning at any cost. If there is a conflict, integrity comes first. So far, though, the conflict has not come. Any senior manager at Amex will insist they can win in their markets without sacrificing an inch of their other values.

Brenda Blake's presentation captured lesson one about moral leadership of any large organization: Effective leadership depends upon the successful integration of moral, social, and business values. You cannot *just* be a moral leader, even as you cannot *just* be a strategic leader. The values that drive an organization do not work in isolation. Choices about moral values are an intrinsic part of the cultural fabric of every organization. Ask great business leaders about their values and you will inevitably hear them mix "integrity" in the same breath as "beating the competition" and "quality" along with "giving back to the community" and with "honesty."

Is There Such a Thing as a Morally Intelligent Organization?

In the last chapter, you considered the concept that the major task of moral leadership is to bring all of an organization's values to life so that employees can connect to them personally and understand how to translate those values into action. With that goal in mind, every aspiring leader will at some time ask, "Is it my job to influence individuals or groups? Does one lead organizations, or does one lead people? Is it even possible to talk sensibly about a morally intelligent organization?"

A morally intelligent organization is one whose culture is infused with worthwhile values and whose members consistently act in ways aligned with those values. A morally intelligent organization's major characteristic is that it is populated with morally intelligent people. After all, if you put enough morally intelligent people in one place, the culture will eventually catch on. But moral leaders realize that their job goes beyond simply hiring others who act in a certain way, just as a morally intelligent organization is more than the sum of its individual members. Moral leaders accelerate and enhance high performance by actively encouraging everyone in the organization to apply their moral principles to their individual actions *while also creating organization-wide policies, practices, and reward systems based on moral values.*

The Morally Intelligent Organization— An Aerial View

PBS periodically airs a program on Italy that consists of nothing more than exquisite video of the Italian countryside shot from a helicopter. No sound track, no plot, just moving pictures of mountains, valleys, and water as the camera followed the curves of landscape from north to south. Unlike the normal tourist's eye view, the video shot from high above the terrain gives a context for understanding the character of the country in a way that would be impossible from the ground.

If we had an aerial view of the ultimate morally intelligent organization, what would we see? First, we would *not* see people being simply moral, or simply social, or simply focused on the technical aspects of their work. We would see moral values lived out in their "natural habitat," interwoven with other social and business values important to a successful large enterprise. We would see leaders who believe that some shared human moral values apply to humankind all over the world and therefore apply both at work and outside of work. We would notice leaders who speak passionately about their beliefs and the values that their company stands for. We would also notice that the leaders are as morally competent as they are strategically gifted.

As we rise higher, so that we can see the entire organization, we would see job candidates scrutinized to ensure that their beliefs and values are consistent with the beliefs and values the company upholds. We would see employees given opportunities to develop competencies that translate values into action. We would see people solving problems and making decisions in ways consistent with the organization's values. We would see managers at all levels sharing their personal values and goals and inviting their peers and employees to hold them accountable to those values and goals. We would watch as employees go the extra mile for their leaders and their company because they feel respected and trusted by their leaders. We would observe employees rewarded, not for being workaholics, but for results. We would see employees who deliver superior results, while reserving adequate time for their families, community service, or other passionate interests. If we look closely, we can even see people make mistakes. We can also see that mistakes are usually treated as normal byproducts of innovation and growth and that people are given a chance to correct them and move on without being negatively branded.

Higher yet, we would see an organization that does not abandon its values when the economy sours, or a disruptive technology threatens, or a natural disaster strikes. We would see a company that has a long track record of profitable growth. We would see the organization dedicate a certain amount of its resources to helping others in the larger communities where it is located.

If our vantage point were high enough, we would see in the global organization the intertwined threads of moral, social, and business values reaching across countries and continents to join together people of different languages, social customs, and traditions in pursuit of a shared dream of individual and professional performance.

Morally Intelligent Policies

McKinsey co-founder, Marvin Bower,[1] observed that virtually every successful company codifies its culture, rather than letting it grow through an inevitable self-molding process. Many effective leaders have discovered the wisdom of this advice. A senior management team of a defense laboratory attended a session on managing conflict during an especially stressful period of organizational change. Its workshop leader suggested that one way to prevent conflict in organizations was to develop a "social contract"—a code of behavior that everyone in the organization would agree to. The management team thought that was a good idea. It asked its employees to get together in small groups and talk about what should be in the "social work contract."

Managers admit they were somewhat apprehensive. Most of the laboratory's employees had worked there for decades. They had seen management fads come and go. Would they be cynical about the idea of a social work contract? But when the groups met, it was thoughtful and engaged. When it came time to merge the results of the small groups into a social work contract for the whole laboratory, the managers were surprised and relieved to see that the small groups' proposals were remarkably similar.

They didn't call it a statement of moral values, but what they developed was clearly a shared moral guidance system. With the support of their leaders, they did the collective work of codifying how they wanted to be treated and how they believed they should treat one another. Many months later, it is clear that the words still mean something to this group. Employees display copies of the contract in their cubicles and on corridor walls—reminders of how they want to be at their best. In a year of massive change and unremitting workload, when people are overtired and tempers could easily unravel, there have been no meltdowns. The people in the laboratory have kept their act together. The social work contract has been a powerful influence on the laboratory's capability to weather the organizational changes that continue to surround them.

The Principles That Matter Most

Earlier, we described the universal principles we believe are key to leadership effectiveness—integrity, responsibility, compassion, and forgiveness. These same principles are essential to organizational effectiveness. The organizations whose values reflect these principles are the most likely to be successful over the long term. Companies that embed these principles into their cultures succeed because they keep more than their fair share of the world's most talented employees. These are the principles that resonate strongly with employees so that they want to stay and are inspired to give their best efforts to the organization. But if integrity, responsibility, compassion, and forgiveness are absent from the life of an organization, there is dissonance between what the organization stands for and its employees' hopes and beliefs. If employees' moral compasses don't line up with a company's code of conduct, it is unlikely that they will give the company their best.

Cultivating Organizational Integrity

Companies should assign four to eight values as their "core values"—including among them the principle of integrity. Based on these core values, organizations can use three key strategies that promote and demonstrate integrity. The first is for senior management to plot a communications strategy in which it engages with its employees and the public at large to identify and promote its organization's values. Ideally, the CEO leads this strategy: She should talk about the company's values—the core of the corporate culture—at every possible opportunity.

Second, the senior team needs to practice what it preaches and enforce adherence to the company's declared values. Managers in many companies fail in this regard. They may not be guilty of fraud or terrible dishonesty but of a common white lie: It is common for managers to give annual performance reviews that fail to confront poor performance or behavior not aligned with core values. We've all heard stories of companies giving someone a bonus on Friday for "outstanding performance" and then firing them on Monday, but this behavior pattern has a high cost: Everyone in the company can see that their management does not practice integrity or really believe in it.

The third strategy is for senior management to invite their workforce to hold them accountable. An example of how to establish accountability is to set up a Leadership Alignment Task Force, a group of no more than 12 people from all layers of the organization—from Joe in the mail room to Debbie, a marketing director, or Sam, the head of production—to join this task force on a volunteer basis. The task force is charged with giving the CEO and the senior team an annual "alignment review." During the alignment review, the task force offers feedback from their workforce on their perceptions of how well the CEO's and senior managers' behavior is aligned with the organization's values. Alternatively, companies can use intranets to collect confidential feedback from their workforce on senior management practices and their integrity.

Integrity produces substantial rewards for organizations who embrace it. All stakeholders—employees, vendors, investors, and business partners—prefer doing business with organizations that have strong integrity. It is simply easier to engage with an organization that is honest, that states its mission and values, and does not diverge from them. It's common sense: Organizations that attract employees and customers by virtue of their integrity are likely to be highly successful in the long run.

The Responsible Organization

There are two hallmarks of the responsible organization. First, it embraces its responsibility for being of service to others. Second, it acknowledges mistakes and failures. With respect to serving others, there are two levels of service. The first level of responsibility is that the organization provides worthwhile products or services. This does not mean that your organization is only a responsible one if it invents the cure for the common cold. It is, however, important that your organization has a socially worthwhile mission.

Hormel Foods is a company that takes its responsibility for being of service seriously. Hormel Foods stockholders have had a lot to celebrate lately, with record sales, earnings, and stock prices in 2010. And there is no question that Hormel is one of the great American companies, having been named to *Forbes* magazine's 400 Best Big Companies List for ten consecutive years. But one of the things CEO Jeff Ettinger is most proud of is Hormel's long-standing commitment to serve others. Following the hurricane disaster in 2005, Hormel Foods donated food and money and encouraged employees and retirees to get involved and help with the recovery efforts. Now Hormel is focusing on combating hunger in developing countries. As Jeff explains

We've been active in giving back to the community for years, doing pro bono work and making contributions to

relief efforts. But about two years ago we launched a project to create a new protein item, SPAMMY, designed to overcome malnutrition. Right now we are focused on relieving hunger in Guatemala, where we are partnering with Food for the Poor and Caritas. Guatemala has some of the worst malnutrition rates for children in the world, and SPAMMY was designed to help address this chronic problem. We will distribute over one million cans to the needy in Guatemala in 2011, with larger goals for the future, including expanding distribution of the product to other countries.

There is an undeniable relationship between Hormel Foods' history of being a responsible company and its financial success. But the benefits of being responsible for serving others go well beyond the bottom line. A company's commitment to serving others enables it to attract and retain talented and engaged employees. When Jeff Ettinger initially unveiled SPAMMY at a sales meeting, he noted

The product was only 5 minutes or so of my presentation, but eighty percent of the questions and comments afterward related to that. People want to know that the company is doing the right thing. We are using our heritage of innovation on a pro bono basis and our people are really proud of that. It's interesting that this program, while we have invested some dollars in it, clearly more than pays for itself in increased employee engagement and productivity. This is not the reason we do these programs, but it is an interesting side benefit.

In contrast to Hormel's focus on making products that benefit others, companies that make dangerous products or provide questionable services put their long-term performance at risk. They may be profitable for a time, but eventually will falter. Phillip Morris is an example of a company that struggles with the tension between a dangerous core product and its desire to be socially responsible. Phillip Morris sells cigarettes.

No one can ignore the dangers of its core product. But Phillip Morris also sponsors antismoking advertising aimed at children and contributes generously to charitable causes. Admittedly, Phillip Morris's social responsibility efforts were court-ordered as a result of litigation. You could argue that the company has not been as aggressive as it should in diversifying its holdings so that cigarettes are no longer its only revenue stream. You might dismiss Phillip Morris' efforts to be responsible as nothing more than a public relations smokescreen. You might be right. But it is possible that Phillip Morris genuinely wants to behave responsibly, rather than creating the disaster for shareholders that an abrupt exit from their core business would provoke.

Another example of a company dealing with adverse consequences of some of its products is Kraft Foods, maker of Oreo cookies, Oscar Meyer bacon, and Easy Mac macaroni and cheese. In 2003, Kraft announced that it would stop selling high-fat foods to schools and launched a series of initiatives to promote healthy eating. As of 2003, it had spent more than $17 million to increase the amount of fruits and vegetables distributed by U.S. food banks. You might conclude that Kraft was simply trying to forestall the kind of litigation first seen by fast-food chains by some obese customers who blame the food purveyors for their health problems. Hopefully, Kraft is making a good faith effort to ensure that its products are used in ways that do no harm. Whatever its full range of motives, Kraft does serve its broad customer base by encouraging people to make wise nutritional choices.

Although companies such as Phillip Morris and Kraft try to be responsible without altering their core product, other companies demonstrate responsibility by literally changing their product into one that better serves their customers. Harvey Golub did just that as CEO of IDS, a financial advisory company. He transformed IDS from a transactional services company to a company that offered objective financial planning services. To understand how profound a change that was, recall that the 1970s and 1980s were a time when the financial services industry had a well-deserved reputation for questionable transactions.

Consider the comments of one person who worked for a brokerage house:

It was a hectic noisy place with stockbrokers crowded together talking on phones and calling out across the room to one another. Right in front of me, I saw a man on the phone put someone on hold, then yell out, "What do we have for a buck with a half?" Someone yelled back, "XYZ stock." The man got back on the phone and proceeded to extol the virtues of XYZ stock. As I left, I asked my friend to tell me what a buck with a half meant. He told me that it is a stock for which you pay a dollar for the stock with a fifty cent load—meaning the customer paid a dollar for a stock that was only worth fifty cents. It was obvious that the guy who promoted XYZ stock didn't care about gouging his customer and was only interested in maximizing his earnings.

It is no wonder people were suspicious of brokers, many of whom were more interested in lining their own wallets than helping their customers. It was the "me generation," an era of excess, a time when Wall Street was synonymous with greed. Enter Harvey Golub, a McKinsey consultant called in by American Express to analyze a promising potential acquisition in the financial advising business. Golub examined IDS, a small company in Minneapolis that focused on creating wealth for its clients by offering long-term investment and insurance products. Golub's studies showed that IDS advisors gave good financial advice. Clients could benefit from their advice, even if they decided to purchase financial products elsewhere. They didn't use hard-sell tactics. Their first priority was helping clients reach their financial objectives. Golub thought IDS had the right idea. IDS was small, but its principles were scalable. So, he recommended that American Express buy IDS.

American Express agreed, but on one condition—that Golub take over as CEO. Golub grew IDS (eventually American Express Financial

Advisors) by putting its customers front and center. He made a commitment that the financial planning documents prepared for clients would
be objective. IDS's recommendations would not be biased toward IDS
products. They would recommend IDS products that fit client objectives
but also acknowledge that clients could do well if they chose to go to
another company to purchase financial products. He also insisted that
financial planning had to be independent from the sale of products, even
though he knew the company wouldn't be profitable if it sold only
financial planning services. But Golub said, "We are going to be a
financial planning company and help customers make financial decisions prudently and carefully." It was curious advice at a time when the
financial industry's high flyers were just "doing deals."

A lot of industry insiders thought IDS would fail, especially after
his predecessor lowered the sales charge customers paid for each transaction. There was a revolt in the ranks of the sales force. Many advisors
threatened to quit. But Golub was confident it was the right thing to do,
so IDS lowered its sales load. It lost some advisors, but, important, kept
those who understood the values that drove Golub's strategy.

Although pundits had their doubts, Golub's values-driven strategies
paid off spectacularly. From 1984 until 2000, IDS (later renamed
American Express Financial Advisors, which now is an independent
company, Ameriprise Financial) increased profits by at least 15% every
quarter, taking the company from 60 million to more than one billion
dollars in gross earnings. Before being spun off as Ameriprise Financial
in 2005, AEFA helped keep American Express profitable through the
worst of the post 9/11 doldrums. Providing a valuable service and being
a responsible organization is no doubt the morally right thing to do, but,
as the success of Ameriprise demonstrates, values-based business practices are also strategically smart. At Ameriprise, financial advisors feel
energized by providing a worthwhile service for their clients. Most
financial advisors would hate having to pressure their clients to buy a
product. Clients, in turn, value solid advice that helps them achieve
their financial goals. Being a responsible, service-oriented organization

resonates powerfully with employees and customers alike. Not surprisingly, Ameriprise, led by CEO Jim Cracchiolo, performed especially well following the stock market's slide in 2008 and 2009. By January 2011, its stock price had risen to over $60 after having fallen to nearly $10 just two years earlier.

There is a second dimension that marks the responsible organization: its willingness to admit mistakes and failures. If admitting mistakes is crucial to maintaining employee commitment, it is essential to maintaining customer loyalty as well. Some companies seem to know this in their bones; others go down in flames trying to hide the truth about their mistakes. Taking responsibility for mistakes may be painful in the short run, but admitting failure and taking steps to compensate for errors cements customer loyalty. Customers know that they can trust an organization that tells them the truth. Mark Sheffert, chairman and CEO of Minneapolis-based Manchester Companies, illustrates the business value of admitting mistakes:

> **One of the more meaningful experiences for me was when I became chairman and CEO of First Trust, then part of First Bank Systems and now US Bank. I knew we had some problems I was going to have to help deal with, but I quickly discovered it was more serious than I had expected. Our statements for people with 401k plans were all wrong. If you can believe it, we were $8 billion out of balance. When I met with the managers and asked what we should do, the answers were far ranging. Some thought we should finesse the situation until we fixed it, essentially through misinformation [and] essentially lying. I took the position we were going to our clients and we were going to tell the clients the truth and that the data on their employee statements would not be right for 90 days or so. I personally went to our clients, including companies such as 3M, General Mills, and Medtronic. I told them we had a problem, and I said**

"I need your help." I've learned those four words are so powerful and use them all the time still to this day with my clients, employees, and virtually everyone. We asked them to hang in there with us, and we would fix the problem. I told them "I guarantee that not one nickel will be lost." These clients could have said "We're taking our business elsewhere." I knew the financial implications for us were huge, but I also really believed if we stood on solid moral ground they would stick with us, and they did. We demonstrated that by being honest and forthright the vast majority will respond well. We lost only one small piece of business. The regulators, clients, and employees were all thrilled. First Trust went on to become the largest corporate trust company in the world.

One of the most dramatic instances of the importance of admitting corporate mistakes came in 1982. The fate of Johnson & Johnson was in the balance when bottles of Tylenol capsules were laced with cyanide, killing seven people. James Burke, CEO at the time, knew exactly where to look for direction—the company's 40-year-old "Credo," a single-page document that began with these words: *We believe our first responsibility is to the doctors, nurses, and patients; to mothers and fathers; and all others who use our products and services.* Johnson & Johnson ordered an unprecedented recall of all 30 million bottles of Tylenol capsules in circulation. It immediately stopped production of the capsules and replaced them with tamper-resistant caplets. It communicated constantly with the public and the media, and it was its openness and concern for public safety that that helped Johnson & Johnson to overcome its initial losses and recover its market share within a matter of months.

More recently, in 2004, drug manufacturer Merck & Company voluntarily withdrew its widely used arthritis pain medication Vioxx after a three-year clinical trial showed a higher incidence of heart attacks and strokes among users of the drug. Merck has a reputation for concern for those who use its products. It developed and distributed at no cost a drug that cures river blindness in underdeveloped regions of the world. According to Thomas Donaldson, Wharton professor of legal studies and ethics,[2] Merck "has always emphasized, in effect, that the company puts the health care of the customer first, and if we do that, we will make money. If we ever just put making money first, we will lose our business." Donaldson adds, "You can question the extent to which Merck follows this, but it's not something that just appears [once in a while]. It is repeated fairly consistently."

Contrast Merck and Johnson & Johnson's handling of product defects with Firestone Tire's handling in 2000 of the recall of tires that were implicated in fatal SUV accidents. Firestone was initially reluctant to replace the defective tires, claiming that it was the vehicle rather than the tire that was at fault. The media later discovered that Firestone had prior knowledge of the problem and did nothing. It was also reported that Firestone had earlier refused to recall another defective tire sold in Saudi Arabia because a recall would mandate reporting the problem to the U.S. National Highway Traffic Safety Administration. Instead, it had launched a quiet replacement program that left the NHTSA in the dark. The result? Daniel Eisenberg, reporting on Firestone's tire debacle for *Time* magazine, concluded, "Thanks to a generally dreadful crisis management, marked primarily by silence and denials, the Firestone brand has very little credibility left. The public is becoming increasingly skittish about any of Firestone's tires—the vast majority of which are safe."

To promote responsibility, CEOs should carefully consider what it means to be a "responsible person," communicate this to managers, and encourage the promotion of responsible people within the organization. A company made up of responsible people is a responsible company. CEOs can assess managers according to the following "responsibility checklist."

Responsibility Checklist

Taking responsibility for personal choices

When I make a decision that turns out to be a mistake, I admit it.

When I make a mistake, I take responsibility for correcting the situation.

When things go wrong, I do not blame others or circumstances.

Admitting mistakes and failures

I always own up to my own mistakes and failures.

I am always willing to accept the consequences of my mistakes.

I use my mistakes as an opportunity to improve my performance.

I discuss my mistakes with coworkers to encourage tolerance for risk.

Embracing responsibility for serving others

I believe and show through my actions that an important aspect of my leadership approach is to find ways to serve and support others.

I pay attention to the development needs of my co-workers.

I spend a significant amount of my time providing resources and removing obstacles for my co-workers.

Rather than simply use this as a tool for self-examination, CEOs should discuss this checklist with senior management and ask them to rate their own responses on a scale from 1 (never does this) to 10 (always does this). The CEO should then discuss his expectations with management: which statements are the most important, which need to be adhered to the most closely, and work with them to improve their scores if necessary. The managers can then, in turn, work on responsibility within their individual departments.

The Compassionate Organization

When it's business as usual, acts of compassion are small or subtle in the great organizational scheme of things. But when a major crisis strikes, it is easy to see the difference between the truly compassionate organization and one that gives lip service to values. Aaron Feuerstein is the former president and CEO of Malden Mills, a company best known for producing the revolutionary fabric Polartec. On a cold December night in 1995, a devastating fire tore through his factory in Lawrence, Massachusetts. In a time of corporate downsizing, many of his peers urged him to re-open operations overseas—a decision that would lead to the loss of 3,000 jobs at home. Shunning their advice, Aaron pledged instead to rebuild the mill at home—*and* to pay his employees during the three-month reconstruction. "I think it was a wise business decision, but that isn't why I did it. I did it because it was the right thing to do," says Feuerstein.

Malden Mills battled insurance companies and government officials not just to rebuild the plant, but also to spend the additional money necessary to build the safest textile plant possible and to take care of his employees while the new plant was under construction. By 1997, just two years later, he had proved to the doubters that it was the right thing to do. Malden Mills was recording $400 million in annual sales—more than it ever had before the fire. Although Feuerstein's sometimes controversial decision making led to financial problems and a bankruptcy filing, the company emerged from bankruptcy intact.

Sometimes, though, despite a company's best intentions, layoffs must be made for the good of the company—its customers, its shareholders, and its remaining employees. The way an organization handles layoffs says more about its corporate character than any other activity. It is a test of its capability to weave moral, social, and business values into an effective whole. Answering the call of compassion in isolation

might tempt an organization to avoid a layoff at the cost of fiscal survival. But a moral organization that doesn't attend to its bottom line
won't be around long enough to keep any of its workforce gainfully
employed. So the task of a moral leader facing serious financial difficulties is not necessarily whether to reduce the size of the workforce, but
how to do it in a compassionate way that provides a soft landing for
those affected and in a way that preserves key talent.

In our high-achieving business culture, self-recrimination is common. We often find that our executives are far more critical of themselves (and less forgiving) than their bosses. One of the best ways a
morally intelligent leader can show compassion is to challenge the
executives about their excessive self-criticism. Of course, this implies
that the leaders have enough interpersonal skills and rapport with the
subordinates to find out what their critical self-talk is all about. Yet, this
challenge can be a superb way to embrace compassion and make it central to your organization. To the extent that employees spend their precious energy engaging in negative and self-critical inner dialogue, they
are *not* giving it to the company in pursuit of the strategic plan!

Finally, compassionate companies make it a priority to help others
beyond their own organizations For instance, Larson Manufacturing
sponsors extensive volunteer work in the community, including Habitat
for community and the Boys' and Girls' Club. Larson matches all
employee contributions to the local United Way, and in 2010 Larson
employees' pledges amounted to more than 25 percent of its community's United Way campaign goal. In addition, the Larson Family
Foundation funded the building of the Children's Museum of South
Dakota that opened in 2010. Another example of compassionate organizations comes from ID Media, which has found a particularly clever
way to help fight cancer. It sponsors a company coffee bar staffed by a
professional barista with a full complement of coffee drinks and par-
faits, for which employees pay bargain rates of $1 and $2, respectively.
ID Media donates all proceeds to Gilda's Club, a worldwide group of

centers providing support for people with cancer, and the American Cancer Society.

The Forgiving Organization

Organizational forgiveness is an organization's capacity to accept mistakes and failures among its workforce. Forgiveness is critical for two reasons. First, employees need to know that they have room to fail. If mistakes are invariably punished, the emotional climate of the organization will be unattractive to your best employees, who will go elsewhere in search of a more favorable work environment. Second, forgiveness is fundamental to innovation and growth. Innovation entails venturing into the unknown, where no formulas exist. Risks will be taken; mistakes will be made. Some things will work, and some things will fail. Organizations cannot pioneer new territory unless they accept that they will spend some time going around in circles or down dead-end paths.

When asked whether 3M's reputation for innovation is legitimate, Ray Langer, a 3M project engineer, says, "Yes, it really is. We're encouraged to try new things in our projects, and if they don't work out, no one is punished. As a result, we have created many, many engineering processes that no one else in the world comes close to."

Interestingly, the United States Marine Corps is an organization that has institutionalized forgiveness. "Most managers like to say they give their subordinates room to fail," says David Freedman, author of *Corps Business: The 30 Management Principles of the U. S. Marines*,[3] "but the Marines practice failure tolerance to a degree that would raise most [managers'] hair. To a certain extent, they *demand* failure: A Marine who rarely fails is a Marine who isn't pushing the envelope enough, goes the logic."

A final incentive to practice forgiveness is that without a climate of risk tolerance, employees will be too intimidated to acknowledge mistakes or offer feedback, thus perpetuating problems that may be costing your company millions each year. Nancy Jones, CMO for Allianz Life Insurance Company of North America understands the importance of creating a mistake-tolerant culture:

> **I have a philosophy of "No surprises." I don't want my boss, the CEO, to find out a mistake from someone else or in the wrong way, so I admit when I or my team makes a mistake and what we're going to do about it. I lead my people the same way. I tell them that admitting mistakes is not a sign of weakness. It's actually a sign of strength. It's the difference between a fear-based culture and a solutions-based culture. An example of this is when I had a director who came to me very upset about a costly mistake she had discovered. She figured out the cause and the solution, and took full accountability even though it was a vendor mistake. I told her she did the right thing. She felt supported and what I got back was loyalty and support. She continued to do great work and no longer feared bringing a mistake to my attention.**

Although the most forgiving companies are often the best innovators, these companies also know how to set limits. If you want to increase forgiveness at your company, establish "curbs" for innovative behavior—for example, set out the percentage of work time team members can use to engage in innovative projects that are their own or their team's creation or set budgetary limits, allowing employees to spend a certain percentage of their department's budget on innovation. But then, if you want to establish a truly forgiving company, make sure you celebrate this activity—not just the positive results. Honor your team members' mistakes as learning episodes. Edison is quoted as saying something like, "I didn't make any mistakes. I just tried ten thousand things that didn't work;" if you want to build an organization of budding

Edisons, celebrate the innovation process and the failures that come with it, not just the results.

Another way to encourage your organization to increase forgiveness is for you to establish a learning organization (rather than a punitive organization). Praise your team members for embracing the learning process. Allow mistakes to be forgiven and analyzed and not punished harshly.

But, as with all values, forgiveness cannot be practiced in isolation. Peter Georgescu of Young & Rubicam recalls a time when some young employees discovered racist jokes on the Internet and began passing them around. In all likelihood, they did not intend to offend anyone; they were just completely thoughtless. Georgescu struggled and worried over this. Anyone could make a mistake, he realized, but the company also had a policy of zero tolerance for such activity. People's lives and self-respect were at stake. In a move that he judged to be not only best for his business, but also for the moral development of the two employees, he let them go. It was an action that won acclaim throughout the business community. By understanding the implications of each possible choice, Peter demonstrated moral intelligence. By taking the action he did, he demonstrated moral competence. As Peter showed, the leaders who consistently puts both skills into practice creates resonance with those whom they lead.

Recruiting for Values

The basic unit of your organization is its people. Your organization's capability to engage in principled actions rests squarely on its people. Hiring the right people—the ones who already share your company's values and have a track record of acting consistently with those values—is the most important lever you have in creating a morally competent organization.

Jim Collins, author of *Good to Great*,[4] found that hiring the right people was a key differentiator of companies that had significantly outperformed the S&P over many years. When *FastCompany.com* asked him what his research suggested was the best way to respond to economic slowdown, he said this:

> **If I were running a company today, I would have one priority above all others: to acquire as many of the best people as I could. I'd put off everything else to fill my bus. Because things are going to come back. My flywheel is going to start to turn. And the single biggest constraint on the success for my organization is the ability to get and to hang on to enough of the right people.[5]**

Don't delegate recruitment to your human resources department. Take charge of your own hiring process as much as you can while still conforming to employment law. When possible, avoid anonymous newspaper ads. Instead, network continuously so that you always have a large pool of potential candidates or referral sources. Let your network know what kind of people you are interested in having work for your company. Don't hesitate to talk about your organization's values. Recruiting from your personal network is likely to lead to a significant jump in the retention rate and contribute positively to your organization's performance. Why? Because new jobholders who know you or are connected to you through your network are much more likely to share your values and to stay when things get a little rocky.

Reinforcing Values Starts at the Top

In *Primal Leadership: Realizing the Power of Emotional Intelligence*, Daniel Goleman, Richard Boyatzis, and Annie McKee describe their model of leadership.[6] The best leaders, they say, are resonant leaders. Resonant leaders use their emotional intelligence to create a positive emotional work climate in which the best work happens. To that equation, we would add this: The best leaders create resonance through their moral intelligence and their emotional intelligence. People naturally want to follow leaders who demonstrate commitment to moral principles and values. When people believe that their organization and its leaders practice the values they preach, they become energized. When people work in an organization that operates from a set of beliefs that resonate with their own, they are naturally inclined to give their best efforts to their work.

In the real world of organizations, we never have the luxury to work with a fully morally competent workforce. Maintaining organizational alignment with values is just as challenging as it is for any individual. That is why leaders should look for any opportunity to reinforce values. Training is key to reinforcing values and enhancing moral competencies. Senior executives may act allergic to training sessions in the misguided belief that they are finished products who don't need further education. But values start at the top, so senior level managers need to hone their moral judgment just like the rest of the workforce.

The Power of Formal Rewards

Psychologists tell us that people do what gets rewarded. It is critical that organizational reward systems reinforce morally competent behavior and goal attainment. Unfortunately, corporate reward systems that violate the principle of integrity are not unusual. Media reports of fired CEOs laughing all the way to the bank, CEOs who get multimillion dollar bonuses despite staggering year-end losses, and pyramid compensation systems that routinely reward executives far in excess of their relative contributions are common. Contrast that with former Best Buy CEO Brad Anderson (now retired) who declined 200,000 stock options in 2004. At the time he already owned company stock worth roughly $78 million dollars and asked that the declined options be distributed to nonexecutive employees.[7] Anderson's action was an effort to create more equity in the distribution of corporate rewards, although no one—Anderson included—would argue that he felt too much of a pinch. But his recognition that he did not need more sent a powerful message to other companies' executives about corporate excess—while creating a richer source of rewards for rank and file employees who do the right things.

Paul Clayton is insistent about sending positive messages through meaningful rewards. Paul recalls a time when he was president of Burger King North America and had to convince his executive team that he was serious about rewarding employees.

At Burger King, we had a recognition program for the top general managers. Once a year, we brought them to our world headquarters in Miami. During the recognition ceremony, 600 headquarters employees would give the award winners a standing ovation. As they entered the main rotunda, their pictures went up on our "Wall of Fame." As we were giving out awards, it struck me that one GM in particular had been the top performer for five years running. I turned to the HR person next to me and said that we should give him a car. The HR person replied, "We can't do that because we don't have budget and I don't have authorization." I reminded him that I was the president and that I thought that I could authorize the expenditure. When I presented the idea to the finance team, they thought it was fine but suggested an inexpensive car that wouldn't cost too much. "He'll never know the difference," one finance person said. But I had a different idea. I told them, "I'm thinking about a BMW. I don't care about the budget. I want people to know that we are sincere about the contribution they make." So when I took the stage to announce that I was rewarding the top GM with a fully loaded series 3 BMW, the place went crazy. The GM's wife ran up on stage to hug me and her husband. Then the GM ran off the stage to call his grandmother.

Success Stories

Given that moral values are embedded and intertwined with other values in the conduct of your business, how do you link moral values to performance? American Express does it by storytelling. The Amex team in Australia had just won the prestigious "Chairman's Award." The country manager wasted no time assembling his team to congratulate them. He did it in a way that explicitly linked Amex values to their success. He told stories about how individuals acted on Amex's values and how that contributed to their getting the Chairman's Award. This manager celebrated not only their accomplishments, but also the values that led to their success. Leaders in morally competent organizations never take values for granted. They promote them, they apply them, and they make sure that their people see how values translate into business performance.

Ideal Versus Real

Even within an organization committed to values, you can always find managers who fail to apply them. Wherever there are imperfect managers, there are cynical employees who look at them and say, "He, or she doesn't live the values, so…why should I follow the values if my boss ignores them?" Or "…why should I go the extra mile for a management that doesn't respect me?" If employees complain about someone who works for you, it is your responsibility to deal individually with unacceptable behavior. It is also critical that you convey the message that Ken Chenault gives to his employees: "There is no excuse for personal behavior inconsistent with Amex's values. You can't wait for everyone to behave in alignment with values before you do. The only way for people to start acting on values is to do it independently of whether others do. Do not expect perfection from leaders."

Values and the Global Organization

More and more companies not only do business internationally, but also are actually global companies with offices throughout the world, employing local workforces in numerous countries. Imagine how difficult it would be to communicate with a multinational workforce in the absence of some shared beliefs. Without common values, business would be impossible. Common values, based in the universal principles, can knit together a diverse global workforce. In an era marked by international conflict, we believe it will be in the world of business—rather than in the political arena—that people from different ethnic, racial, and religious heritages will discover their common path.

Endnotes

1. Marvin Bower. *The Will to Lead: Running a Business With a Network of Leaders*, Boston: Harvard Business School Press, 1997.

2. Quoted in "Death of a Drug: The Aftermath of Merck's Recall," *Knowledge at Wharton*, October 6, 2004.

3. David Freedman. *Corps Business: The 30 Management Principles of the U. S. Marines*, New York: HarperBusiness, 2001.

4. Jim Collins. *Good to Great: Why Some Companies Make the Leap...and Others Don't*, New York: Harper Collins, 2001.

5. Jim Collins, Web-Exclusive Interview, "Good Questions, Great Answers," Fast Company.com, October 2001. http://pf.fastcompany.com/magazine/51/goodtogreat.

6. Daniel Goleman, Richard Boyatzis, Annie McKee. *Primal Leadership: Realizing the Power of Emotional Intelligence*, Boston: Harvard Business School Press, 2002.

7. Reported in Patrick McGeehan, "Making a Point By Taking Less," *The New York Times*, May 24, 2004. Also reported in the article was that James Parker, Southwest Airlines' chief executive, had requested that his salary be significantly lower than suggested by its compensation consultant.

12

Moral Intelligence for the Entrepreneur

Starting from scratch. Imagine this: You have a great business idea, eager investors, and a prime location for your new company. With every resource at your disposal, you now have the chance to realize your fondest hopes and ambitions. You also have the power to create a high-performance culture from the ground up. No legacy employees, no unnecessary bureaucracy, no history to overcome. How would *you* begin? Would you use your newfound power to build a company based on universal principles, with socially noble goals and a morally competent workforce? Entrepreneurs rarely launch their ventures with an explicit moral focus. They make mistakes, and the most costly missteps are frequently moral, not strategic or operational. When entrepreneurs lack a consistent level of moral competence, their businesses usually falter or fail completely. Even exceptional business models can't survive without morally competent leadership. Entrepreneurs who want to succeed must master not only their business challenges, but must also align their businesses with the principles of integrity, responsibility, compassion, and forgiveness.

Morally clueless in Minneapolis. In the 1970s, a group of entrepreneurs started a telemarketing business named Minneapolis
Circulation, which primarily sold subscriptions to *Minneapolis* magazine. Its arrangement with the magazine was that Minneapolis
Circulation would own the subscriptions and would pay the magazine
$1 for every $5 subscription it sold. The company was creative about
marketing subscriptions, but the partners' greed and irresponsibility
doomed it to failure. The partners failed to recognize that the magazine
publishers would come to resent their meager share of the profits, and it
was only a matter of time before the publishers found a way to dry up
the telemarketing company's pipeline and pave the way for a better deal
with another telemarketer. When the entrepreneurs got the squeeze, they
didn't have the financial reserves to retool their strategy. They had
naively thought of the company as their cash cow, and any money they
made after expenses went straight into their personal bank accounts.
Because their vision of the business was so limited, Minneapolis
Circulation's owners didn't even think about their responsibility to their
employees or to the sustainability of the business.

Poorer, but wiser, or so one owner thought, he launched another
company, Twin Cities Telemarketing, with a new business partner. He
had learned his lesson about trying to own subscriptions, so his new
enterprise sold subscriptions for a fee. Its first client was *Twin Cities
Woman*, a struggling newspaper look-alike. When *Minneapolis* magazine got a new publisher and a new name, *Minneapolis St.Paul
Magazine*, Twin Cities Telemarketing acquired its subscription sales
business, too. Then it went after business with *Twin Cities* magazine, a
publication *that Minneapolis St.Paul Magazine* viewed as a competitor.
Twin Cities Telemarketing knew that it could sell both magazines effectively. It recognized that a lot of customers, such as hotels and professional offices, subscribed to both. Its game plan was to help both clients
succeed. But it carefully didn't mention its relationship with either magazine to the other. That was a fatal flaw. When the *Minneapolis St. Paul
Magazine* publisher found out that Twin Cities Telemarketing was

working for its arch rival, he pulled the plug. The owners of Twin Cities Telemarketing never thought of themselves as dishonest, but they were. Integrity would have dictated that they do their best to convince both magazines that representing the two was a win-win scenario—before taking on the second magazine.

Both of these ventures demonstrate that business savvy relies as much on moral intelligence as it does on a good business plan. Both start-up companies were initially successful businesses that unraveled because of gaps in integrity and responsibility. Like most entrepreneurs, it took several false starts for this group to learn the importance of principles and values. Those early business failures also point out just how critical moral competence is to a small business. Failures of integrity or responsibility might not be terminal in a large business that has the resources to absorb a certain number of mistakes. But for most small organizations, the distance between solvency and bankruptcy is painfully short.

Driving without a steering wheel. KRW International, one of the first executive coaching firms in the country, was founded in 1990 to offer premium consulting services to Fortune 500 executives. KRW's owners were strong on integrity and responsibility where their clients were concerned, but those principles were not always extended to their own organization. In the first few years, the owners' attitude was, "Let's have fun and make money." When demand for their services started growing beyond what they could handle, the partners did not think proactively about the kind of organization and workforce they needed. Instead, they reacted to the needs of the moment. They hired contract consultants and discovered that they didn't stick around long. They hired administrative staff at fairly low wages and worked them hard. They didn't stay long either. It took some time for KRW's partners to realize that if they didn't act responsibly toward their employees, employees would have no reason to feel responsible to them.

Luckily, KRW hired an administrative head, Kelly Garramone, who became its moral champion. More than once, Kelly confronted the owners, "There is too much work, too few people to do it, and deadlines are impossible." She successfully challenged the company to create work processes that both consultants and administrators could live with. Business grew consistently until 1994 when a major client company abruptly canceled its contract. KRW's owners were so shaken that they immediately decided they had to lay off most of their employees to preserve the owners' financial resources. That decision was ill-considered, both on business and moral grounds....

It was a beautiful fall day when KRW employees were gathered for the company's annual Octoberfest celebration. When the owners walked into the room, employees expected the festivities to commence. Instead, the owners announced a major downsizing. Soon, people were crying and running out of the room to call their spouses and friends. KRW's owners *were* open and honest, but their approach was a lot like surgery without anesthesia. It turned out to be unnecessary surgery. Everyone was given a good severance package. But soon most employees were rehired as independent contractors because KRW still had work in the pipeline. Before long, its major client reinstituted the contract, and KRW rehired all but a few of its former employees. One employee never missed a paycheck, but she got a windfall—three months off. KRW's owners ended up losing more money by thinking of themselves first than they would have if they had stepped back to take everyone's needs into account.

The mistakes KRW made during its 1994 downturn were the result of destructive emotions and a moral virus. KRW's owners had started their business with the goals to "make money and have fun." As soon as something happened that threatened both goals, fear took over, and they lost their ability to be reflective and self-aware. Further, because their goals were not aligned with a deeper purpose, there was no overriding sense of responsibility that could overcome their impulse to take care of themselves first.

KRW weathered that crisis and soon regained considerable momentum, so much so that during a 1998 company meeting, Kelly Garramone and her administrative staff once again announced that they were so overworked and stressed that if the company didn't make major changes, many would quit. KRW owners and consultants finally got the message. It was a turning point. The strong feelings of the administrative staff prompted the group as a whole to question why it was in business. It became clear that financial rewards were only part of the motivation for working at KRW. Some employees said that their ideal purpose was "to make the world a better place." Many employees resonated strongly with that purpose. Others worried that KRW would lose business if hard-nosed senior executives got wind of such a pie-in-the sky mission statement. Eventually, their collective desire to do something ambitious and wonderful won the day. In subsequent months, Kelly led the effort to define the organizational values that sprung from their newly articulated purpose. "If we are going to be an organization of moral integrity," insisted Kelly, "then we need to behave consistently with our purpose." Eight years after starting the company, "doing the right thing" became an explicit part of the KRW culture. Little did KRW's owners realize that within a few short years, KRW's collective commitment to a shared purpose would mean the difference between extinction and survival.

KRW took a steep trajectory as it gathered media recognition for its approach to CEO coaching and senior executive development. In 2000, it increased its revenues by 27%, expanded its consulting staff by one-third, doubled its office space, and was actively recruiting for additional staff to support anticipated further growth. By June of 2001, business bookings were so strong that one overwhelmed owner instructed the consultant group to stop marketing until further notice. Only three months later, in the wake of September 11, KRW's revenues crashed. This time, the moral lessons of the past came to the fore. The owners, despite enormous pressure, vowed to keep the company going. They cut their own salaries, mortgaged their houses, and did everything they could to keep the staff together for as long as possible. Each week, they updated their employees on the financial status of the company. For months, the news was grim. Everyone could see the handwriting on the wall, but when two rounds of selective layoffs finally came, laid-off employees were grateful for the lead time they had been given to prepare for their job transition. Employees who remained had almost as tough a time as those who left. Consultant salaries were cut, and administrative employees were given reduced hours. Owners suspended their salaries. With half of the staff gone, the offices looked—and felt—like a ghost town. But no one left who had the choice to stay. Maybe they stayed because the job market was dismal. But if you ask KRW employees why they stayed, they will tell you, "I believe in what KRW is trying to do." If you ask former KRW employees if they would go back if asked, the answer is almost always, "Yes." KRW returned to profitability within a year. Quite a few consulting firms did not survive the economic downturn of 2000–2002. KRW might have started by driving without a steering wheel, but it learned the value of guiding principles along the way, and those values steered it safely through its darkest hours.

Moral Values in Small Organizations

The moral values highlighted throughout this book are crucial to organizations of all sizes and stripes, big and small, for-profit and nonprofit. Integrity, responsibility, compassion, and forgiveness are undeniable values, no matter what the venue. Although the four core principles are the same, the moral challenges that dominate an organization are often size-dependent.

Poll a cross-section of employees who work for small organizations, and you begin to see differences in the character of small versus large organizations. Small company employees typically place a premium on decision-making freedom. Some value risk and adventure, whereas others value the small-town intimacy or the potential to have a larger impact. Another difference lies in the visibility of leadership in small organizations. The entrepreneurs or small company CEOs live in a fishbowl—everyone can see everything they do. The beliefs and goals that drive leader behavior are just as clear. So, moral competence is particularly crucial to the small company leader because moral gaps cannot be hidden—and bad choices lead to more than a slap on the wrist. They could spell the end of the business.

Challenges of integrity. For small organizations, internal integrity comes more easily than external integrity. Small companies by virtue of their size promote more direct and honest communication. Your boss might be sitting at the desk in the next cubicle, rather than sequestered in a remote executive suite. Fortunately, good information flow is easier to come by in a small company because without it, a small enterprise could go belly up in a matter of weeks. Actifi's Spenser Segal says this about the business value of honesty: "When we started, financial viability was not a given, and we felt everyone had to feel responsible for our success. To do that, they had to be able to manage the risk they were personally taking on. So we instituted a policy of sharing detailed financial information on a weekly basis. Now everyone knows how much cash is in our account, what is coming in, and what our pipeline looks like. Instead of managers and employees speculating and worrying, everyone knows what's going on and works together to help us find solutions."

Some hierarchical organizations, on the other hand, produce cultures of intimidation that discourage effective communication. Employees of large corporations often feel pressured to keep distant superiors happy, even if it means concealing a painful truth about poor performance. Ironically, when difficult truths are finally uncovered, the consequences might not be so dire because large profitable companies usually have the cash reserves to weather fallout from internal dishonesty.

Although internal honesty might come more readily to small companies, integrity can be challenged when small companies must put on a good face to the outside world. Capitalization is a perennial issue for many small companies. They need to borrow; they need to sell equity shares, or both. As one start-up founder points out, "It is very tempting to hide the truth from potential investors about the health of the company. But resisting temptation is essential. We have to be open and as transparent as possible about what the issues are. If you're getting people to really commit—whether they are employees or investors, then you have to be honest about what is working and what isn't."

Challenges of responsibility. Unlike large companies, which usually are focused on increasing profits, many new or small companies are trying to reach the point of making a profit. Small companies don't have the luxury of irresponsibility. Taking too long to admit a mistake can make the difference between black ink and red ink. But admitting failure can be hard, in part because individuals who work for small companies often feel more intense ownership for the decisions they make and want to keep plugging away to make it work. Unfortunately, that can spell doom for an emerging business. New companies are successful, not because they don't make mistakes, but because they know how to make a lot of mistakes quickly. The sooner the organization acknowledges a mistake, the sooner it can change course.

ActiFi's Spenser Segal reflects on the cost of denying mistakes: "In a small business that doesn't have a long history of results, it is critical that you stay firmly grounded in reality without giving up hope for the long term. We initially developed some sales assumptions for our first product. Our projections exceeded our results by a factor of five. It was four months before we were ready to reexamine our assumptions. The truth was staring us in the face, but no one said anything—maybe because I was a big part of making the mistake. Fortunately, we were able to recover, but we lost three months of valuable time by not admitting that our assumptions were flawed and our targets were unrealistic."

Spenser then adds a note about the benefits of admitting mistakes: "Because we had a very experienced management team, we were over-confident about our business model and our projections. After we admitted our miscalculation, we got better at admitting that we don't know what we don't know and therefore could look at things more like experiments. That took a lot of pressure off of everyone thinking that everything had to succeed."

Contrast ActiFi's rocky start with giant American Express, which had the financial resources to stay with a troubled business venture that its executives mistakenly thought would work—eventually. American Express finally closed the business at a loss, but the company as a whole was never at risk of going out of business because it delayed coming to terms with a bad business decision. Executives of large companies might produce higher profits if they heeded the lessons of responsibility that come from small organizations.

Small Companies Teach Some Big Lessons About Responsibility

In large organizations, we often encourage people to take lateral assignments that broaden their experience. Companies would be even smarter to encourage their high potential managers to spend a year or two working in the small business world. What they would learn would make them far more disciplined financial managers. They would know how to pay more attention, when to maintain support, and when to pull the plug on a struggling business. They would be more responsible with the company's resources. They would appreciate that five million dollars is a lot of money and should not be squandered.

Challenges of compassion. Compassion comes more easily in a small organization. Within the walls of a small enterprise, you know people better, and you are likely to know all your co-workers. In a small organization, no one is anonymous. Small companies more closely resemble the interdependent tribal groups that were so important to survival of our human species. Membership in smaller working groups seems to activate our hard-wired tendency for altruism. We take interest in our co-workers. We feel bonded to them. We see their success and ours as interconnected. When they need help, we want to help them. That does not mean that smaller organizations are immune from rivalry or deception or dislike. No human community is perfect. We may see the dark side of connectedness when we work in a small organization, but we rarely see indifference. If the small company headquarters is big enough to have an elevator, it will not be a silent ride.

But compassion is a double-edged sword. Too little compassion—as in the hard-edged and ultimately unnecessary lay-off in KRW's early days—and business may suffer. Too much compassion, as in KRW's post-9/11 protracted subsidy of employees, and business may also suffer. Business judgment without compassion can be as equally damaging as compassion without business judgment. Just as in the last chapter when we emphasized the fabric of values, skillfully interweaving business and moral values is even more critical for the small organization that commonly lacks the financial cushion to absorb mistakes and downturns.

Challenges of forgiveness. Because small organizations rely on their capability to cycle rapidly through mistakes, it is equally important for small organizations to forgive mistakes. Spenser Segal believes that forgiveness is critical to the success of a new business, adding, "Every startup makes tons of mistakes. We have built our business model assuming mistakes and bad assumptions. By being aligned around our mission and core values, we are able to look at various strategies as tests and hypotheses that we are seeking to prove or disprove. By ensuring that an environment fosters trying new things and doesn't cause bad feelings when tests or hypotheses fail, we are able to learn much more quickly—and that results in much better business models going forward. We need to learn to avoid four-month mistakes. It's better to make lots of small mistakes than any big ones." Amazon.com credits its growth from small online bookseller to e-commerce giant to its encouragement of innovation. David Risher, former SVP of Marketing with Amazon.com, describes what the company did to foster innovation:

> **Three times a year, we presented the "Just Do It" award. We wanted to explicitly reward people who have pride in doing something innovative. It had to have been well-thought through—not just something silly—truly innovative and focused on customer need. But it didn't have to work! And [one-third] of the time they didn't. The reward? A used Nike sneaker—the bigger the better.**

When it comes to letting go of mistakes and failures, small organizations have an edge. It can be hard to forgive a stranger. Forgiveness works best when you and I know each other and therefore are willing to give each other the benefit of the doubt when we make mistakes. Therefore, letting go of mistakes and moving beyond them happens more easily in a smaller organization—luckily so. In a small organization, you work in close quarters with all the people who might do something to hurt you. When you are angry at someone who has done you harm, or when you have done something to hurt another, there is nowhere to hide. Without the capacity for forgiveness, you would be surrounded by the tension of the unresolved hurt. Not only would a tense work environment prevent you from giving your best efforts, it would keep you from taking advantage of the resources your colleague would normally offer. In a small organization, it is difficult to work around a contentious relationship. For example, when you are in conflict with your colleague who is the company accountant, there is usually no department full of other accountants you can go to for help. In small companies, we are stuck with one another. That is ultimately a good thing. Knowing and accepting the foibles and failings of our co-workers sets the stage for "getting over it" and moving forward.

The moral impact of small organizations. Small businesses (companies of 500 employees or less) represent more than 99% of U.S.

employers, employ about half of the private sector workforce,and generate a majority of the innovations that come from United States companies.[1] Although as of 2010, small business growth has slowed, perhaps because of pessimism caused by the depth of the recent financial crisis; during prior economic recessions, such as the one between 2001–2003, job growth surpassed job losses among small companies. During the first quarter of 2002, 36% of jobless managers and executives started their own businesses, with a majority of laid-off managers moving to small companies.

Some workers, disenchanted with the legacy of mega-company scandals, or simply weary of large corporate bureaucracies, look to smaller organizations to provide a greater sense of meaning and purpose. KRW's former Chief Financial Officer Don Waletzko is a case in point. Don left an executive finance position when he couldn't approve his former employer's plan to go on an acquisition binge that would produce substantial layoffs. Don's moral compass wouldn't allow him to be the financial architect of a strategy that he feared would cause great personal disruption to his fellow employees. His former company's loss was KRW's gain. Don arrived with a financial pedigree that a small company such as KRW could ordinarily never have afforded. Fortunately, salary was not Don's top priority. He wanted to work for a company whose values reflected his own, and he found that in KRW's commitment to leadership development as a way to improve human lives. When the aftermath of 9/11 threatened KRW's survival, Don's steadfastness and financial savvy saved the day. He was a key player in the reorganization and recapitalization that stabilized KRW on its way back from the brink.

Don is one of many managers who believe they can have more positive impact on people and organizations by working in a small business. The large organization, such as a lumbering ocean liner, can be hard to turn in the direction of increased moral competence. In contrast, small organizations, such as a 25-foot sailboat, can turn quickly and efficiently when the compass and prevailing winds dictate. Small companies are fertile ground for shaping a morally intelligent culture—one that provides value simultaneously to its customers, employees, owners, and the community it inhabits. For those of us who are concerned about the welfare of all the world's peoples—small ventures offer great hope for the future. The path of economic development isn't from the sweatshop to the boardroom. It is from poverty to small locally based sustainable businesses. Everyone who invests in a new venture or small company has a golden opportunity to infuse the business world with more principled, more humane, and ultimately, more financially stable businesses.

Five maxims of moral entrepreneurship. Start-ups are excellent laboratories for moral leadership. Because resources are tight, mistakes have more immediate consequences. If you falter, there is no elaborate infrastructure to cushion you from disaster. American Express can write off millions in bad junk bond debt without going out of business. The owner of a new company does not have that luxury.

Entrepreneurs by definition choose paths to success that are both risky and rewarding, both exhausting and exhilarating. Your success as an entrepreneur, like that of any leader, depends on following the same four principles of integrity, responsibility, compassion, and forgiveness that underlie any sustainable enterprise. Following are five additional pieces of advice:

1. **Build a business that helps others. If your product or service doesn't make the world a better place, why bother?**

   Frankly, the world just doesn't need any more pet rocks, reality TV programs, or 2,500-calorie cinnamon buns. Starting a business is hard work. Doesn't it make sense to unleash your passion on something that will improve the safety, security, or comfort of fellow humanity? Knowing that you are building a socially worthwhile business can sustain you and your workforce through the rockiest times. Consider this model of a profitable business that exists to help others. Mark Oja runs ACTIVEAID, Inc., the medical devices manufacturing company founded by his father 45 years ago. ACTIVEAID is a small company by most standards But to long-time customers such as the Mayo clinic, and to the 37 employees in the small town of Redwood Falls, Minnesota (population 5,459), it is a big business. Employees know what their work means to customers—disabled people who rely on its products for mobility, comfort, and dignity. Quality is paramount. Everyone takes pride in that what they do helps people in their daily lives. This level of employee engagement is a big part of the reason why the company has continued to grow significantly despite a historical recession.

Modern Survey is another small enterprise with service at its core. Early on, its founders discovered that its real product was not the business information software solutions it provided, but the service it offered its customers. According to co-founder, Don MacPherson, "Service to others is very important. That's what we do as a company. It's helped our business effectiveness because if we put our clients' goals first, we achieve our goals. We have loyal clients, and we do virtually no advertising.

Even if your business fails—most entrepreneurs do fail several times before finally developing a successful venture—you will have the satisfaction of knowing your intentions were good. When you ultimately succeed—by staying true to universal principles and following the maxims of moral entrepreneurship—you will reap the combined rewards of service and profit.

2. Choose your partners wisely.

If you work in a large organization, your professional relationships tend to form through networks of work associates, industry colleagues, mentors, bosses, and acquaintances. If you work in a small organization, your professional relationships often overlap with personal networks of family and friends. Small business entrepreneurs are more likely to enter into partnership arrangements with family members, friends, and friends of friends. Choosing friends as business partners carries a host of dangers. No matter how objective you think you are, it is hard to evaluate a friend or relative's moral strengths and weaknesses. The success of your partnerships depends on shared principles and values. Looking at close personal associates through the rose-colored glasses of your affection, you may not notice moral gaps that could spell doom for your mutual venture. Rowland Moriarty, noted chairman of the Board of CRA International, Inc., said this about a previous business partner. "I made a 25-year commitment to a friendship [and] then watched him take actions that led to the collapse of our company."

Choosing a friend as a business partner can make it difficult to address the business problems created by one or the other. What *do* you do when a partner-friend betrays your trust by putting the business at risk? Though it's hard to contemplate, your best response would be to remind yourself of your friend's ideal self. By considering how your friend wants to behave ideally, you can give your friend the benefit of the doubt and avoid being overcome by destructive anger. When you believe that your partner and friend shares your values, you can discuss and jointly recommit to your vision and goals for your business. You forgive, and then you move on. You try again. You trust again. Keep in mind, however, that shared values lose meaning when ongoing behavior is inconsistent with those values. Forgiveness is not synonymous with stupidity. You can't look the other way when a partner continues to violate your mutual commitment. It's bad for your bottom line, and it sends the wrong message to employees who see that you are afraid to confront deceptive behavior. Remember that your emotional blinders are even stronger when your partner is a family member. Consider the experience of Janet Smith. Twenty years ago, her husband started a home renovation company. Business was booming, but cash flow was tight. Janet, a bright special needs teacher and mother of two, did not know that her husband was keeping his employees' social security and tax withholdings, until the IRS summons arrived. Janet and her husband declared bankruptcy, but that did not protect her from the legal liability to the IRS. They avoided imprisonment but ended up with massive penalties that took many years to repay. Meanwhile, her husband started a second small construction company, after assuring his wife that he had learned his lesson and would faithfully make employee tax payments. A year and a half later, Janet discovered that her husband had once again failed to make the proper employer payments to the IRS. Angry but still desperate to believe in her husband, Janet agreed to become his partner in a new business that designed, produced, and sold diagnostic equipment for chiropractic offices. The company had some success, was on the way to profitability, and had attracted the interest of a potential buyer. But the succession of business pressures had taken its toll on their marriage, and Janet and her husband finally divorced. Only after he signed over the business to her, did she discover that the potential investor was a phantom, and her husband had saddled her a third time with a set of enormous tax liabilities. Janet was an intelligent woman with good analytic skills. But her overwhelming desire to trust her husband blinded her to his persistent ethical lapses. Ten years after her divorce, she is a successful financial advisor to small businesses, having built a second career out of the painful lessons of her business partnership with her former husband.

Because start-ups are so fragile, it's especially important to choose partners who share your values. "I can't say enough about this," says Spenser Segal. "Understanding that the first few years would be filled with adversity, it was critical that we hired a leadership team that shared common values and believed that working on something they believed in was the best possible use of their time. By coming together with a team who shared that commitment, they were assured of personally being *successful even if the business failed.*"

3. Hold on tight to your core values.

Small business entrepreneurs need to be vigilant about maintaining their alignment with core values. Most entrepreneurs we know are highly morally intelligent. They are notably articulate about the principles and beliefs that guide them. ACTIVEAID's Mark Oja, for instance, endorses the importance of remaining true to one's principles. His moral compass is deceptively simple. "Honesty and family are the values that mean the most to me," says Mark, adding "If you don't mean it, don't say it. If you know or think or feel that something is improper, immoral, or illegal, don't do it." But even though Mark is strongly committed to those values, business pressures can begin to lure a company away from its moral foundation. "It can be tough competing with companies who go offshore for their products. When we had an opportunity to sell a low-priced cane that came from outside the U.S., we took it. Then our distributors complained about how bad the canes were. Our distributors and customers count on us for high-quality products, and we had violated their trust. When we realized what we had done, we canceled the deal. It took some time to repair the relationships that had been completely trusting before."

4. Surround yourself with employees who share your values.

When it comes to human talent, do not confuse the "best" with the "brightest." Values fit is a stronger contributor to performance than technical skill. We all have known "values misfits" who were expert in their fields but couldn't advance because they did not operate effectively within a particular organizational culture.

Mark Oja recounts this experience: "One time, we knowingly hired someone we didn't trust. We needed a certain skill that was in short supply in our area. Our only skilled candidate in this small town was a man with a minor rap sheet and a reputation for bad relationships. But we felt desperate, so we thought we could handle him. We were wrong. He was impossible to work with, and we had to let him go."

KRW International is obsessed with hiring employees who resonate with its purpose and values. Before job candidates are invited for an interview, their technical credentials are carefully scrutinized. Then the real vetting begins. Candidates run through a gauntlet of individual and group interviews in which the spotlight is almost exclusively on "fit" and values. The KRW community as a whole must agree that the candidate shares key values and will effectively represent them to customers and stakeholders. An owner once violated the recruitment protocol by hiring a consultant who had not run the full interview gauntlet. His colleagues were angry, and the unwitting new consultant wondered why some of his new associates were less than friendly.

Although resonance with organizational values is key for successful hiring, be sure to preserve diversity. Organization cultures have strengths and weaknesses, and if you hire only clones of your current workforce, you lose the opportunity to energize your company with new employees who bring novel approaches to your products and services.

5. **Put your people—and your organization—first.**

The United States Army has a saying, "The leader eats last." *The New York Times* offered an illustration of this maxim a few years ago when it published a photograph of an Army general serving Thanksgiving dinner to his combat troops in Afghanistan. Army leaders know what every entrepreneur needs to know. Followers must absolutely trust their leaders to do what is best for the unit.

Putting people first also means investing in the development of employees. Small businesses are notorious for neglecting to invest in employee development. Their financial struggles usually leave little cash reserve, and it's easy to drop the ball when it comes to "overhead" expenses such as training. Studies indicate that large company employees are more than twice as likely as small company employees to be offered employer-subsidized educational programs.[2] Given the lower average wages offered by small companies,[3] it is even less likely that employees of small companies will have the financial resources to maintain and update their job skills. Bucking this trend is ACTIVEAID's Mark Oja, who used the productivity increases generated by a new production system, not as an excuse to downsize, but as an opportunity for employee development. Several years ago, ACTIVEAID transformed its manufacturing process from batch production to packet production—essentially, it changed to a just-in-time production method. Mark knew that packet production would be more responsive to their customer, but it also meant there would be times when employees were not occupied making inventory during the transition. When employees were first told not to make products, they were worried, fearing that down time would mean layoffs. But Mark had no intention of laying people off or reducing work hours. Today, when orders come in, production gets busy. When no inventory is needed, employees use the time for training. Mark is firmly convinced that the investment in training creates not only more skilled employees but also a more motivated workforce that can enhance their business performance in the months and years to come.

Last Words About Business Start-Ups

Despite many differences in the culture and operations of small and large enterprises, the basic requirements of moral leadership are the same. Moral skills are intrinsic both to successful entrepreneurship and successful management of established companies. If you are an entrepreneur, it may seem more difficult to stay true to principles when the stakes are high and the cash flow is low. But your new venture simply cannot survive unless it is anchored in core principles. Moral competence is essential for the small business leader. The small organization rarely has the excess resources to weather a major moral lapse, nor does it typically offer the golden handcuffs that could keep employees tied to a morally bankrupt enterprise.

So in the end, the small organization and the large have this in common: Doing what is right morally and doing what is right for the business are inseparable. No matter the size of the territory, the morally competent leader weaves business and moral values together—and that makes all the difference. Just as it's true that buildings built to last need a strong foundation, it is also true that businesses built to last need a strong foundation. Moral principles and moral competencies are that foundation.

Endnotes

1. U.S. Small Business Administration Office of Advocacy, September 2009.
2. U.S. Bureau of Labor Statistics, Employee Benefits Survey, 2008. http://www.bls.gov/ncs/ebs/benefits/2008/ownership/civilian/table26a.htm.
3. U.S. Bureau of Labor Statistics, "National Compensation Survey: Employee Benefits in Private Industry in the United States, March 2006." http://www.bls.gov/ncs/ebs/sp/ebsm0004.pdf.

Becoming a Global
Moral Leader

Undoubtedly, you want your business to succeed, *and* you want to do the right thing. The good news of this book is that you are not alone. A large number of business leaders want to do the right thing and believe doing the right thing leads to organizational and personal success.

Like many leaders, you feel a deep responsibility for your businesses and your workforces. Your challenge now is to accept an even larger responsibility. Whether you realize it, the future of our planet is in your hands. Why? Because you are part of the most powerful social force on the planet today. In the last half-century, the corporation has assumed a central role as *the* iconic institution of many cultures across the globe.

Business is rapidly assuming a role as *the* most influential force in the lives of the world's 6.9 billion people. Religions, families, ethnic groups, and governments still matter and thankfully will continue to matter, but unless business leaders and their workforces bring moral values to work, none of those other institutions will matter enough. If you are not sure just how influential you are, consider the importance of the consumer economy to the well-being of your friends, family, employees, and the world.

As a business leader, you are a de facto moral educator. The moral lessons you and your company teach are lessons more powerful and more pervasive than that of churches, schools, and families. If you do the right thing, you can teach moral behavior to your employees. If you cook the books, fire someone unfairly, or use deceptive business practices, you teach others to do the same thing, or you mislead others into believing that's just how business is done.

Your workforce learns right and wrong at your workplace and learns that "right" is sustainable and "wrong" is not. If we want current and future generations to care about the welfare of others and the prosperity of the business and the survival of the planet, we who lead today's businesses need to show them the way. When it comes to moral values in the workplace, a lot needs to be said, and more needs to be done!

You may not have signed up to be a global moral leader, but you are. And with the inescapable power of your role comes a daunting responsibility. It is a responsibility that includes and yet goes beyond profitability. It is a responsibility that encompasses and goes beyond more obvious notions of corporate social responsibility.

Raising the Stakes

This book argues that moral intelligence and moral skills are critical to sustainable business performance. It proposes a set of essential moral skills and highlights the moral mechanics of interacting with the usual organizational stakeholders, especially customers, employees, and owners. Like most leaders, you recognize that you are accountable to those three groups, but another constituency is equally important—the communities beyond your organization.

Every organization lives within at least one community: whether it is the neighborhood surrounding the corner grocery store or the world community in which a major multinational corporation operates. How well do you serve the community that hosts your business? Consider these three different levels of responsibility you have for your external communities:

- The responsibility to do no harm

- The responsibility to add current value

- The responsibility to add future value

Watch Your Wake

Boaters entering harbors are often greeted by signs saying, "Watch Your Wake." Traveling too fast creates lines of turbulence—the wake of the boat—that can capsize smaller vessels. You also need to watch your wake. You need to understand the potential negative consequences of your presence in the communities where you operate. Some of the most admired corporations in the United States and in the world have been slow to acknowledge the catastrophic side effects of their business processes.

Businesses have knowingly and unknowingly polluted oceans and rivers and lakes. As Erik Peterson and Jay Farrar from the Center for Strategic and International Studies[1] have pointed out in their presentation on the "Seven Revolutions" that will shape the world in the next 25 to 50 years, strategic resource management of food, water, and energy will become an even greater challenge as the overall population of the world balloons to 8.8 billion by mid-century, while simultaneously the population of developed countries contracts.

Too few of the world's biggest companies take seriously their responsibility to do no harm." A research report published by

AccountAbility, a UK-based social responsibility institute found that the world's 100 largest companies have a poor record of accounting for their impact on society and the environment.[2] Had traditional philanthropy and community involvement been included in the report, big companies would have been rated more highly. Nevertheless, their relatively poor showing illustrates large companies still need to be convinced to do no harm to the environment.

Although environmental protection is an obvious responsibility for business organizations, other more subtle forms of pollution need to be remedied, and other challenges need to be addressed. If you work in the media industry, you may need to watch your wake in the behavioral messages you send to children and adults. Just about every business needs to be concerned with the potential negative consequences on family life of a 24/7 work culture.

Give Back

In addition to doing no harm, you also have a responsibility to "give back" to your communities in exchange for the varied resources that they provide—desirable locations, good employees, attractive living conditions, raw materials for manufacturing, customers, and so on. Business-sponsored social responsibility programs are one good way to add value to your communities at large. Your personal efforts and contributions of time and money are another.

You and your business have likely contributed positively to your local communities in many ways—perhaps by supporting programs in education, the arts, and health/well-being or by mentoring programs for at-risk youth or fundraising for medical research. If you and your organization add value in these and other ways, good for you and good for your company.

Giving back is more than a public-relations tool. It is vital for maintaining thriving local, regional, and world communities and the more you can do, the better. As the world's economy continues to globalize and as communication and travel technologies continue to "shrink" the world, each of us and the businesses we lead and work in have the opportunity to become even better at giving back.

Create the Future

Your third level of responsibility, to add future value, is the most challenging. Accepting responsibility for the future can be difficult in a business environment that is so attuned to the short term. It is relatively easy to contribute to the cause of the month because the need and the benefits are usually obvious. Figuring out how to add future value is less intuitive. Caring about the future impact of your business on the community and the world requires a different mindset. Consider this illustration of the kind of mindset that we would have to cultivate: At the 1998 State of the World Forum (founded in the mid-1990s by Jim Garrison and Mikhail Gorbachev), participants had the fascinating experience of participating in a ceremony led by a Polynesian tribal chief from Hawaii. After the ritual, the chief was asked, "What is your advice for those of us in businesses who are concerned about both the short term and the long term? There is a lot of pressure on quarterly and annual results." The chief answered, "You need to understand how we think about responsibility and accountability. In our culture, we help people realize they are *accountable to the three generations that preceded them and responsible for the seven generations that follow them.* When we make decisions, we take into consideration the impact of that decision on someone seven generations from now."

Imagine what your company's strategic plan would look like if Polynesian decision-making criteria were incorporated into your analyses. We have seen the harm done by managers who optimize for the short term. What kind of good could your company do if its performance objectives were designed to contribute to results a hundred years down the road?

A Global Business Opportunity

Ironically, the global economic crises we have been facing during the last several years make our opportunities to "do well by doing good" even more obvious. Caroline Stockdale, SVP and chief talent officer of medical device maker Medtronic offers this perspective:

> The globality of the [economic] crisis has made this crisis significantly different from any previous downturn. This is still a very difficult time, and we can see it in countries like Greece and Ireland and even here in the US. The crisis has impacted so many lives. Everyone knows someone who has been personally hurt. What is interesting to me is what lead to this perfect storm at the macro level was a lack of moral intelligence and a preoccupation with self-interested behavior. At the micro level we saw people living far beyond their means. People had so much faith in the economic institutions in America, and that faith has crumbled, and those institutions have lost respect. But the crisis also brings opportunity and puts on the map some of the emerging markets, such as the emergence of China and India. Serving the need of new markets creates new opportunity.

Like all the moral competencies discussed in this book, serving your external communities is not only morally right, but also essential for sustainable business success. The business case for global moral leadership is strong. There are profits to be made. Here lies the opportunity: As you provide the people of the world with good jobs and fair pay for their work or fair prices for their products and services, you simultaneously expand the opportunity for yourself and your business.

Global business is less about expansive holdings and more about expansive thinking. Consider this: *Businesses that work to increase the welfare of the global community simultaneously increase the market for economic goods and services.*

A *Business Week* article chronicled how new technologies could help alleviate chronic poverty in India. It pointed out that "many of the educated elite responsible for the success of India's tech and software houses—or who have helped U.S. multinationals prosper—decided to turn their energies to helping India's poor."[3] They see both the opportunity for *compassion* and the business opportunity for profit that comes from helping the poor move up the economic ladder.

The article quotes management strategist C.K. Prahalad, who says, "If you can conceptualize the world's four billion poor as a market, rather than as a burden, they must be considered the biggest source of growth left in the world."[4] Every person on the planet is a potential customer or partner or supplier or employee. Large companies today may compete aggressively for a dominant share of a ten-million customer market or for a relatively small number of highly educated and technically competent prospective employees, when the actual potential market and the potential workforce is the entire world's population.

Today, markets are constrained by the economic status of regional populations, and education and development is typically available only for those who can afford it. But people lacking education are not dumb, and people without economic means still have material needs and the intelligence to create economic value (through jobs) in exchange for the ability to buy products that will satisfy those needs. Many people in underdeveloped regions can't afford the consumer products they are hired to produce. (Think designer athletic shoes.) Wouldn't it be good for business if they could? Henry Ford asked that question about an infant American car industry more than half a century ago. Henry Ford may not have been a saint in many respects, but he knew how to do well by doing good. He figured out how to create customers for his new-fangled automobile by paying his workers well above the going rate. He wanted people making the Model T to be able to afford one. He created a market for his products through enlightened self-interest. Henry Ford's workers won, and Ford won.

Prosperity need not be a zero sum game. Why couldn't we increase our markets by financing business start-ups in third-world regions? The micro-lending movement is a good example of the economic effectiveness of business creation in undeveloped regions. But those economic experiments are largely the province of academics and nonprofits. Why aren't those of us in the for-profit sector doing more to develop communities that will, in turn, sustain us and our businesses through the balance of this new century and beyond?

We need to stop thinking that we can only win if others lose. Ultimately, none of us will do well unless all of us do well. We may be feeling quite comfortable in our plush executive suite or on the porch of our summer home. But our grandchildren and great-grandchildren will not have the benefit of our well-appointed lives if we don't help all the world's people do better.

Conclusion

Mark Twain once said, "It is curious that physical courage should be so common in the world and moral courage so rare." It is time for moral courage to take center stage in business and for business to accept the responsibility that comes with its prominent position in the world. The ball is in our court.

Endnotes

1. As presented at http://www.csis.org.
2. AccountAbility, The State of Responsible Competitiveness 2007, http://www.accountability.org/images/content/0/7/075/The%20State%20of%20Responsible%20Competitiveness.pdf.
3. "The Digital Village," *Business Week*, June 28, 2004.
4. Ibid.

A

Strengthening Your
Moral Skills

Think of moral skill building as a learning process like any other. Richard Boyatzis, noted leadership development expert, offers a particularly useful way of understanding how we build leadership capabilities.[1] Boyatzis argues that we don't learn to be better people or better leaders by attending training programs. We build our human and leadership capabilities through actual life experiences. Though experience is the best teacher, we don't have to leave what we learn to chance. Boyatzis proposes that we can put ourselves in charge of our learning using a structured five-step process:

1. Understand your ideal self—The person you want to be.

2. Recognize your real self—Your actual strengths and weaknesses in the context of who you want to be.

3. Decide how to build on your strengths and reduce the gaps between your real and ideal selves.

4. Experiment with new behaviors and feelings.

5. Develop trusting relationships with people who will support your learning process.

Developing moral skills follows the same cycle of self-directed learning. In Chapter 3, "Your Moral Compass," you had an opportunity to complete the first step of the process—you examined the contents of your principles, values, beliefs, and your goals, all of which make up the raw material of your ideal self. So you're now ready for the next step to understand your real self—by assessing your moral strengths and weaknesses. With a full picture of your ideal self and real self, you can then be in position to craft a moral learning plan. Your moral learning plan can be your road map for gaining the moral skills that are most important to you *and* that promote the highest levels of business performance.

A Look in the Mirror

Most of us have some idea of our moral strengths and weaknesses. Our conscience might give us a pang if we exaggerate a business accomplishment. A friend could take us to task for being thoughtless. Or we may feel secure in our unswerving fairness to our employees. But our data about our own moral performance is usually anecdotal and incomplete. To help you identify your moral strengths and weaknesses, we have developed the Moral Competency Inventory (MCI). See Appendix B, "Moral Competency Inventory (MCI)."

Using the MCI

The MCI is a 40-item survey that you will find here and in Appendix B. It is a self-report survey; that is, you are the person who rates yourself on each item, and you are the person who decides the meaning of the results. Take the MCI when you have an hour to spend. It will take about 20 minutes to complete the survey, about 10 minutes to score, and another 30 minutes to reflect on your results.

The MCI is a self-development tool, not a test, so it does not have the scientific precision of, say, the SATs or an IQ test. But leaders who have used the MCI tell us that it helps them capitalize on their moral strengths and strengthen moral skills that are difficult for them.

It is important for the user of the MCI to understand that this instrument does not have validity as a selection tool nor as a personality test. Thus, it should be used for personal reasons only and not for any professional use by human resource professionals.

The Right Frame of Mind for Completing the MCI

The MCI items are all worded in a positive way, so there is no attempt to hide what the survey would consider to be positive behavior. Because you are rating yourself, the value of the MCI will be enhanced if you are as honest with yourself as possible. That means trying to avoid two kinds of self-rating errors:

- The tendency to give yourself a high rating on most items because they sound like positive things to do

- The tendency to give yourself low ratings on many items because you are typically hard on yourself (self-critical)

Scoring and Interpreting Your MCI

You will find scoring instructions in Appendix C, "Scoring the MCI," and interpretation guidelines in Appendix D, "Interpreting Your MCI Scores."

There are several different ways to look at your MCI scores. You will have an opportunity to consider your overall moral competency profile, and you also can examine specific areas where you have strength or need development. No single interpretation is correct, and no "test" is the last word on your capabilities. If any part of your MCI scores don't ring true to you, keep in mind that you know yourself best. But if you are dissatisfied with your scores, we ask only that before dismissing them, you use your results as a springboard for honest reflection about your strengths and weaknesses.

Prioritizing Your Moral Development Efforts

There are two paths to improving your performance in any arena of life. You can concentrate on removing weaknesses, or you can focus on using your strengths. When you focus on your weaknesses, you try to improve your performance by undoing old behavior and practicing new skills or competencies. When you focus on your strengths, you try to improve performance by finding new ways to use the skills and competencies you already have.

Which path do you think is more effective? We believe you can reach higher levels of performance by capitalizing on your strengths than by trying to remove your weaknesses.

Which path do you think most organizations follow? Most organizations try to improve the performance of their workforce by concentrating on deficiencies. Our experience has been that most of the performance feedback many employees receive is negative, that is, information about perceived gaps. Organizations assume that negative feedback will create awareness of gaps that employees will then seek to improve. Ironically, negative feedback often produces the opposite effect. Studies have shown that performance often gets worse following negative feedback. It can take weeks for performance to recover to previous levels and months, if ever, to see positive gains in performance. Even though managers regularly observe that negative feedback can be counterproductive, most organizations continue to provide an excess of feedback about performance gaps. Focusing on gaps is a well-worn path, but one that rarely leads to the highest organizational performance.

The Road Less Traveled

Most organizations treat positive feedback, that is, recognition of strengths, like a scarce resource. Employees are expected to perform well, and when they use their strengths to accomplish positive results, it often passes without comment. Organizations who fail to acknowledge strengths miss out on a tremendous performance multiplier. That is unfortunate because most employees perform best by spending most of their time leveraging their strengths. It is in our strengths that we most resemble our ideal selves, and the more time we spend using our strengths, the more closely we approach our ideal self. Focusing on strengths may be "the road less traveled," but it is the path that makes the most difference to creating high performance.

The 80/20 Rule

Management consultant Roy Geer, offers this advice: Spend 80 percent or more of your time developing and leveraging your strengths and 20 percent or less of your time "pumping air into your priority flat spots (weaknesses)."

Look for ways to leverage the moral strengths you already have. Actively use those aspects of yourself that are closest to your ideal self. For example, Marietta Johns is a senior executive who knew she was weak in the financial management aspects of her job. But she didn't spend a lot of time trying to learn what she didn't know. She got help from a corporate financial guru and concentrated on doing what she did best—connecting with her people and inspiring them to produce enviable financial results.

Moral development is largely a process of developing and leveraging your strongest moral competencies. You can get the most performance equity from using your strengths, but you can also benefit from spending up to 20% of your development time dealing with your gaps. By concentrating primarily on your strengths, you can also avoid the discouragement of trying to remove gaps that are part of your basic personality and difficult to change. So don't ignore your gaps. Allocate your time wisely on the path to your ideal self.

Your Moral Development Plan

A moral development plan helps you boost your performance by increasing the odds that you will actually do the things that increase your moral competence. A moral development plan records your moral development goals and outlines specific actions you will take to become increasingly morally competent. This need not be a separate plan from a professional development plan. If you work in an organization or for a boss open to discussing principles, values, and beliefs, you may find it useful to include moral development as part of your overall development plan. The important thing is to write down the moral and emotional competencies on which you want to focus and detail the steps you will take to use those competencies. Goals for moral development, like any goals, are more likely to be achieved when you commit to them in writing.

Step 1: Describe Your Ideal Self

Moral development planning makes sense only in the context of who you want to be. Recall the principles, values, and beliefs that form your moral compass. Given that set of beliefs, what kind of person would you be if you were at your absolute best?

Step 2: Document Your Goals

Again, moral development is only important if it helps you accomplish your most important goals. Recall your goals frame. What are the most significant things you want to accomplish in all of the important areas of your life?

Step 3: Identify the Moral Competencies You Need the Most

Reflect on the moral and emotional competencies that you need the most to reach your goals. If you used the alignment worksheet presented earlier, you have already completed this step.

Step 4: Leveraging Your Strongest Moral Competencies

Now recall your strongest moral and emotional competencies:

- In the course of the next six months, how can you use those competencies to get closer to your goals?

- Can you use your strengths in a new situation?

- How might you become even stronger in your use of some of those strengths?

- If it were possible to use your strengths and use them well enough, how many gaps would you actually have?

Step 5: Reducing Moral Gaps

- In the next six months, what could you do to strengthen those moral competencies in situations that are important to you?

- If you strengthened one competency, what impact would that have on your ability to accomplish your goals?

Finally, consider any other moral or emotional competencies that are highly important to accomplishing your goals:

- In the next six months, what could you do to strengthen those moral competencies in situations that are important to you?

Step 6: Your Moral Development Short List

Putting this all together, what are the three to five most important actions you can take to boost performance by developing your moral competence? Put this on a note card, enter it into your planner, or record it anywhere that you can keep it handy as a reminder of what you plan to accomplish.

Putting Your Moral Development Plan into Practice

Now that you have your short list, moving forward should be easy. But actually doing what you think is important requires that you clear the road ahead. We need to keep our behavior on course with our beliefs and goals. If you recall the alignment model, unproductive behavior is usually the result of *disconnectors*—those moral viruses or destructive emotions that get in the way of positive and aligned actions. So changing behavior begins with *recognizing* your personal disconnectors and then *reprogramming* yourself to stay in alignment even when moral viruses or destructive emotions threaten you.

Breaking Bad Habits

Although moral viruses and destructive emotions are major causes of misalignment, another common cause of misalignment between goals and behaviors is simply a matter of bad habits. Changing our behavior so that we do what we need to do to accomplish our goals usually means overcoming the inertia of doing things the usual way. Anyone who has tried to quit smoking or lose ten pounds knows that reprogramming behavior is not easy. Developing moral competence usually means that you have to change habits that get in the way of being moral.

Realize that doing something different will not feel natural. Don't wait until something feels right. Do the right thing until it feels right. Expect a new behavior to feel strange or uncomfortable. Be willing to do it no matter what for *x* days. Build in reinforcement to tide you over until the behavior becomes second nature.

Reward Yourself for Positive Change

The best way to reinforce a new behavior is to reward yourself for doing something new. This doesn't mean that you need to sign up for a golf or spa vacation to reward yourself for doing the right thing. It's more along the lines of waiting for dessert until you have eaten your peas. Take the pleasures that are already part of your life and make them contingent on succeeding in the behavior changes that are part of your moral development planning. Celebrate your new behavior by going to that Friday night movie. If you have ignored your development plan for the week, stay home and pay your bills. When setting up your reward system, be sure that you use an optional activity, not a necessary activity such as exercise. You don't want to compromise your health or well-being if you suffer a setback in your change efforts.

Surround Yourself with Positive People

Because we are wired for interdependence, we need help from others to do our best. Within Boyatzis' theory of self-directed learning is the discovery that "you need others to identify your ideal self or find your real self, to discover your strengths and gaps, to develop an agenda for the future, and to experiment and practice." Everyone needs the support of trustworthy friends and colleagues to help them stay true to their goals. Make sure you establish at least a few relationships with people who will tell you the truth about yourself, even when you might not want to hear it. Find trusted people who know your values and goals and will let you know when you are not living up to them. When you are attempting new behavior, let them know what changes you are trying to make and ask them to tell you if they see you falter.

Do I Really Need to Change?

Like any worthwhile activity, living in alignment takes some effort. You might wonder if you really need to change. You are, after all, a decent human being with a good track record of career accomplishment. If you are an experienced manager, you may even believe that you already know all you need to know and don't need to learn anything new. If you are a senior manager, it has probably been a long time since you have gotten any critical feedback about your leadership skills. So why go to the trouble of trying to enhance your moral competence? Developing moral competence is every person's job because when it comes to human behavior, there is no standing still. If you don't continuously work on your moral development, you will lose moral competence. Think about any activity you used to enjoy that you have dropped over the years. It is not quite true that there are some things you never forget how to do, such as riding a bicycle. Get on a bike after 20 years, and you will probably gain your balance, but you certainly won't be able to go as fast, or as far, or turn as smoothly as you did when you were young. You might still be able to pedal, but your performance won't be what it could if you had kept on biking all those years. Maintaining and developing moral competence happens only when we keep pedaling. We need to use our strengths consistently, day after day, in pursuit of our ideal self. As our real self comes to look more and more like our ideal self, we will see the results in our personal lives and in our leadership of others.

Resist the urge to think of yourself as a finished product. Don't let anything stand in the way of becoming your ideal self. Invest time in activities that build on your strengths and enhance your moral competence. You are in charge of your moral development, but don't think you have to go it alone. Take advantage of personal development resources that you might not have considered in the past.

Books, Audio, and Video Media

There are many worthwhile books on the topic of principled leadership and personal growth. Reading such books is one good way to reflect on what is most important to you. For the busy manager with a long commute, books on tape are a useful way to de-stress and maintain alignment.

Workshops

Look for seminars on leadership, emotional intelligence, and values. Many senior managers think they don't need "training." Recognize your human fallibility and invest the time in active learning where you can benefit from the expertise of the presenters and the support of your fellow participants.

Personal Counseling

Some of us find that our moral viruses are so severe that they are seriously limiting our personal and professional effectiveness. The worst moral viruses usually arose out of traumatic childhood events. If some aspect of your life is not working for you, despite your best efforts, find a counselor or psychotherapist who can help you understand the source of your difficulties and work with you to develop more effective behavior.

Executive Coaching

Executive coaches are a particularly helpful resource for high-potential managers who want to accelerate their leadership development and for seasoned managers with moral or emotional blind spots. An executive coach understands the demands of your leadership role and the politics and culture of your organization. A coach can help you get the kind of honest feedback you need to build a development plan, keep you focused on your goals, and advise you on how to increase your leadership effectiveness. Many of the best-known Fortune 500 CEOs have benefited from their use of executive coaching services.

Endnote

1. Dan Goleman, Richard Boyatzis, Annie McKee. *Primal Leadership: Realizing the Power of Emotional Intelligence*, Boston: Harvard Business School Press, 2002.

B

Moral Competency Inventory (MCI)

- Please choose one rating in response to each statement by circling the number that corresponds to your rating.

- You will get the most value from this assessment if you respond honestly. It may be tempting to give yourself a high rating because the statement sounds positive, but please do your best to rate yourself accurately in terms of how you really behave.

---

1. I can clearly state the principles, values, and beliefs that guide my actions.

1 = Never
2 = Infrequently
3 = Sometimes
4 = In most situations
5 = In all situations

2. I tell the truth unless there is an overriding moral reason to withhold it.	1 = Never 2 = Infrequently 3 = Sometimes 4 = In most situations 5 = In all situations
3. I will generally confront someone if I see them doing something that isn't right.	1 = Never 2 = Infrequently 3 = Sometimes 4 = In most situations 5 = In all situations
4. When I agree to do something, I always follow through.	1 = Never 2 = Infrequently 3 = Sometimes 4 = In most situations 5 = In all situations
5. When I make a decision that turns out to be a mistake, I admit it.	1 = Never 2 = Infrequently 3 = Sometimes 4 = In most situations 5 = In all situations
6. I own up to my own mistakes and failures.	1 = Never 2 = Infrequently 3 = Sometimes 4 = In most situations 5 = In all situations
7. My colleagues would say that I go out of my way to help them.	1 = Never 2 = Infrequently 3 = Sometimes 4 = In most situations 5 = In all situations

8. My first response when I meet new people is to be genuinely interested in them.	1 = Never 2 = Infrequently 3 = Sometimes 4 = In most situations 5 = In all situations	
9. I appreciate the positive aspects of my past mistakes, realizing that they were valuable lessons on my way to success.	1 = Never 2 = Infrequently 3 = Sometimes 4 = In most situations 5 = In all situations	
10. I am able to "forgive and forget," even when someone has made a serious mistake.	1 = Never 2 = Infrequently 3 = Sometimes 4 = In most situations 5 = In all situations	
11. When faced with an important decision, I consciously assess whether the decision I want to make is aligned with my most deeply held principles, values, and beliefs.	1 = Never 2 = Infrequently 3 = Sometimes 4 = In most situations 5 = In all situations	
12. My friends know they can depend on me to be truthful to them.	1 = Never 2 = Infrequently 3 = Sometimes 4 = In most situations 5 = In all situations	
13. If I believe that my boss is doing something that isn't right, I will challenge him or her.	1 = Never 2 = Infrequently 3 = Sometimes 4 = In most situations 5 = In all situations	

14. My friends and co-workers know they can depend on me to keep my word.	1 = Never 2 = Infrequently 3 = Sometimes 4 = In most situations 5 = In all situations
15. When I make a mistake, I take responsibility for correcting the situation.	1 = Never 2 = Infrequently 3 = Sometimes 4 = In most situations 5 = In all situations
16. I am willing to accept the consequences of my mistakes.	1 = Never 2 = Infrequently 3 = Sometimes 4 = In most situations 5 = In all situations
17. My leadership approach is to lead by serving others.	1 = Never 2 = Infrequently 3 = Sometimes 4 = In most situations 5 = In all situations
18. I truly care about the people I work with as people—not just as the "human capital" needed to produce results.	1 = Never 2 = Infrequently 3 = Sometimes 4 = In most situations 5 = In all situations
19. I resist the urge to dwell on my mistakes.	1 = Never 2 = Infrequently 3 = Sometimes 4 = In most situations 5 = In all situations

20. When I forgive someone, I find that it benefits me as much as it does them.	1 = Never 2 = Infrequently 3 = Sometimes 4 = In most situations 5 = In all situations
21. My friends would say that my behavior is consistent with my beliefs and values.	1 = Never 2 = Infrequently 3 = Sometimes 4 = In most situations 5 = In all situations
22. My co-workers think of me as an honest person.	1 = Never 2 = Infrequently 3 = Sometimes 4 = In most situations 5 = In all situations
23. If I knew my company was engaging in unethical or illegal behavior, I would report it, even if it could have an adverse effect on my career.	1 = Never 2 = Infrequently 3 = Sometimes 4 = In most situations 5 = In all situations
24. When a situation may prevent me from keeping a promise, I consult with those involved to renegotiate the agreement.	1 = Never 2 = Infrequently 3 = Sometimes 4 = In most situations 5 = In all situations
25. My co-workers would say that I take ownership of my decisions.	1 = Never 2 = Infrequently 3 = Sometimes 4 = In most situations 5 = In all situations

26. I use my mistakes as an opportunity to improve my performance.	1 = Never 2 = Infrequently 3 = Sometimes 4 = In most situations 5 = In all situations
27. I pay attention to the development needs of my co-workers.	1 = Never 2 = Infrequently 3 = Sometimes 4 = In most situations 5 = In all situations
28. My co-workers would say that I am a compassionate person.	1 = Never 2 = Infrequently 3 = Sometimes 4 = In most situations 5 = In all situations
29. My co-workers would say that I have a realistic attitude about my mistakes and failures.	1 = Never 2 = Infrequently 3 = Sometimes 4 = In most situations 5 = In all situations
30. I accept that other people will make mistakes.	1 = Never 2 = Infrequently 3 = Sometimes 4 = In most situations 5 = In all situations
31. My co-workers would say that my behavior is consistent with my beliefs and values.	1 = Never 2 = Infrequently 3 = Sometimes 4 = In most situations 5 = In all situations

32.	I can deliver negative feedback in a respectful way.	1 = Never 2 = Infrequently 3 = Sometimes 4 = In most situations 5 = In all situations
33.	My co-workers would say that I am the kind of person who stands up for my convictions.	1 = Never 2 = Infrequently 3 = Sometimes 4 = In most situations 5 = In all situations
34.	When someone asks me to keep a confidence, I do so.	1 = Never 2 = Infrequently 3 = Sometimes 4 = In most situations 5 = In all situations
35.	When things go wrong, I do not blame others or circumstances.	1 = Never 2 = Infrequently 3 = Sometimes 4 = In most situations 5 = In all situations
36.	I discuss my mistakes with co-workers to encourage tolerance for risk.	1 = Never 2 = Infrequently 3 = Sometimes 4 = In most situations 5 = In all situations
37.	I spend a significant amount of my time providing resources and removing obstacles for my co-workers.	1 = Never 2 = Infrequently 3 = Sometimes 4 = In most situations 5 = In all situations

38. Because I care about my co-workers, I actively support their efforts to accomplish important personal goals.	1 = Never 2 = Infrequently 3 = Sometimes 4 = In most situations 5 = In all situations
39. Even when I have made a serious mistake in my life, I can forgive myself and move ahead.	1 = Never 2 = Infrequently 3 = Sometimes 4 = In most situations 5 = In all situations
40. Even when people make mistakes, I continue to trust them.	1 = Never 2 = Infrequently 3 = Sometimes 4 = In most situations 5 = In all situations

C

Scoring the MCI

If you are using the paper version of the MCI that appears in this book, you now need to use the following scoring sheet to produce your survey results:

1. Transfer your ratings for each item to the scoring sheet. Your item 1 rating should be placed next to the number "1" in column A. Your rating for item 2 should be placed next to "2" in column B, and so on. Continue until you have transferred your ratings for all 40 items.

2. Add each column and place the total in the box indicated.

3. Add columns A through J and place the total in the box indicated. Columns A through J are subscores for each of the 10 moral competencies discussed in Chapters 5–7.

4. Divide the total from columns A–J (step 3a) by 2 and place in the box indicated. This is your total MC (Moral Competency) score. The maximum MCI score is 100.

5. Using the Moral Competencies Worksheet below the scoring sheet, transfer your scores for each column—A through J—to the corresponding list of competencies listed after each corresponding letter.

MCI Scoring Sheet

Item A	Item B	Item C	Item D	Item E	Item F	Item G	Item H	Item I	Item J	3a. Add columns (A–J)
1	2	3	4	5	6	7	8	9	10	
11	12	13	14	15	16	17	18	19	20	
21	22	23	24	25	26	27	28	29	30	
31	32	33	34	35	36	37	38	39	40	
Add Col A	Add Col B	Add Col C	Add Col D	Add Col E	Add Col F	Add Col G	Add Col H	Add Col I	Add Col J	

4a. Divide by 2

MCI Score

Moral Competencies Worksheet

_____ **A.** Acting consistently with principles, values, and beliefs

_____ **B.** Telling the truth

_____ **C.** Standing up for what is right

_____ **D.** Keeping promises

_____ **E.** Taking responsibility for personal choices

_____ **F.** Admitting mistakes and failures

_____ **G.** Embracing responsibility for serving others

_____ **H.** Actively caring about others

_____ **I.** Ability to let go of one's own mistakes

_____ **J.** Ability to let go of others' mistakes

Highest Moral Competencies	Lowest Moral Competencies
1.	1.
2.	2.
3.	3.

What Your Total MCI Score Means

Your total score is a measure of alignment. If your score is high, it is highly likely that you typically act in ways consistent with your beliefs and goals. If your score is low, it is likely that your typical behavior is out of synch with what you believe and what you want for yourself. Table C.1 shows the distribution of MCI scores from very low to very high.

Table C.1   Total MCI Score (Alignment Score)

Score	Ranking
90–100	Very High
80–89	High
60–79	Moderate
40–59	Low
20–39	Very Low

D

Interpreting Your MCI Scores

There are quite a few different ways to look at your MCI scores. No single interpretation is correct, and no "test" is the last word on your capabilities. We recommend that you reflect on each of these aspects of your MCI scores to see whether they trigger the self-awareness that is so crucial to ongoing moral development. We think you will find your results to be interesting and illuminating. If aspects of the MCI interpretation are confusing or don't make sense to you, we trust that in the final analysis, you know yourself better than any paper-and-pencil assessment. That said—here are some ways to interpret your scores.

Total MCI Score (Alignment Score)

Score	Ranking
90–100	Very High
80–89	High
60–79	Moderate
40–59	Low
20–39	Very Low

- The maximum possible score is 100. A score of 100 would mean that you answered every item on the MCI with a "5" and would indicate that you believe you are completely competent in all 10 moral competencies assessed by the inventory. Because no human being is perfect, a perfect score on the MCI might mean that you have some difficulty acknowledging areas of weakness.

- The minimum score is 20. Most people have some degree of moral competency; therefore, low and very low scores may reflect excess self-criticism rather than genuine moral incompetence. In our experience, scores below 60 are extremely rare, most likely because corporate leaders do not succeed without some degree of moral competency.

- MCI scores fall most frequently in the moderate range (between 60 and 79).

- Your total MCI score is simply a snapshot of your overall moral competence. If you take the MCI every year or so, your total score can help you see whether your overall level of moral competence is increasing.

Highest and Lowest Competency Scores

- Most people who complete the MCI have one or two moral competency scores that stand out as higher or lower than the bulk of the scores. When you completed the MCI worksheet, you identified your highest and lowest scores in each competency area. Take a look at them now.

- Do your highest scores fit your understanding of your own strengths? If so, these are the competencies that you know how to use to maintain alignment and promote high performance. Are there any high scores that surprised you? If so, they may represent areas of strength that you had not been aware of and are competencies that can further help you to achieve your goals.

- Do your lowest scores fit your understanding of where your weaknesses lie? If so, you have an opportunity to develop your competencies if you decide that improvement in those competencies is important to you. Are there any low scores that surprised you? If so, they may represent blind spots that are keeping you from reaching your goals.

Individual Item Scores

- Go back to the scoring sheet and look for very high and very low scores. If you have a few scores of "5," those items may be areas of particular strength that you should recognize, appreciate, and use. If you have a majority of "5"s, you may be extremely morally competent across the board, but you also may have over-represented your strengths. People with very high scores across the board may need to solicit feedback from others to confirm the accuracy of their scores.

- If you have some scores that are "2" or "1," what weaknesses do those items represent? Given that most people who take the MCI have very few item scores below "3," low item scores usually represent wonderful opportunities for removing obstacles to high performance.

- Take a look at the item scores for your highest and lowest competencies. Was your lowest competency score a result of midrange scores for each of the four related items, or was your competency score low because of one very low item score? If so, you might find that paying attention to that single aspect of the competency could greatly boost your competence in that area.

Reality Testing

How much do you trust your self-assessment of your moral competencies? Most of us have some degree of difficulty seeing ourselves as other see us. As a reality test, we recommend that you share your MCI scores with one or two trusted friends or colleagues. Here are some questions you can ask them:

- How well do my strengths as reported on the MCI reflect your perception of my strengths?

- How well do my weaknesses as reported on the MCI reflect your perception of my strengths?

- Are there other moral competencies that you see as my strengths?

- Are there other moral competencies that you see as weaknesses?

- On a scale of 1 to 10, how would you rate me on integrity?

- On a scale of 1 to 10, how would you rate me on responsibility?

- On a scale of 1 to 10, how would you rate me on how well I show compassion?

- On a scale of 1 to 10, how would you rate me on my capacity for forgiveness?

Do Your Scores Matter?

- All the competencies included in the MCI are important, and all act synergistically. But realistically, we are all human and need to concentrate on developing the competencies that will have the most impact on us and our organizations.

- You already have decided whether your scores accurately reflect your areas of moral strength and weakness. At a deeper level, how well do your scores represent competency areas that are important to you? After all, you can be good or bad at things that you don't care about. So, we encourage you to think about the extent to which the competencies identified are consistent with your moral compass and your goals that you explored in Chapter 3, "Your Moral Compass." Completing the *Alignment Worksheet* helps you to decide how much effort to put into developing specific emotional and moral competencies. In the first column, you see the list of competencies.

- In the second column, record your relative scores. (For example, was it your highest, lowest, or midrange score for each scale.)

- In the third column, rate each competency in terms of its importance to your personal guidance system. For example, is "admitting mistakes and failures" high, medium, or low in its importance to your principles, values, and beliefs?

- In the fourth column, rate each competency in terms of its importance to accomplishing your goals. For example, is "actively caring about others" high, medium, or low in its importance to your
  ability to accomplish your goals?

Now What?

By completing the alignment worksheet, you have prioritized competencies in terms of their importance to you. You have identified

- Areas of strength and weakness that are important for alignment.

- Areas of strength and weakness that are less important for
  alignment.

- Competency areas that are neither strengths nor weaknesses that
  are important for alignment. Your scores for a competency may
  be mid-range, but because it is a highly important competency
  for maintaining alignment with your guidance system or to
  accomplish your goals, it is worth your effort to enhance that
  competency to the fullest.

As an aside, if your rating of a competency's importance to your guidance system is different from your rating of its importance to goal
accomplishment, you might have a disconnect between your moral
compass and your goals that needs to be considered.

Armed with this understanding of your moral competency levels
and their importance to your moral compass and goals, you can map
out a straightforward approach to enhance your moral and emotional
competence.

Alignment Worksheet

Moral Competencies	MCI Score (High, Midrange, Low)	Importance to My Principles, Values, and Beliefs (High, Medium, Low)	Importance to Accomplishing My Goals (High, Medium, Low)
A. Acting consistently with principles, values, and beliefs			
B. Telling the truth			
C. Standing up for what is right			
D. Keeping promises			
E. Taking responsibility for personal choices			
F. Admitting mistakes and failures			
G. Embracing responsibility or serving others			
H. Actively caring about others			
I. Ability to let go of one's own mistakes			
J. Ability to let go of others' mistakes			

Index

A

ABACUS 2007-AC1, 12
Aberman, Rick, xxxi, 175
ACA (ACA Management LLC), 12
ActiFi, 59, 73, 229-230
actions, 79
active listening, 149-151
ACTIVEAID, Inc., 236, 239-241
Adelphia Communications, 6
admitting mistakes/failures,
  117-121, 209
adrenal gland, 51
adrenaline, 51
AdvisorNet Financial, 14
AEFA (American Express Financial
  Advisors). *See* Ameriprise
  Financial Services
Alcatel, 6
Alignment Worksheet, 281-283
alignment. *See* living in alignment
Allianz Life Insurance Company of
  North America, 27, 216
Amazon.com, 108, 232
American Atheists, Inc., 36

American Express, xxvi-xxvii,
  145, 182-185, 197-198, 221,
  231, 235
American Express Financial Advisors
  (AEFA). *See* Ameriprise
  Financial Services
American Honda Motor Co., Inc.,
  18, 108
American Humanist Association, 37
American Partners Bank, 106
American Portfolio, 107
Ameriprise Financial Services, xxv, 25,
  124-126, 144, 208
amygdala, 49-51, 161
Anderson, Brad, 219
approachability, 154-155
Arnold, Roger, xxix, 157-158

B

bad habits, 258-259
Baker, Douglas, xxviii, 18, 145
balance, 144-146
Bank of America, 11
Bar-On, Reuven, xxxi

basal ganglia, 49
Bastian, Rich, 60
Bear Stearns, 10
behavior, 75
    actions, 79
    emotions, 77-79
    thoughts, 76-77
beliefs
    acting consistently with, 98-99
    explained, 68
    identifying your top ten beliefs,
        68-69
    sharing, 192-193
Bell, David, 85
Benson, Herbert, 146, 171
Best Buy, 219
Best Corporate Citizen companies, 26
big picture, reflecting on, 172-173
Blackwell, Lawana, 125
Blake, Brenda, xxx, 197-198
Blanchard, Ken, 120
Bower, Marvin, 201
Boyatsis, Richard, xxxi, 23, 218,
    251-252, 262
Bradley, Walt, xxx, 98
brain, moral anatomy of, 41-46
    danger system, 51
    emotional center, 49
    fMRI (functional magnetic
        resonance imaging), 45
    habit center, 49
    lessons from brain-injured
        individuals, 42-45
    neuroscience of moral
        decision-making, 48-52
    plasticity of brain, 52-53
    rational center, 49
    reward system, 52
    simplified model of brain, 48
breaking bad habits, 258-259
Brettler, Dan, xxviii
Bronfman, Sam, xxx, 184
Brown, Donald E., 36
Brushaber, George, xxx
Burger King North America, 103, 220
business success, impact of moral
        intelligence on, 25-27

C

Campbell, David, 72
Camus, Albert, 142
Cannon, Kate, xxxi
Caplan, Robert, xxxi
Cardinal Health, 188
Carlson, Cindy, xxx
Carlson Companies, 119
Cayne, James, 10
cerebral cortex, 49
change
    recognizing need for, 260-261
    rewarding yourself for, 259
Chapman, Peter, 10
Chenault, Kenneth, xxvi-xxviii,
        182-183, 221
Cherniss, Cary, xxxii
childhood, moral development in
    empathy, 39-40
    importance of early childhood
        experiences, 41
    neonate responsive crying, 38
    responsibility, 40
choices, taking responsibility for,
        115-117
Churchill, Winston, 142
Clayton, Paul, xxviii, 103, 220
Clevette, Rick, 119
coaching, 190, 262
Coca-Cola, 189
cognitive behavior, 76-77
cognitive intelligence (IQ), 19
Collins, Jim, 218
collision of values, 195
communities
    giving back to, 246-247
    responsibility to, 244-245
compassion, 126-128
    defined, 22
    misplaced compassion, 149-151
    in morally intelligent organizations,
        213-215
    in small organizations, 231-232
competing drives, 47-48
competitiveness, 47
confidences, honoring, 110-111
confirmation bias, 169
conflicts (values), 67-68
Connolly, Michael, xxx

consistency, 98-99
consumers, influence of moral
        intelligence on, 29-30
core values for small businesses, 239
corporate accounting scandals, 5-7
*Corps Business: The 30 Management
        Principles of the U. S. Marines*
        (Freedman), 215
cortisol, 51
Coughlan, Jay, 16
counseling, 261
Countrywide, 8-10
Covey, Stephen, xxxii, 37
Cracchiolo, Jim, 209
Cuomo, Andrew, 11

D

Dalai Lama, 125
danger system (brain), 51
Dardis, Stan, xxviii
Darwin, Charles, 46
Dautheribes, Therese M., 36
DDB Worldwide, 136
decision-making
    4 Rs
        explained, 159-162
        practicing, 162-163
        recognition, 163-170
        reflection, 170-173
        reframing, 174-175
        responding, 175-178
    neuroscience of, 48-52
    and values, 65-66
destructive emotions, 89-91
diagnosing moral viruses, 86, 88
The Diary of Anne Frank, 104
differences, appreciating, 152-156
differentiating competencies, 19
disconnectors, 258
Distribution for Wealth Enhancement
        Group, 157
documenting goals, 257
Dodd, Christopher, 10
Dolber, Lon, xxviii, 107
Donaldson, Thomas, 211
dopamine, 52, 78
Druskat, Vanessa, xxxii
Ducks Unlimited, 126
Dylan, Bob, 113

E

Ecolab, Inc., 18, 145
Edison, Thomas, 216
Edwards, Dave, xxx, 197
80/20 rule, 255-256
Eisenberg, Daniel, 211
Emmerling, Robert, xxxii
emotional center of brain, 49
emotional competencies, 77-79
        compared to moral intelligence,
                23-24
        destructive emotions, 89-91
        empathy, 148-149
        emotional health, nurturing, 143-147
        explained, 19-21, 83-85, 135-137
        getting along with others, 154-156
        influence on life success, 22
        interpersonal effectiveness, 147
        misplaced compassion, 149-151
        nurturing emotional health, 143-147
        personal effectiveness, 141
        positive self-talk, 141-142
        recognizing emotions, 139, 169-170
        respecting others, 151-153
        self-awareness, 137-139
        self-control, 142-143
        understanding your thoughts, 140
*Emotional Intelligence: Why It
        Can Matter More Than IQ*
        (Goleman), 20
empathy, 38-40, 148-149
employees
        coaching, 190
        communicating belief in
                employees, 191-194
        development, 189-191
        mutual accountability, 194-195
        providing feedback to, 193-194
        recruiting, 217-219, 239
        retention, 27-29
        reward systems, 219-221
        value differences with, 195-196
Enron, 5, 114
entrepreneurs, 223
        compassion, 231-232
        five maxims of moral
                entrepreneurship, 235-241
        forgiveness, 232-233
        integrity, 229-230
        KRW International, 225-228

moral impact of, 233-235
moral leadership, 242
responsibility, 230-231
Twin Cities Telemarketing,224-225
values, 228
environmental protection, 245-246
epinephrine, 51
Ettinger, Jeff, xxviii, 204
executive coaching, 262
exercise, 146
experiential triangle, 91-93, 137-139,
    163-167

F

failures, admitting, 117-121, 209
familiarity bias, 169
Fantom, Lynn, xxviii, 17, 85,
    128, 132
Farrar, Jay, 245
Fastow, Andrew, 6, 114
feedback, 193-194
feelings. See emotions
Feurstein, Aaron, 213
financial costs of ignoring moral
    principles, xxiii-xxv
financial services industry. See also
    specific companies
    absence of moral competence in,
        7-15
    lack of publish trust in, 29
Firestone Tire, 211
flexibility, 155
fMRI (functional magnetic
    resonance imaging), 45
followers, inspiring, 187-188
Ford, Henry, 249
forgiveness, 128-129
    defined, 22
    forgiving others' mistakes,
        131-134
    forgiving your own mistakes,
        129-131
    in morally intelligent
        organizations, 215-217
    in small organizations, 232-233
4 Rs
    explained, 159-162
    practicing, 162-163

recognition
    of emotional patterns,
        169-170
    experiential triangle, 163-167
    Freeze Game, 166-167
    practicing, 163
    of thinking patterns, 168-169
reflection
    on big picture, 172-173
    making reflection a habit, 171
    practicing, 170
    preparing for, 171
    on values, 171-172
reframing, 174-175
responding, 175-178
Frank, Anne, 104
Fredrickson, Barbara, 20
Freedman, David, 215
Freeze Game, 166-167
Fribourg, Paul, xxviii
Froude, Don, 62
Fuld, Dick, 11
functional magnetic resonance imaging
    (fMRI), 45
fundamental beliefs, 36-37
future-based goals, 74
future value, creating, 247

G

Gage, Phineas, 42
Garramone, Kelly, 226-227
Garrison, Jim, xxxii, 247
Geer, Roy, xxxii, 71, 255-256
Georgescu, Peter, xxviii, 217
Gilda's Club, 214
global business opportunities,
    222, 248-250
global moral leadership, 243-244
    adding future value, 247
    giving back to community,
        246-247
    global business opportunities,
        248-250
    responsibility for potential
        negative consequences,
        245-246
    responsibility to communities,
        244-245
GMAC, 106

Gnazzo, Patrick, 28
goals
    documenting, 257
    explained, 70
    goal alignment test, 75
    identifying life's purpose, 70-71
    identifying most important life goals,
        74
    importance of, 73
    purpose-driven goals, 71-73
    sharing, 192-193
Goldman Sachs, 11-14
Goleman, Daniel, xxxii, 19-20,
        22-23, 161, 218
Golub, Harvey, xxviii, 185, 206-208
Good to Great (Collins), 218
goodness of people, belief in,
        188-189
Gorbachev, Mikhail, 247
Gowing, Marilyn, xxxii
Grace, Patrick, xxx
Grigg, Darryl, xxxii

H

habit center (brain), 49
Hall, Brian, xxviii
Hall, Don Jr., xxix, 109
Hallmark Cards, 109
Harrington, Dick, xxix,
        181-184
HealthSouth, 6
Heath, Brian, xxix, 126, 130
highest competency scores
        (MCI), 279
hippocampus, 51
Hoefer, M'Lynn, xxx
honesty
    exceptions to rule of honesty,
        104-105
    good intentions, 105
    influence on performance, 106
    leading with honesty, 100-103
    in performance reviews, 103
    tact, 105
honoring confidences, 110-111
Hormel Foods, 204-205
*How to Get What You Want and Remain
        True to Yourself*
        (Geer and Lennick), 72
Hubers, David, xxix

Hughes, Mike, xxix-xxx
Hugstad-Vaa, Jennifer, xxxii
Hunt, Harriot K., 97
Hutcheson, Dorothy, xxxii
hypothalamus, 51

I

IBM, 131
ID Media, 17, 85, 128, 132, 214
ideal self, 188, 256
IDS, 206-208
*If You Don't Know Where You're Going,
        You'll Probably End Up
        Somewhere Else* (Campbell), 72
ImClone, 120
IMG, 127
inconsistency, 98
individual item scores (MCI),
        279-280
inspiring followers, 187-188
Institutional Risk Analytics, 14
insula, 51
integrity
    consistency, 98-99
    defined, 21
    honesty, 100-105
    honoring confidences, 110-111
    in small organizations, 229-230
    keeping promises, 109-111
    organizational integrity, 203-204
    standing up for what is right,
        106-109
International Management
        Group, 16
interpersonal effectiveness, 147
interpersonal relationships, 154-156
interpreting MCI scores. *See* MCI
        (Moral Competency Inventory)
Interpublic, 17, 85
IQ (cognitive intelligence), 19
irresponsibility, 114-115

J

Jacobs, Ruth, xxxii
Jamba Juice, 103
Jefferson Bus Line, 105, 127
Jewell, Sally, 101-102
Johnson & Johnson, 210

Jones, Nancy, 27, 216
Jordan, Kathy, 176
JPMorganChase, 10

K

Kaess, Ken, xxix
Kaiser, Lori, xxx, 84, 142
Kant, Immanuel, 104
Kantor, Stuart, xxxiii
Keers, Carol, xxxiii
Kelner, Stephen Jr., xxxiii
Kennedy, Robert F., 68
Kenny, David, xxix
Kernes, Jerry L., 36
Kessler, Gary, xxx, 18, 108
Khuzami, Robert, 12
Kidd, David, xxxiii
Kinnier, Richard T., 36
Kleiner, Art, xxxiii
Kopper, Michael, 6
Kozlak, Diane, xxx
Kraft Foods, 206
Kram, Kathy, xxxiii
Krei, Ken, xxix, 8, 122
KRW International, 225-228, 234, 240

L

Lane, Karen, xxx
Langer, Ray, 215
LaRocco, Mike, xxix
Larson, Dale, xxix, 8, 102
Larson Family Foundation, 214
Larson Manufacturing Company, 8,
      102, 214
Lawrence, Paul, 47
Lawson Software, 16
Lay, Ken, 6, 114
leadership. See moral leadership
Lehman Brothers, 10
Leider, Richard, xxxiii, 70
Lench, Kenneth, 12
Lennick, Doug, xxvi, 71
Lennick Aberman Group, 64, 175
Leohr, Jim, xxxiii
Leuning, Harvey, xxx
Levinson, Ann, xxx
Lewis, Ken, 11

life's purpose
   identifying, 70-71
   setting purpose-driven goals, 71-73
limbic system, 49, 51
listening, 149, 151
living in alignment
   behavior, 75
      actions, 79
      emotions, 77-79
      thoughts, 76-77
   beliefs
      acting consistently with, 98-99
      explained, 68
      identifying your top ten beliefs,
         68-69
      sharing, 192-193
   destructive emotions, managing,
         89-91
   emotional competence, 83-85
   experiential triangle, 91-93
   explained, 57-61, 81-85
   goals
      explained, 70
      goal alignment test, 75
      identifying your life's
         purpose, 70-71
      identifying your most
         important life goals, 74
      importance of, 73
      setting purpose-driven goals,
         71-73
   moral compass, 61-62
   moral competence, 82-83
   moral misalignment, 85
   moral viruses
      common moral viruses, 88
      dealing with, 88
      diagnosing, 86-88
      disabling, 88-89
   preventative maintenance, 93
   staying aligned, 85
   values
      compared to principles, 63
      and decision-making, 65-66
      explained, 63
      identifying top five values, 64
      morality of values, 65
      uncovering values conflicts,
         67-68
loss avoidance system (brain), 51

lowest competency scores
(MCI), 279
Lucent Technologies, 6
Luskin, Fred, xxxiii

M

M&I Bank, 8, 122
MacPherson, Don, xxix, 28, 119, 129, 138, 236
Madoff, Bernie, xxv
Malden Mills, 213
management techniques, 196
Manchester Companies, xxiv, 209
Mangino, Matthew, xxxiii
May, Dan, xxix, 14
Mayer, John, 19
McAfee, 7
MCI (Moral Competency Inventory), 263-270
    interpreting scores, 277
        Alignment Worksheet, 281-283
        highest and lowest competency scores, 279
        individual item scores, 279-280
        reality testing, 280-281
        total MCI score (alignment score), 278
    moral strengths and weaknesses, 252
    scoring, 253-254, 274-275
        Moral Competencies 274
        scoring sheet, 271-272
        total MCI score (alignment score), 274
    as self-development tool, 252-253
    self-rating errors, 253
McKee, Annie, 23, 218, 262
McMahon, Ed, 10
Medtronic, 118, 131, 248
Menttium Corporation, 62, 78
Merck & Company, 210
Merrill Lynch, 11
Microsoft, 108
The Mind and the Brain: Neuroplasticity and the Power of Mental Force (Schwartz), 53
Minneapolis Circulation, 224
Minneapolis magazine, 224
Minneapolis St. Paul Magazine, 224

Minow, Newton, 113
misalignment, 85
misplaced compassion, 149-151
mistakes
    admitting, 117-121, 209
    forgiving
        others' mistakes, 131-134
        your own mistakes, 129-131
Mitchell, Jim, xxxiii
Modern Survey, 28, 119, 129, 138, 236
moral anatomy, 41-46
    danger system, 51
    emotional center, 49
    fMRI (functional magnetic resonance imaging), 45
    habit center, 49
    lessons from brain-injured individuals, 42-45
    neuroscience of moral decision-making, 48-52
    plasticity of brain, 52-53
    rational center, 49
    reward system, 52
    simplified model of brain, 48
moral compass, 61-62
    disclosing to employees, 192-193
    staying true to. See living in alignment
Moral Competencies Worksheet, 274
moral competency. See also emotional competencies
    compared to moral intelligence, 43
    compassion, 126-128
    explained, 83
    4 Rs
        explained, 159-162
        practicing, 162-163
        recognition, 163-170
        reflection, 170-173
        reframing, 174-175
        responding, 175-178
    forgiveness, 128-129
        forgiving others' mistakes, 131-134
        forgiving your own mistakes, 129-131
    identifying competencies you need most, 257

integrity
    consistency, 98-99
    honesty, 100-106
    honoring confidences, 110-111
    keeping promises, 109-111
    in performance reviews, 103
    standing up for what is right,
        106-109
    moral development. *See*
        moral development
responsibility
    admitting mistakes and
        failures, 117-121
    explained, 114-115
    serving others, 121-124
    taking responsibility for
        personal choices,
        115-117
Moral Competency Inventory.
    See MCI
moral development
    in childhood, 39-41
    choosing between competing drives,
        47-48
    moral anatomy, 41-46
        danger system, 51
        emotional center, 49
        fMRI (functional magnetic
            resonance imaging), 45
        habit center, 49
        lessons from brain-injured
            individuals, 42-45
        neuroscience of moral
            decision-making, 48-52
        plasticity of brain, 52-53
        rational center, 49
        reward system, 52
        simplified model of brain, 48
    moral gaps, reducing, 257
    natural selection, 46-47
    nature versus nurture, 38-39
    neonatal empathy, 38
    plan, 256-258
    prioritizing efforts, 254-255
    requirements for, 53-54
    resources
        books and media, 261
        counseling, 261
        executive coaching, 262
        workshops, 261
    responsibility, learning, 40

strengthening moral skills, 251-252
    book and media resources, 261
    breaking bad habits, 258-259
    counseling, 261
    80/20 rule, 255-256
    executive coaching, 262
    MCI. *See* MCI (Moral
        Competency Inventory)
    moral development plan, 256-258
    positive feedback, 255
    prioritizing development efforts,
        254-255
    recognizing need for change,
        260-261
    rewards for positive change, 259
    surrounding yourself with
        positive people, 259-260
    workshops, 261
universal principles, 36-37
moral impact of small organizations,
    233-235
moral leadership, 181-184
    belief in the goodness of people,
        188-189
    communicating belief in
        employees, 191-194
    disclosure of moral compass,
        192-193
    employee development, 189-191
    examples of moral leadership,
        15-18, 257
    inspiring followers, 187-188
    leading with honesty, 100-103
    management techniques, 196
    mutual accountability, 194-195
    power, 185-187
    providing feedback, 193-194
    for small businesses, 242
    value differences with employees,
        195-196
    visibility, 184-185
moral misalignment, 85
"moral positioning system," 25
moral viruses
    common moral viruses, 88
    dealing with, 88
    diagnosing, 86-88
    disabling, 88-89
morally intelligent organizations
    compassion, 213-215
    defined, 199

employee recruitment, 217-219
explained, 199-201
forgiveness, 215-217
global organizations, 222
integrity, 203-204
policies, 201-202
principles, 202
responsibility, 204-212
reward systems, 219-221
small organizations
    compassion, 231-232
    five maxims of moral
        entrepreneurship, 235-241
    forgiveness, 232-233
    integrity, 229-230
    moral impact of, 233-235
    responsibility, 230-231
    values, 228
values, 197-199
Moret, Pam, xxx, 149
Moriarty, Rowland, xxix, 237
Mozilo, Angelo, 8-10
Mungavan, Tom, xxxiii
mutual accountability, 194-195
mutual feedback, 193-194

N

NASA, 109
natural selection and moral
    development, 46-47
nature versus nurture, 38-39
need for change, recognizing, 260-261
negative consequences, responsibility
    for, 245-246
neonatal empathy, 38
neonate responsive crying, 38
brain, moral anatomy of, 41-46
    danger system, 51
    emotional center, 49
    fMRI (functional magnetic
        resonance imaging), 45
    habit center, 49
    lessons from brain-injured
        individuals, 42-45
    neuroscience of moral
        decision-making, 48-52
    plasticity of brain, 52-53
    rational center, 49
    reward system, 52
    simplified model of brain, 48

Nicholson, Nigel, 191
Nicolay, John, xxxiii
Nohria, Nitin, 47
Northwestern Mutual, 18, 140, 147
nurturing emotional health, 143-147

O

O'Hagan, Gary, xxx, 16, 122, 127, 130
Oja, Mark, xxix, 236, 239-241
organizational integrity, 203-204
organizations. *See* morally
    intelligent organizations
Ovations, 59
overconfidence, 169

P

Parker, James, 222
partners, choosing, 236-239
Paulson, Carla, xxx
Paulson & Co., 12
Pavilla, Steve, 64
performance, influence of honesty
    on, 106
performance reviews, 103
Perrine, Tom, xxx, 188
The Personal Advisor Group
    (TPAG), 62
personal choices, taking responsibility
    for, 115-117
personal counseling, 261
personal effectiveness, 141
Peterson, Erik, 245
Peterson, Richard, 52
Phillip Morris, 205
Phillips, Mark, xxx, 59
Phillips, Michael, xxix
physical fitness, 146
Pinnt, Larry, xxix
plasticity of brain, 52-53
policies, 201-202
Pomerance, Hy, xxxiii
positive change, rewarding yourself
    for, 259
positive feedback, 255
positive people, surrounding
    yourself with, 259-260
positive self-talk, 141-142
Positivity (Fredrickson), 21

postponing responses, 177-178
power, leveraging, 185-187
Prahalad, C. K., 249
prefrontal cortex, 52
preventative maintenance, 93
Price, Richard, xxxiii
*Primal Leadership: Realizing the Power
    of Emotional Intelligence*
    (Goleman, Boyatzis, and
    McKee), 23, 218, 262
primary beliefs, 36-37
principles
    acting consistently with, 98-99
    compared to values, 63
    for morally intelligent
        organizations, 202
    principled stands, 106-109
    universal principles, 36-37
prioritizing moral development efforts,
    254-255
professional rewards resulting from
    moral intelligence, 24
promises, keeping, 109-111
purpose-driven goals, 71-73

Q-R

rational center of brain, 49
real self, 188
reality testing (MCI), 280-281
recharging emotional batteries, 146
recognition
    of emotional patterns, 139, 169-170
    experiential triangle, 163-167
    of need for change, 260-261
    of thinking patterns, 168-169
    practicing, 163
recruiting employees, 217-219
reducing moral gaps, 257
reflection
    on big picture, 172-173
    making reflection a habit, 171
    practicing, 170
    preparing for, 171
    on values, 171-172
reframing, 174-175
REI, 101-102
Reiess, Helen, xxxiii
Reinhard, Keith, xxix, 136

relaxation activities, 146
The Relaxation Response (Benson), 146
*Repacking Your Bags: Lighten Your
    Load for the Rest of Your Life*
    (Leider), 70
reprogramming, 258
resources for moral development
    books and media, 261
    counseling, 261
    executive coaching, 262
    workshops, 261
respecting others, 151-153
responding, 175-178
responsibility
    admitting mistakes and failures,
        117-121
    to communities, 244-245
    explained, 21, 114-115
    for future, 247
    learning in childhood, 40
    in morally intelligent organizations,
        204-212
    for potential negative consequences,
        245-246
    serving others, 121-124
    in small organizations, 230-231
    taking responsibility for personal
        choices, 115-117
Responsibility Checklist, 212
retaining employees, 27-29
reward systems, 219-221, 259
Rigas, John, 6
Rigas, Timothy, 6
Risher, David, xxx, 108, 233
Roraback, Pat, xxx
Ruddy, Jim, xxx

S

Sala, Fabio, xxxiii
Salovey, Peter, 19
Samenuk, George, 7
Schinke, Tom, xxx
Schlidt, Joe, xxx
Schlifske, John, xxix
Schwab Bank, 59
Schwartz, Jeffrey, xxxiv, 39, 53, 161
Schwartz, Tony, xxxiv

scoring MCI (Moral Competency
    Inventory), 253-254, 274-275
  Alignment Worksheet, 281-283
  highest and lowest competency
    scores, 279
  individual item scores, 279-280
  Moral Competencies Worksheet, 274
  reality testing, 280-281
  scoring sheet, 295-296
  total MCI score (alignment score),
    274-278
Scrushy, Richard, 6
Seagram Company, 184
SEC Structured and New Products
    Unit, 12
Segal, Spenser, xxix, 59, 73,
    229-232, 238
self-awareness, 137-139
self-control, 142-143
self-forgiveness, 129-131
self-talk, 140-142
selfishness, 47
Seligman, Martin, 37
serving others, 121-124
*The Seven Habits of Highly Effective
    People* (Covey), 37
Sharan, Kim, xxv, xxxi
sharing beliefs and goals, 192-193
Shattuck, Mayo, xxix
Sheffert, Mark, xxiv, xxix, 209
Shefrin, Hersh, xxxiv
Skilling, Jeffrey, 6
Skoglund, Judy, xxxiv, 144
Sleiter, Jay, xxix
small organizations
  compassion, 231-232
  five maxims of moral
    entrepreneurship, 235-241
  forgiveness, 232-233
  integrity, 229-230
  moral impact of, 233, 235
  moral leadership, 242
  responsibility, 230-231
  values, 228
Smith, Ben, xxxi, 106
Smith, Janet, 238
Solomon Brothers, 130
Sontag, Lynn, xxix, 62, 78
Southwest Airlines, 222

SPAMMY, 205
Spencer, Lyle, xxxiv
Sperling, Dale, xxix
spotlight, leveraging, 184-185
standing up for what is right, 106-109
startup businesses, 223
  compassion, 231-232
  five maxims of moral
    entrepreneurship, 235-241
  forgiveness, 232-233
  integrity, 229-230
  KRW International, 225-228
  moral impact of, 233-235
  moral leadership, 242
  responsibility, 230-231
  Twin Cities Telemarketing, 224-225
  values, 228
state of being goals, 74
staying aligned, 85
Steifler, Jeff, xxxiv
Stewart, Martha, 120
Stewart, Thérèse Jacobs, xxxiv
Stockdale, Caroline, xxxi, 118, 131, 248
strengths
  80/20 rule, 255-256
  leveraging, 257
Structured and New Products Unit
    (SEC), 12
success
  impact of emotional intelligence
    on, 22
  impact of moral intelligence
    on, 22-27
surrounding yourself with positive
    people, 259-260
survival of the fittest, 46

T

tact, 105
Tatum LLC, 84, 142
technical intelligence, 19
thinking patterns, 168-169
Thomsen, Jim, xxxi, 3-5, 15, 117, 195
Thomson Corporation, 181-184
Thomson Reuters, 183
thoughts, 76-77, 140
3M, 215
threshold competencies, 19

Thrivent Financial for Lutherans, 3-5, 117, 149, 195
total MCI score (alignment score), 274-278
Tourre, Fabrice, 13
TPAG (The Personal Advisor Group), 62
Truman, Harry, 114
Twain, Mark, 250
Twin Cities magazine, 224
Twin Cities Telemarketing, 224-225
Twin Cities Woman, 224
Tylenol recall of 1982, 210

U

United Nations Declaration of Rights, 37
United States Army, 240
United States Marine Corps, 215
United Technologies Corp., 29
universal principles, 36-37

V

values
    acting consistently with, 98-99
    compared to principles, 63
    core values for small businesses, 239
    decision-making and, 65-66
    explained, 63
    in global organizations, 222
    identifying top five values, 64
    morality of values, 65
    for morally intelligent organizations, 197-199
    recruiting employees for, 217-219, 239
    reflecting on, 171-172
    uncovering values conflicts, 67-68
    value differences with employees, 195-196
Vappie, Kim, xxix
Vioxx recall, 210
viruses. *See* moral viruses
visibility of leaders, 184-185

W

Waletzko, Don, 234
Watson, Thomas, 131
WDYWFY process, 72
weaknesses, 80/20 rule, 255-256
Weiss, Kevin, 7
Wells Fargo, 106
Westar Energy, Inc., 7
Whalen, Christopher, 14
Williams, Redford, xxxiv
Wilson, Larry, xxxiv
Wilson, Michael, xxxi
Winfrey, Oprah, 70
Wittig, David C., 7
Woodward, Mike, xxxi, 126
Woolford, Lauris, xxxiv
workaholism, 186
Working with Emotional Intelligence (Goleman), 22
workshops, 261

X-Y-Z

XATA, 16

Young & Rubicam, 217

Zelle, Charlie, xxix, 82-83, 105, 122, 127
Zore, Ed, 18, 140, 147